Ricardo on the Theory of Value and Money

This book is a renovative research work on Ricardo's theory of value and of money, achieved through analysis of Ricardo's original writings, made available in Sraffa's *Works*.

Takenaga argues that Ricardo's economic theory should be understood as a cost theory of value. He begins by re-reading the first chapter of Ricardo's *Principles*, focusing on the chapter's theoretical structure and definition of labour. He then extends Ricardo's characterisation of the theory of value by situating it in the context of debates with other contemporary economists, namely Torrens and McCulloch. In the third chapter, he argues that Ricardo's theory of money is not a quantity theory, and according to him the causal relation between money's value and its quantity runs from the former to the latter. In the fourth and fifth chapters, he discusses Ricardo's plans to reform the English monetary regime of his time. He closes the book with examination on a particular aspect of Ricardo's theory of money: his view on the relation between monetary issue and economic dynamics.

Providing new insights into essential aspects of Ricardo's economic theory, as well as into the history of economic thought, this book will appeal to economic researchers, particularly those studying the classical English economists.

Susumu Takenaga is an Emeritus Professor of Economics at Daito Bunka University, Japan. He has edited two books on David Ricardo: *Ricardo and the History of Japanese Economic Thought* (2016) and *Ricardo on Money and Finance* (2013, with Yuji Sato). This is his third book on Ricardo.

Routledge Studies in the History of Economics

Adam Smith's Theory of Value and Distribution
Economics as a Moral Science Once Again
Jeffrey T. Young

Arthur Spiethoff and the German Historical School
Continuities and Discontinuities
Vitantonio Gioia

The Economic Thought of Hilaire Belloc
A Christian alternative to the Servile State
Alfonso Díaz Vera

Schumpeter's General Theory of Capitalism
Tristan Velardo
Translated by Katya Long

Slavery and Colonialism in the History of Economic Thought
The Cases of France and Great Britain
Simona Pisanelli

Hegel on Ethics, the State and Public Policy
Comparisons with Immanuel Kant and Utilitarianism
Samuel Hollander

Transaction Economics of John R. Commons
Towards Reasonable Capitalism
Shingo Takahashi

Ricardo on the Theory of Value and Money
Susumu Takenaga

For more information about this series, please visit: www.routledge.com/series/SE0341

Ricardo on the Theory of Value and Money

Susumu Takenaga

Routledge
Taylor & Francis Group
LONDON AND NEW YORK

First published 2025
by Routledge
4 Park Square, Milton Park, Abingdon, Oxon, OX14 4RN

and by Routledge
605 Third Avenue, New York, NY 10158

Routledge is an imprint of the Taylor & Francis Group, an informa business

British Library Cataloguing-in-Publication Data
A catalogue record for this book is available from the British Library

Library of Congress Cataloging-in-Publication Data
Names: Takenaga, Susumu, author.
Title: Ricardo on the theory of value and money / Susumu Takenaga.
Description: Abingdon, Oxon ; New York, NY : Routledge, 2025. |
Series: Routledge studies in the history of economics |
Includes bibliographical references and index. |
Summary: "This book is a renovative research work on Ricardo's theory of value and of money, achieved through analysis of Ricardo's original writings, made available in Sraffa's Works. Takenaga argues that Ricardo's economic theory should be understood as a cost theory of value. He begins by re-reading the first chapter of Ricardo's Principles, focusing on the chapter's theoretical structure and definition of labour. He then extends Ricardo's characterisation of the theory of value by situating it in context of debates with other contemporary economists, namely Torrens and McCulloch. In later sections, he argues that Ricardo's theory of money is not a quantity theory, and according to him the causal relation between money's value and its quantity runs from the former to the latter. He closes the book with a discussion of Ricardo's plans to reform the English monetary regime of his time. Providing new insights into essential aspects of Ricardo's economic theory as well as into the history of economic thought, this book will appeal to economic researchers, particularly those studying the classical English economists"– Provided by publisher.
Identifiers: LCCN 2024040596 (print) | LCCN 2024040597 (ebook) |
ISBN 9781032807362 (hardback) | ISBN 9781032807379 (paperback) |
ISBN 9781003498322 (ebook)
Subjects: LCSH: Ricardo, David, 1772-1823. |
Money. | Monetary policy. | Finance.
Classification: LCC HB103.R5 T34 2025 (print) | LCC HB103.R5 (ebook) |
DDC 332–dc23/eng/20240925
LC record available at https://lccn.loc.gov/2024040596
LC ebook record available at https://lccn.loc.gov/2024040597

ISBN: 9781032807362 (hbk)
ISBN: 9781032807379 (pbk)
ISBN: 9781003498322 (ebk)

DOI: 10.4324/9781003498322

Typeset in Galliard
by Newgen Publishing UK

Contents

Introduction

This book is a collection of my articles on David Ricardo (1772–1823) originally written in Japanese during the last two decades. Only one among them, corresponding to Chapter 3, has been published in English as Chapter 4 in Sato and Takenaga (2013) (see 'References' at the end of the book), reproduced here with the permission of Routledge, the copyright holder.

Among the various fields in his economic theory and thought, I concentrate on the two core pillars: value and money, in which Ricardo was interested for a long time during his career as an economist, for the former as the cornerstone of his entire system of economic theory developed in the magnum opus *On the principles of political economy, and taxation* (1817, 1819, 1821 in Ricardo (1951–2)), and for the latter as the key-concept in the bullionist controversy of the time, in which he actively participated from the beginning till the end of his career.

The claim I bring forward in the whole of this book is contrary to what has been long admitted as 'orthodox' interpretation on Ricardo's economic theory. He did not bring forward a 'pure' theory of labour value to liquidate the ambiguities contained in the theory of Adam Smith. Neither did he adopt a quantity theory of money, determining its value by its quantity injected into circulation. Besides, these two theories have sometimes been considered as contradictory to each other. My contention in this book belongs rather to a dissident minority, claiming that decisive for Ricardo in determining the value of commodities was not the labour carried out by the labourer in the process of production, but the monetary cost spent by the capitalist as his employer, and in the relation between the value and quantity of money, I contend that the causality runs from the former to the latter, not the other way round, the value of money being determined in the same way as the value of other non-monetary commodities.

This book consists of six chapters, the first two are on the subject of value, the rest are on money. They are not necessarily arranged in the order of writing. The following is the gist of each of them. At the end of every chapter are added some concluding remarks, so there is no repetitive general conclusion after the final chapter.

DOI: 10.4324/9781003498322-1

Chapter 1 is an attempt to re-evaluate the first chapter of *Principles.* It focuses on its theoretical structure, in particular on the relationship between the first half and the second half, the former is currently interpreted as his 'pure theory of labour value', whereas the second is a regression from it admitting a number of its 'modifications'. An attentive reading of Ricardo's text reveals the true meaning of the concept of labour in his theory which is, above all, the monetary cost (wages) paid for employing a worker, or even the worker himself, and at the same time as well as the labour in Marx's theory. His theory of value can be characterised, on the whole, as a cost of production theory, instead of a labour theory.

In Chapter 2, I attempt to give the same characterisation to Ricardo's theory of value, in examining his discussions and debates on the notion of value with his contemporary economists, namely Torrens and McCulloch. His theory of value can be thus characterised also in the historical context of economic thought. Torrens pointed out to Ricardo the ambiguities and theoretical difficulties of the notion of 'durability of circulating capital', one of the elements which were to lead Ricardo to admit in some cases the 'modifications of labour value'. On the other hand, McCulloch was strongly opposed to the notion itself of 'modifications of labour value', in insisting on his particular view on 'labour' to be allegedly recognised even with regard to the activities of non-human factors of production.

Chapter 3 tries to show two points. First, in his theory of money the quantity of money in circulation is regulated by the value of money determined in the same way as the other commodities. Secondly, the quantity theoretic determination of the value of money with the causal relation running from quantity to value appears only in some special contexts of his theory of money. During the time when Ricardo was active as an economist, the domestic circulation was entirely made up of inconvertible paper money issued by the Bank of England. Then, the value 'inherent' in it (virtually null) could never determine or regulate its quantity in circulation. Its value moves up and down only in accordance with the quantity issued. This is precisely the situation akin to that in the quantity theory of money.

Chapter 4 takes up and examines some other more concrete aspects in Ricardo's theory of money, i.e., his plans for the reform of the monetary regime intended to overcome the difficulties contained in the English monetary regime during the Bank Restriction Period (1797–1821). In the last few pages of 'Appendix' added at the end of the last fourth edition of his first pamphlet *High Price* published in 1811, Ricardo showed for the first time the plan in which he proposed a payment in bullion instead of in specie. In 1819, he succeeded, as a member of Parliament, in getting it integrated into a bill. It is worth paying attention to the fact that a concept of establishing a national bank in place of the Bank of England dates back to this period before the enactment of Peel's Bill, four years prior to his last manuscript of

1823. This chapter examines the processes of his thinking and actions up to this moment.

Chapter 5 traces the following processes, ending with his sudden death in 1823. Once his plan of bullion payment aiming at an entire paper circulation was to be implemented, unforeseen difficulties arose, and Ricardo had to continue to struggle with them during the rest of his lifetime. The Bank of England immediately began to recover part of its banknotes issued to contract its domestic circulation, resulting in an inflow of foreign gold. For Ricardo, these acts of the Bank were at the origin of the increase in the value of money and of the spread of coin in place of paper circulation. He saw in them sufficient reasons for claiming the Bank's liquidation. During the summer of 1823, he drafted his final manuscript, 'Plan for the Establishment of a National Bank', in the situation of the factual failure of his initial plan of bullion payment allowing a return to the metallic circulation.

Chapter 6 sheds some light on other aspect of Ricardo's theory of money in examining his reactions to the arguments brought forward by Thornton, etc. They advanced the theory of 'forced saving', according to which the increase in monetary issue has some real effects, consisting in expanding production through a redistribution of wealth and modifications in the relative price system. Ricardo, on his part, makes an impressive discussion on the relation between the rate of interest and the variation of bank loans in a passage of *Principles*, ch. 27. It is on this passage that the arguments of those who estimate Ricardo as a precursor of the cumulative process theory of Wicksell are based. In this chapter, we examine what Ricardo brings forward concerning the continued expansion of monetary issue with the level of the rate of interest as a fundamental factor, taking into account the theory of Thornton.

The texts of most of these chapters were presented in the national and international conferences of 'The Japanese Society for the History of Economic Thought (JSHET)' and 'The Ricardo Society' in Japan, and of 'The European Society for the History of Economic Thought (ESHET)' in Europe. On these occasions I have benefitted from discussions with participants from various countries, while not giving here their names. I am grateful to them for comments and constructive criticisms, encouraging me to go further in the research on Ricardo's economics.

I must also express my gratitude to the three anonymous referees for their helpful suggestions and advice, which permitted me to make the book more readable. Of course, the usual disclaimer applies here.

In particular, I owe much to my colleagues of 'The Ricardo Society', founded in 2000 and continuing to organise biannual conferences, alternately national and international. It has published up to the present the results of these activities in the form of several collections of articles in English, some of which are written by authors from foreign countries invited to our international conferences. This may be said to be unprecedented for the research work carried out in Japan. Without these activities, the publication of this book would be impossible.

On the other hand, I have written some texts in fields other than value and money in Ricardo, like his theory on foreign trade, ground rent, etc., not included in this book. They are to be reserved for future occasions.

1 Structure of David Ricardo's theory of value

1.1 Foreword

The aim of this chapter is to characterise Ricardo's theory of value as a whole, by examining the theoretical structure of the first chapter of *Principles of Political Economy, and Taxation* (1817–21, hereafter *Principles* for short)[1].

In the following, we will elucidate the particular construction of the theory of value of the first chapter of the third edition of *Principles*, this theory will then appear neither as an improved version of the theory of Smith, nor as a germinal version of that of Marx. To show this point we will try to emphasise the theoretical framework into which Ricardo puts his theory of value in each stage of its development, and the method he adopts to develop it (by giving special attention to the relation between the first three sections and the following two sections. The fundamental character of the theory of value of Ricardo as a whole will emerge from this attempt).

As Sraffa explains in detail in the introduction of the editor (Ricardo (1951–2), vol. I, p. xiii–lxii, hereafter I/xiii–lxii, the same for all the writings of Ricardo in the whole of this book), chapter one on value constitutes one of the parts which underwent the most extensive revisions during the preparation of the second and third editions. In the first edition it was not subdivided into sections. It was in the second edition that the subdivision into five sections and the subtitles for each section were introduced. It was only in the third edition that it was again divided into seven sections. On the basis of its composition in the third edition, the theory of value of Ricardo has often been interpreted as being made up of three parts (embodied labour theory of value, modification of value, invariable measure of value), of which the first would occupy the central place. In other words, in spite of various problems in Ricardo's theory of value (insufficiencies, contradictions, gaps...), its essence would lie in the determination of the quantity of value of the commodities by the quantity of labour bestowed on its production (the first three sections being the core of his theory[2]). In opposition to such a point of view, we will examine the reason why Ricardo adopted the theoretical construction mentioned above, which may justify the interpretation according to which his theory of value would

DOI: 10.4324/9781003498322-2

consist of 'three domains'. This examination will lead to a characterisation of his theory of value enabling us to understand it as a whole.

One of the principal reasons for which Ricardo adopted for his theory of value the construction mentioned above is its opposition to the theory of Smith. From the subtitle of section one, Ricardo makes clear his point of view opposing him to Smith, not accepting the theory of parallel movement of wages and the price of commodities[3]. During the development of the first chapter, the theory of Smith undergoes explicit critical examinations only in section one with the subtitle quoted in note three above, but the substantial critique of Smith continues beyond this section. Smith noted in chapter 6 of his *Wealth of Nations* that the determination of value by embodied labour (rule determining the ratio of exchange between commodities) is no longer valid after the appearance of 'the accumulation of stock and the appropriation of land'[4]. This is because the incomes on these means of production (profits and rent) which have become private properties constitute the components of the value of commodities together with the wages for workers. Ricardo tries to subject each one of these elements to critical examinations. Such were the original objectives of section three and the following sections (concerning profits) and of chapter two (concerning rent)[5].

In chapter 5 of *Wealth of Nations*, Smith develops his theory of value in the setting of a so-called 'simple commodity production' model. But, in moving to chapter 6, Smith leaves the 'simple commodity production' model and considers as his new object of theory commodity production in modern capitalism composed of three classes (landowners, capitalists, wage labourers). Then he advances that the determination of value by embodied labour is no longer valid there. In his theory of the determination of the value of commodities, at the outset Ricardo adopts seemingly the model of simple commodity production in the wake of Smith ('early stages of society', I/12), and after that introduces the capitalist relations. But, contrary to Smith, Ricardo does not recognise any fundamental difference between these two theoretical models and proposes that the passage from one to the other does not at all change the determination of value. However, this concerns only the external appearance of the theoretical development, caused by the attempt of Ricardo to build his theory by criticising Smith, at the same time being based himself on the method of development of Smith. It is for this reason that there often exist gaps between the letter and the contents of the text. It becomes essential then, in order to decipher the text of the first chapter, to clearly realise the theoretical framework adopted at each stage of the development of the chapter. Without entering in detail, one can say that the first edition of *Principles* adopts initially the model of simple commodity production and then passes to the model of capitalist production on the basis of an aspect of the development of Smith, who follows literally the historical passage. It is from the 'early and rude state of society' to the state with 'accumulation of stock and appropriation of land', cf. note 4 above. But the third edition presupposes from the very outset capitalist relations and brings theoretical operations of abstraction to these relations. In chapter one of the third edition, there is initially an abstract and simplified model for the determination of value and then this simplification will be relaxed to develop the determination of value under less abstract conditions[6]. Significant modifications brought to the details of text in the second and third editions can be interpreted by reference to the *de facto* change in the principle of development of the chapter. This also applies to the elimination of the three paragraphs indicated above, which weakened the aspect of critique of Smith and made the theoretical construction of the third edition a positive development of the theory of Ricardo according to his own certain method. In the subtitle of the first section referred to in note 3, it is clearly indicated that the theory of Ricardo explicitly presupposes from the very beginning the commodities produced in capitalist relations, and that therefore it aims at the determination of their values.

These are preliminary remarks on the whole of chapter one. We will examine below some significant points successively to grasp the fundamental character of the theory of value of Ricardo.

1.2 Critique of Smith's commanded labour theory of value

At the very beginning of the development of his theory of value, Ricardo quotes the text of Smith. Thus, Ricardo builds his own theory by criticising the theory of Smith while at the same time resting on this. After having limited the scope of the theory of value to reproducible commodities under the conditions of unlimited competition following the example of Smith, Ricardo formulates his determination of the value of commodities as follows.

> In the early stages of society, the exchangeable value of these commodities, or the rule which determines how much of one shall be given in exchange for another, depends almost exclusively[7] on the comparative quantity of labour expended on each. ... If the quantity of labour realised in commodities, regulate their exchangeable value, every increase of the quantity of labour must augment the value of that commodity on which it is exercised, as every diminution must lower it.
>
> (I/12–3)

What Ricardo asserts here, is of course the theory of embodied labour value, i.e., the determination of value by the quantity of labour 'bestowed', 'realised' in the commodities. Ricardo does not attribute this principle of the determination of value to his own originality, instead he formulates it by giving his approval to what the authority Smith had already stated. The text of Smith to which he refers here concerns what regulates the relations of exchange of commodities within a theoretical framework in which the workers carry out the production only with their hands, without capitalist relations or means of production, and in which the workers having manufactured these commodities only with their labour appropriate them and offer them in exchange (tacit presupposition of the model of simple commodity production). And this state of society is compared to the 'early stages of society' which historically precede the 'accumulation of stock and the appropriation of land'. There is no knowing whether Ricardo consciously adopted this theoretical framework of the determination of value of Smith when formulating his theory of value as quoted above. But it can at least be said that the restrictive phrase 'in the early stages of society' put at the beginning of the text was added under the influence of Smith.

But, in the subtitle put before the body of text of section one which starts with the determination of value we have just seen, capitalist relations are explicitly presupposed in which the 'labour' was in fact that of employees who work in exchange for wages advanced by their employers. An abrupt change would thus intervene in the presupposed state of society between this subtitle and the beginning of the body of text of *Principles*, in which the determination of value by embodied labour is brought forward, if one takes literally the restrictive phrase 'in the early stages of society'. In addition, the criticism of Smith's measure of value by commanded labour (that Ricardo mistakes for the measurement of value by wages) precisely turns around the category of wages characterising capitalist relations. Here the model of simple commodity production is thus abandoned, which means a return to the presupposition of the state of society in the subtitle. In addition, for this criticism, Ricardo develops argument from the determination of value by the embodied labour he advanced in relation to 'the early stages of society'. If one literally took the restrictive phrase in question, the text of Ricardo would be full of confusions.

In fact, 'almost exclusively' mentioned in note seven was 'solely' in the first and second editions. One would think from this that Ricardo took for his theoretical model the simple commodity production which existed literally in the historical past, and the restrictive phrase 'in the early stages of society' remains intact. But the fact that he changed 'solely' into 'almost exclusively' in the third edition seems to suggest the possibility of another interpretation. That is, the state of society of historical past is not the object of the theory of Ricardo even at the initial stage of the determination of value by embodied labour, his object of theory being the capitalist relations just as in the subtitle. But he formulates the theory of embodied labour value only in disregarding the existence of the means of production and the employed labour (the fact that labour is that of employees and that the workers are not those who appropriate the results of their labour). But, even under these conditions, Ricardo could not completely remain unaware of the existence of the differences in the conditions of production, which will be at the origin of the problems of modifications of value. He had thus to say that the quantity of value depends not 'solely' but 'almost exclusively' on the amount of embodied labour. Therefore, what is in question here is not the primitive state of society itself, but a simplified model set up in bringing certain methodological operations to commodity production under capitalist relations, the proper object of Ricardo's theory.

The method Ricardo adopts implicitly in the third edition consists in successively building a theory of value on the same theoretical object while introducing step by step in accordance with the development of his argument the factors he had disregarded at the beginning. We will see this in detail hereafter.

We have noted that the theory of Ricardo which determines the quantity of value by the quantity of labour which was 'bestowed', 'carried out', to be materialised in commodities is advanced by disregarding capitalist relations and the means of production. We see below how Ricardo criticises the theory of commanded labour value of Smith on the basis of his own determination of value.

For Ricardo, the essence of the theory of value of Smith lies in the principle of the determination of value such as it was formulated in the two texts referred to above. Ricardo supports his own theory of embodied labour value by giving assent to the theory of Smith. But, according to Ricardo, Smith was not consequent on this point and halfway introduced another measure of value incompatible with the aforementioned principle of the determination of value. It is there that he begins his criticism.

> Adam Smith, who so accurately defined the original source of exchangeable value, and who was bound in consistency to maintain, that all things became more or less valuable in proportion as more or less labour was bestowed on their production, has himself erected another standard measure of value, and speaks of things being more or less valuable, in proportion as they will exchange for more or less of this standard measure. Sometimes he speaks of corn, at other times of labour, as a standard measure; not the quantity of labour bestowed on the production of any object, but the quantity which it can command in the market: as if these were two equivalent expressions. (I/13–4)

For commanded labour and embodied labour to be equivalent, it should consequently be supposed that what the employed person produces in capitalist relations and the remuneration which is given to him would quantitatively coincide, or these two constantly keep the same proportion by some reason. It is for Ricardo a completely improbable assumption. It is on this point that he bases himself to criticise the theory of Smith.

But actually, Ricardo does not correctly understand the theory of commanded labour value of Smith, so that they understand altogether different things by the same term commanded labour. And what Ricardo attacks is fundamentally a misinterpreted theory of Smith. We will show the difference of commanded labour which each of them understands (i.e., that Ricardo did not understand the problems of Smith) and ask ourselves about the meaning of what Ricardo wanted to affirm positively by this incorrect criticism.

Let me see concretely how Ricardo mistakes the text of Smith. His argument turns around the key category of 'value of labour'. Ricardo quotes the following text of Smith and adds to it comments to refute Smith's thesis on the invariability of the 'value of labour' and to show that this value is prone to as much variation as that of any other commodity.

Here is Smith's text Ricardo quotes.

> As labour may sometimes *purchase* a greater, and sometimes a smaller quantity of commodities, it is their value which varies, not that of the labour which purchases them, 'and therefore', labour *alone never varying its own value*, is alone the ultimate and real standard by which the value of all commodities can at all times and places be estimated and compared.
>
> (I/16–7, drawn from Smith, ibid., pp. 50–1. the italics are Ricardo's)

Ricardo transfers this text of Smith into the context of his own theory completely differently from that of Smith. For the point of view of Ricardo, what Smith advances in this text is the determination of the value of commodities by 'the comparative quantities of commodities, which are given to the labourer in exchange for his labour' (I/17). And it is precisely in this point that the error of the theory of value of Smith resides, says Ricardo.

Ricardo relies, to highlight Smith's error, on the variations in the value of (the force of) labour (in particular its falls) by the rise of productivity in the branches of production of consumer goods for the workers. According to Ricardo, what determines the value of labour is not the values themselves of the consumer goods, but the physical quantities of these consumer goods required by the workers to subsist 'under normal conditions'. These quantities are not of fixed value, but their value varies with the productivity of labour. Ricardo thus makes use of these variations, from which even the 'value of labour' cannot be free, as the basis for criticising Smith's thesis that the 'value of labour' is not prone to any variation and that one can thus adopt commanded labour as the invariable measure of value.

But in fact, in this thesis Smith does not mean the measurement of value by the amount of wages as Ricardo understands it. According to the idea Smith advances in his text quoted by Ricardo above, the reason why the labour is constantly of an invariable value is that it is a sacrifice, price independent of the quantity of commodities that the worker (in Smith's theory he is not always an employed person) receives from nature in exchange for his labour. From Smith' point of view, it is for this that labour and not some product of labour constitutes the invariable measure of value. Smith bases himself on the structure of the original exchange between man and nature to advance his measure of value. The capitalist relation is not always implied there. For Ricardo, on the other hand, the capitalist relation is the only one conceivable relation of labour and thus for him any remuneration given in exchange for labour means, necessarily, wages. From this it follows quite logically that the determination of the value of commodities by the value of labour is identical to that by wages. Ricardo's criticism of Smith's 'value of labour' was thus completely misplaced.

As we have seen, to criticise the measure of value by commanded labour, Ricardo based himself on variations of value (understood in terms of embodied labour) of commanded labour (in the meaning of employed labour). In other words, Ricardo examines the relevance of commanded labour as the invariable measure of value from the point of view of embodied labour, which is for him the only possible measure. This results in confusion about the meaning of commanded labour in Smith, and on the questions which he raises with this concept. For Ricardo, the 'value of labour' is nothing other than the value of the consumer goods the worker receives as wages. Taking in this way the meaning of the 'value of labour', Ricardo restructures the whole theory of commanded labour value of Smith.

Our examination up to now of the criticism made by Ricardo of Smith's theory arrived at a rather negative conclusion, highlighting the confusion on the part of Ricardo. It is still necessary, independently of the question of relevance of this criticism, to consider what Ricardo positively advances through this criticism. In the context of his criticism of Smith's theory, Ricardo says:

> If the shoes and clothing of the labourer could, by improvements in machinery, be produced by one fourth of the labour now necessary to their production, they would probably fall 75%; but so far is it from being true, that the labourer would therefore be enabled permanently to consume four coats, or four pairs of shoes, instead of one, that it is probable his wages would in no long time be adjusted by the effects of competition, and the stimulus to population, to the new value of the necessaries on which they were expended.
>
> (I/16)

Therefore, in the long run, wages remain constant in physical terms of the quantity of wage goods, independently of the variations in the productivity of labour. And the value of these constant real wages expressed in terms of embodied labour varies in inverse proportion to the productivity of labour. That is, the wages are not the share allotted to the employed workers in what they produce. But the value of wages is given in a process other than the production process in which these employed persons engage themselves. It is given in their life process determining the amount of wages expressed in terms of their consumer goods, and the production process of these wage goods determines the value of the wages. The causes of the variations of the value of wages are thus elsewhere than in the production process in which these employees work. If it is legitimate to interpret thus the text quoted above, one could say that Ricardo gives here *de facto* the essentials of his concept of wages. In other words, Ricardo gives, at the very outset of his theory of value, the fundamental points of his wage determination. We saw above that the theory of embodied labour value of section one of chapter one is made up on an extremely simplified model, disregarding capitalist relations and all the means of production. What Ricardo positively advances through his criticism of Smith in this same section one, is this essential of his concept of wages based on his determination of value. We will see later regarding section three, the meaning of this essential of the concept of wages given in section one of the chapter on value. According to its subtitle, section three aims at advancing that the total value of commodities is determined by the sum of past labour and present labour. But the real contents of this section are discussions on the relation of distribution between the capitalist and the employee by explicitly introducing into the arguments the means of production and capitalist relations (and thus profits). That is, the theory of value of Ricardo is, from its fundamental structure, inseparable from the theory of relation of distribution. To section one is *de facto* allotted the role of determining beforehand the category of wages necessary for the argument in section three. We will see this in detail hereafter. In any case, it seems to us that the points Ricardo has advanced positively through his critique of Smith can be situated as above in his theory of value.

1.3 Framework of Ricardo's theory of value as a theory of distribution

We have seen that the determination of value by embodied labour, such as it had been advanced at the beginning of *Principles* before the criticism of Smith's theory of commanded labour value, rested on an extremely simplified model. In that model, disregarding capitalist relations and all the means of production, independent workers would produce with bare hands, so to speak. It is obvious that normally human labour is not carried out in this manner, that it needs necessarily means of production, whatever they may be. To ensure the validity of the determination of value given at the beginning within an extremely abstract theoretical framework, it is therefore necessary to introduce into the argument the means of production. Section three has the subtitle 'Not only the labour applied immediately to commodities affect to their value, but the labour also which is bestowed on the implements, tools, and buildings, with which such labour is assisted'. Then its explicit objective is to show that the determination of value by embodied labour as given in section one does not undergo any change, even if taking into account the means of production. The reason for this is that the value of these means of production (among the means of production enumerated above are not included raw materials, always neglected by Ricardo) is embodied, according to its quantity and their durability, as much of past labour, together with the immediate labour of the workers into the value of their products and thus transferred to them. Because of Ricardo's proper view on history, which projects the capitalist relations of the time on all past societies and identifies every means of production with capital, the introduction of the means of production into the argument was for him tantamount to that of capitalist relations. Section three consequently has as its aim not only the transfer of the value of the means of production to the product, but at the same time the production and distribution of the value of products under the conditions of capitalist relations. In other words, Ricardo develops in this section the fundamental structure of his theory of value, which is in fact also a theory of distribution. It is because of this that, in addition to the concept of wages given already in section one, here is given also the essential of the concept of profits in opposition to wages. Ricardo thus exposes the broad outline of his theory of production and distribution under the conditions of capitalist relations such as he conceives them. And Ricardo repeats in this section three that the determination of value by embodied labour undergoes no change within the theoretical framework of this section three, more concrete than that of section one, a statement which stands in remarkable contrast to the subsequent sections. We will see hereafter in detail the provenance of this contrast.

By introducing the division of society into classes of capitalists and employees, Ricardo says as follows to affirm that the value of the commodities produced under these conditions is always determined as before by the quantity of labour necessary for their production.

> All the implements necessary to kill the beaver and deer might belong to one class of men, and the labour employed in their destruction might be furnished by another class; still, their comparative prices would be in proportion to the actual labour bestowed, both on the formation of the capital, and on the destruction of the animals. Under different circumstances of plenty or scarcity of capital, as compared with labour, under different circumstances of plenty or scarcity of the food and necessaries essential to the support of men, those who furnished an equal value of capital for either one employment or for the other, might have a half, a fourth, or an eighth of the produce obtained, the remainder being paid as wages to those who furnished the labour; yet this division could not affect the relative value of these commodities[8].
>
> (I/24)

It seems to us that the text quoted above can be regarded as the clearest development of Ricardo's theory of value, consisting of a theory of production and distribution of value under the conditions of capitalist relations. The proposition Ricardo advances is that the determination of value by embodied labour remains unchanged under the conditions in which the product of labour does not belong entirely to those who have produced it, but is distributed between two different classes in the form of profits and wages. In short, he claims here the non-influence of distribution on value. Now let us examine Ricardo's theory of distribution (in the framework of the model of two classes excluding rent and landowners) by an analysis of the text quoted above.

It is necessary first of all to notice the theoretical order of the categories of distribution, i.e., the fact that the argument starts from the side of wages, profits coming thereafter. The concept of wages is the same as that we have seen during the examination of section one. Here two determining factors of the wages are given: (1). 'different circumstances of plenty or scarcity of capital, as compared with labour'; (2). 'different circumstances of plenty or scarcity of the food and necessaries essential to the support of men'. Item one relates to the relation of supply and demand on the labour market, which determines the amount of real wages (expressed in terms of physical quantities of wage goods). According to Ricardo, these wages are subject to the process of long-term adjustment by the variation of the working population, and can be regarded as a given and constant amount. Item two is, in other words, the difficulty of production of this constant amount of wage goods, i.e., the value of wages, which varies (increases in particular) along with the price of corn as the (raw material of) bread, staple food. The amount of wages is given previously to and independently of the production process, and the amount of cost for capitalist (input) is determined in accordance with that. The deduction of this input from the output (produced value) leaves the profits in the hands of the capitalist.

It is the level of wages which determines the distribution beforehand, the profits varying in turn only in a passive way in inverse proportion to the movement of wages. If the determination of the level of wages in Ricardo's theory is as above, there is in this determination no factor particular to any branch of production. The wages must thus be theoretically at the same level throughout all the branches of industry, including agriculture. If a capitalist employs for a certain number of days a certain number of workers with the investment of a certain amount of capital, the value produced must be the same in any branch. The deduction of the same amount of cost from this produced value must leave for remainder the same amount of profits. According to Ricardo's assumption, the uniformity of the level of wages thus implies that of the rate of profits in all the branches (presupposition of the general rate of profit[9]).

In the text quoted above, Ricardo stresses the constant validity of the determination of value by embodied labour in spite of the division of the product of labour between two classes. But here he does not mention any investment of capital for the means of production (fixed capital according to the terminology of Ricardo) monopolised by one of two classes, and its recovery. That is, he appears to neglect completely the starting point which was at the origin of his statement in this text. If it is only the concentration of the means of production in the hands of a part of society and the production with them that allow the categories of distribution (wages and profits) to exist as such, this apparent neglect seems very mysterious. In section three of chapter one Ricardo asserts, in agreement with the subtitle, two points. First, the amount of the whole of the value of product is the sum of the immediate labour done by the employees and of labour already embodied (realised) in the means of production. Secondly, therefore the determination of the value by embodied labour is maintained without reserve, insofar as the amount of the totality of the value of product is concerned. On the other hand, when he comes to speak about the distribution of the value of product, he concentrates only on the part of the capital invested as circulating capital and does not question the fixed capital, in spite of the fact that the distribution comes from the existence of the fixed capital, equivalent to the means of production for Ricardo. We have said, just after the text quoted above, that Ricardo's theory of value and distribution is most clearly stated in section three. This clarity is due, it seems to us, to the fact that Ricardo *tacitly* disregards the part of the fixed capital when he speaks about distribution[10]. We will enter below in detail of what this can mean.

When speaking about Ricardo's theory of value and distribution, it is absolutely necessary to mention the 'inverse relation between the wages and the profits'. Ricardo says on this point in section three as follows.

> The proportion which might be paid for wages, is of the utmost importance in the question of profits; for it must at once be seen, that profits would be high or low, exactly in proportion as wages were low or high.
>
> (I/27)

This text certainly seems to advance the opposition of interest between wage labour and capital. But, if one remembers how the wages were conceived by Ricardo, the rivalry between these two classes does not seem inevitably to be the essential point that he asserts here. Since the wages are for him rather of an amount given in physical terms, it would be legitimate to consider that he lays stress on the movement of the value of this constant amount of real wages in opposition to profits. This opposition does not concern the relation between wages and capital, but it is rather about an opposition between capital and landed property, the interest of wage labour not taking part in it. In Ricardo's theory, the amount of real wages does not in itself oppose the interests of wage labour against those of capital. This opposition does not seem to be the object of his economic theory. If one interpreted immediately the text of Ricardo describing the opposite movement of wages and profits as he underlines here the opposition of the interests of two classes, one would deviate from Ricardo's problems in his theory of distribution and would incorrectly interpret his theory after the manner of the theory of surplus value of Marx.

I say incorrectly, because Marx affirms class opposition based on his theory of surplus value in his analysis of the production process of capital, altogether absent in Ricardo's theory. The process of valorisation of capital, which is the production of surplus value as a capitalist form of exploitation, is made possible only by a *prolongation beyond a certain point* of the working day.

> If we now compare the two processes of producing value and of creating surplus-value, we see that the latter is nothing but the continuation of the former beyond a definite point. If on the one hand the process be not carried beyond the point, where the value paid by the capitalist for the labour power is replaced by an exact equivalent, it is simply a process of

> producing value; if on the other hand, it be continued beyond that point, it becomes a process of creating surplus-value[11].

That is, to recognise the surplus value, it is necessary as a preliminary condition to realise that the duration of the working day is determined by nothing other than by the relation of force between capital and wage labour. Ricardo supposes a working day of given duration without giving particular reasons. And in his theory real wages remain constant, as long as the equilibrium between the increase in the demand for labour and the growth of workers population is maintained during the process of capital accumulation (which Ricardo supposes as a long-term tendency). Consequently, nothing can exist that must be decided through the class struggle between wage labour and capital. This is the fundamental character of the capitalist relation such as is conceived by Ricardo. For Ricardo surplus does not result from class struggles. Therefore, Ricardo's theory concerning the inverse relation between wages and profits are not of a nature to be assimilated directly to the theory of surplus value. It rather concerns the opposition between capital and landed property, caused by the variations (increases in particular) of the value of wages fixed in physical terms, variations caused in their turn by the degradation of arable soil, with which the accumulation of capital is 'naturally' accompanied.

Ricardo had advanced, at the beginning of *Principles*, the determination of the value of commodities by embodied labour. According to this determination, the amount of value is fixed by the quantity (length) of the *time of labour* necessary for production. When Ricardo speaks about this labour time, it is always a 'working day (day's labour)' which constitutes the unit of it. Under the condition in which the intensity and the skill of labour are given, one working day as a unit always expresses the same quantity of labour (thus it goes without saying that the number of working hours per day is given and constant. It seems to us that for Ricardo this is too obvious to be in need of explanation). If the amount of wages per day per worker is given, the amount of capital spent to employ workers can thus be recognised as the index of carried out and embodied labour. As we have seen, Ricardo expressed the amount of wages by the term 'value of labour'. This 'labour' would probably correspond to Marx's 'force of labour'. That is, in Marx's terminology, Ricardo does not distinguish clearly 'living labour' (the amount of which is expressed by the duration of working time in the production process) and the 'commodities sold to the capitalist by the worker' (the value of which is expressed by the amount of wages). And together with the fact that for Ricardo the amount of the part of capital assigned to the payment of wages is tantamount to the index of carried out and embodied labour, 'labour necessary for the production' as the factor determining value can mean equally both 'living labour required for the production' and the 'amount of wages *required to employ* this living labour'. This is revealed only in section three in which the capitalist relation (the relation between wages and profit) is explicitly introduced. As we will see below, this is of decisive importance in considering the fundamental character of Ricardo's 'theory of embodied labour value'.

1.4 Method of chapter one of *Principles*: relation between the first half and the second half

In section three of chapter one Ricardo developed, in an extremely clear way, his theory of the determination of value inseparable from his theory of distribution under the conditions of capitalist relations, and he seems to have succeeded in getting rid of the ambiguity included in the theory of value of Smith. But, as we have seen, Ricardo develops here the determination of value within a wholly abstract theoretical framework, supposing a capitalist production without any means of production. If he could advance embodied labour as the only factor determining value and affirm that 'no alteration in the wages of labour could produce any alteration in the relative value of these commodities' (I/28), this was in fact possible only inside this theoretical framework.

In the history of economic thought, the merit to have gotten over the confusion of the two determinations of value in Smith's theory and developed in a pure form the embodied labour theory of value is not rarely attributed to Ricardo. This 'pure' theory[12] would be realised in the first half of chapter one while the latter half of it would reveal the weakness or defect of his theory and there he had to make modifications to his principle of the determination of value because of the insufficiency of his abstraction[13]. Or, Ricardo, just like Smith, would suppose initially a 'primitive state of society' in which he could make embodied labour the only principle of the determination of value, and, in passing to the developed capitalist relations he could no longer retain the validity of this principle and fell into a fallacy similar to that of Smith (recognition of the influence of the variations of wages on the determination of value).

In opposition to these two points of view on chapter one we intend to show, in the light of what Ricardo himself says about the passage from (until) section three to section four (and five), that there is no cleavage between the first half and the latter half of chapter, i.e., modification of the principle of the determination of value or change of the object of theory (historical passage). And we will also show that between them there exist only differences of theoretical procedure in the framework of one and the same approach to the same theoretical object (setting of a restrictive hypothesis and releasing the restriction, although Ricardo does not make this procedure explicit in the form of a methodology).

For the first time in the last paragraph of section three, he makes an allusion to the fact that his theory in this section has validity only under certain restrictive conditions:

> A rise of wages would not raise them (commodities) in money value, nor relatively to any other commodities, the production of which required no

> additional quantity of labour, which employed the same proportion of fixed and circulating capital, and fixed capital of the same durability.
>
> (I/29)

Ricardo recognises thus implicitly that it is never without condition that wage increases, another factor than embodied labour, remain without influence on the value of commodities. Two elements are evoked here: the 'proportion of fixed capital and circulating capital' and the 'durability of the fixed capital', Ricardo has disregarded them *de facto* up to now. And he acknowledges so to say that the theory of value and distribution of section three is valid only under the special condition that these two elements are 'the same' in each branch of production. The 'modifications of value' in sections four and five relate to problems that the releasing of this special condition raises on the determination of value. Corresponding to the text quoted above, Ricardo raises the problem in the first paragraph of section four:

> This difference in the degree of durability of fixed capital, and this variety in the proportions in which the two sorts of capital may be combined, introduce another cause, besides the greater or less quantity of labour necessary to produce commodities, for the variations in their relative value – this cause is the rise or fall in the value of labour[14].
>
> (I/30)

If Ricardo is always interested in the influence of the variations of wages on value, it is obviously because he is always conscious of the theory of Smith mentioned in the subtitle of section one, a theory leading to the conclusion that 'the wage increase raises the prices of commodities'. The arguments on the 'modifications of value' advanced in sections four and five are motivated partly by Ricardo's intention to refute this theory of Smith. In this sense, it could be said that it is starting from section four that the subtitle of section one of chapter one of *Principles* will be given grounds. But, as we will see, sections four and five have a more positive significance as a component part of Ricardo's theory of value, at the same time as they are the development of a critique of Smith's theory.

If the proportion between fixed capital and circulating capital and the durability of fixed capital are different according to branches of production, the variations of wages intervene together with embodied labour as a determining factor of value. In this way, the unitary determination of value by embodied labour is 'modified'. We will hereafter examine the concrete contents of these 'modifications of value'. Here we quote the three paragraphs in which Ricardo seems to make methodological reflections on the relation between the first half and the latter half of chapter one. These paragraphs come just after the definition of fixed capital and circulating capital given at the beginning of section four.

> If men employed no machinery in production but labour only, and were [sic] all the same length of time before they brought their commodities to market, the exchangeable value of their goods would be precisely in proportion to the quantity of labour employed.
>
> If they employed fixed capital of the same value and of the same durability, then, too, the value of the commodities produced would be the same, and they would vary with the greater or less quantity of labour employed on their production.
>
> But although commodities produced under similar circumstances, would not vary with respect to each other, from any causes but an addition or diminution of the quantity of labour necessary to produce one or other of them, yet compared with others not produced with the same proportionate quantity of fixed capital, they would vary from the other cause also which I have before mentioned, namely, a rise in the value of labour, although neither more nor less labour were employed in the production of either of them.
>
> (I/32–33)

These paragraphs precede the explanation of the 'modifications' of the determination of value by embodied labour, an explanation Ricardo gives concretely using numerical examples. He clarifies here concisely the theoretical framework set in section one, section three, and sections four and five, and thus the method of development Ricardo follows in his theory of value. Let us say in advance that the first paragraph explains the theoretical framework of section one, the second that of section three, and the third that of sections four and five, and that Ricardo presupposes the capitalist relations and the general rate of profits in all these paragraphs. That is, the general profits were already presupposed from the (pure) embodied labour theory of value of section one, where a model was adopted apparently similar to simple commodity production with independent producers working with their bare hands. Only the theoretical framework specific to this stage of theoretical development neutralised this general profit and made it invisible. Having confirmed these points, let us examine the text paragraph by paragraph.

The presupposition of the first paragraph is that only circulating capital is employed in all the branches of production and the time which elapses until commodities are brought to market is also the same everywhere. It is a presupposition of capitalist relations without use of any means of production, or any raw material. One could not regard such relations as really existing. At all events, values of all the commodities 'would be precisely in proportion to the quantity of labour employed'. Here the totality of capital is spent for the payment of wages. Consequently, the amount of capital directly expresses the quantity of labour employed (number of workers multiplied by the number of working days). And the quantity of labour employed is in direct proportion to the quantity of labour bestowed and embodied, the working day being a given and constant length. And also, the value is supposed to be proportional to this quantity of embodied labour. From all of this, the following equations are obtained. Ratio of embodied labour = ratio of employed labour = ratio of amount of capital invested = ratio of amount of values. We will see below the importance of these equations. We have said that the profits at a general rate are already implicitly presupposed in the first paragraph quoted above expressing the theoretical framework of section one. The ground for this is as follows. The two conditions which allow the equations above to hold are that the whole of the capital consists of circulating capital, and that this circulating capital has the same durability in all the branches of production. These conditions mean that the general profits are already implicitly presupposed, which is in proportion to the two factors, i.e., the quantity of invested capital and the time elapsing between the investment and recovery. But, since the part which makes up these general profits is in the same proportion for the capital of every branch, these general profits are compensated and disappear from the surface on the level of the relative ratios of the values of the commodities. This is why the equations above hold without taking into account profits, and profits do not intervene in the argument of section one in spite of being *de facto* presupposed.

Let us pass on to examine the second paragraph. The use of fixed capital is explicitly introduced here, but it is supposed to be of the same value, of the same durability in all branches. These are the presuppositions that were made *de facto* in section three. In this case also, the relative values of each commodity are given only by the 'quantity of labour employed on their production' and therefore the equations above hold. The same reason mentioned concerning circulating capital of the same durability also explains why the conditions added here again do not create an obstacle for these equations to hold. The use of fixed capital does not have any influence on the relation between the first term and the second term of the equations, so that the first equal sign remains valid. The fixed capital occupying the same proportion in all branches, the relations between the sums of invested capital expresses directly the relations between those of circulating capital. The intervention of fixed capital does not at all change the relation between the second term and the third term of equations, therefore the second equal sign remains valid too. The validity of the third equal sign can be justified as follows. From now on part of the value of fixed capital will be transferred to the produced value and will reappear in it. According to the presupposition of the second paragraph, the part of the produced value coming from the fixed capital for each period of production is equal to the value of the fixed capital ÷ durability × (1 + general rate of profits), this part occupies the same proportion in the sum of the produced value. It follows that the ratios of the values of commodities between the branches remain the same as if the fixed capital were not used. The use of fixed capital presupposed in the second paragraph does not change the values of the third term and the fourth term. Therefore, the third equal sign remains valid. Here also, as in the first paragraph, the general rate of the profits is presupposed.

It is for the first time in the third paragraph that differences in the conditions of production are introduced as an object of examination into each branch which operates using fixed capital. Not the relative values of the commodities of all the branches, but only those of the commodities which satisfy the requirements given in the two preceding paragraphs are determined only by 'the quantity of labour necessary to produce one or other of them'. With regard to the commodities between which these conditions are not satisfied (this is rather the general case), 'the relative value of commodities was regulated by two causes instead of by one'[15]. These two causes are 'labour employed in the production' and 'value of labour' (value of real wages). This third paragraph describes the theoretical framework of sections four and five, relating to the problems of 'modifications of value'. Since here the proportion of fixed capital and its durability is admitted to vary between branches, the second and third equal signs of the equations given above do not hold any more. These equations hold only in particular cases.

As examination above of the three paragraphs of section four show, the passage from the first half to the latter half of the theory of value of chapter one of *Principles* can be interpreted as the process of the setting of a restrictive hypothesis and the releasing of the restriction, the capitalist relations and the general rate of profit being presupposed from the very outset. There is therefore not, between first half and latter half of this chapter, a transition in the object of theory from the primitive state of society to developed capitalism, nor a relation between the 'right' determination of value by embodied labour and the limit or defect of Ricardo's theory. We think on the contrary that the whole of chapter one constitutes the theoretical considerations on the same object according to a coherent method.

Ricardo says in the third paragraph quoted above that value is regulated by the two causes. The regulation of value by the two causes results in the 'modifications of value'.

1.5 'Modifications of value'

To consider the variations of value by 'two causes', Ricardo uses five numerical examples in sections four and five. These examples refer to the difference with regard to the three points: (1) composition of fixed capital and circulating capital; (2) durability of the circulating capital or the time which elapses until commodities are brought to the market; (3) durability of the fixed capital. Ricardo considers that variations of value can be caused by these three factors jointly with the quantity of embodied labour, and he examines each of these factors in each numerical example. Needless to say, actually all these factors operate together. But the variations of value by these three factors independent of the variations in the quantity of embodied labour are reduced in fact to the same problem (presupposition of the general rate of profits).

We will then examine only the second numerical example (I/33–5), in which Ricardo treats successively the two phases distinct from the problem of the 'modifications of value' by supposing a difference in the proportion between fixed capital and circulating capital. The characteristics of what Ricardo calls the 'modifications of value' are expressed in this procedure.

In this numerical example, Ricardo examines, before tackling the problem of the variations of value according to those of wages, the difference in the amount of values produced in two branches which employ just the same quantity of labour, which constitutes the precondition for the examination of the influence of the variations in wages on value.

Let us suppose two branches which produce respectively corn and fabric. The first branch employs, with £5,000 of capital, 100 workers during one year (Ricardo expresses in this way the 'quantity of labour employed in the production'. And, in this case, £5,000 composing the whole of the invested capital, the production must be carried out without means of production or raw material, at least bought on the market as commodities). The annual rate of profits is supposed to be 10%. All the reasoning of Ricardo is based on the premise of the general rate of profits given *a priori* and left unexplained[16]. The value of capital one year after will be £5,000 (1+0.1) = £5,500. This amount is determined by the original amount of capital and the rate of profits, not directly by the quantity of labour carried out by the workers employed by this capital. The capitalist of the first branch continues the production in the second year on the same scale and according to the same method. The sum of the value produced during two years in this branch will be thus £5,500 + £5,500 = £11,000.

On the other hand, in the second branch which produces fabric, the capitalist employs in the first year 100 workers during one year by investing the same quantity of capital (£5,000) to make them manufacture a machine he will employ thereafter for the manufacture of cloth (Ricardo supposes here the manufacturing of a machine only with labour). The value of the machine completed at the end of the first year will be, as in the first branch, £5,000 (1 + 0.1) = £5,500. But, in the second year, the capitalist employs with £5,000 of capital 100 workers, who produce fabric using the machine produced in the previous year (production with machine but without raw material). The amount of investment in the second year will be thus £10,500 (= £5,500 + £5,000). According to the presupposition of the general rate of profit at 10%, the value the capitalist will obtain at the end of the second year will have to be equal to £11,550 .

Ricardo draws from above the conclusion that the equal quantity of labour results in unequal amounts of value if the proportion of fixed capital in the whole of the invested capital varies according to branches. 'Here then are capitalists employing precisely the same quantity of labour annually on the production of their commodities, and yet the goods they produce differ in value on account of the different quantities of fixed capital, or accumulated labour, employed by each respectively' (I/34).

The proposition Ricardo maintained until section three that the amount of value is given only by the quantity of labour bestowed on the production, must thus be 'modified' in the following way: whenever fixed capital intervenes, it becomes an independent element exerting its influence on the determination of value, the amount of value is not always given only by the quantity of bestowed and embodied labour.

Below is a schematic representation of Ricardo's numerical example.

	First year	Second year
Branch I	$A \rightarrow A(1 + r)$	$A \rightarrow A(1 + r)$
Branch II	$A \rightarrow A(1 + r)$	$A + A(1 + r) \rightarrow A(2 + r)(1 + r)$

Where A means the value of the invested capital, r the general rate of profits. The left term of each arrow indicates the input of each year, the right term the output. All the invested capitals are supposed to consist only of circulating capital, except those of branch II in the second year which consist of circulating capital A and fixed capital $A(1 + r)$.

The sum of the value produced during the two years is $2A(1 + r)$ in the first branch and $A(2 + r)(1 + r)$ in the second branch. The difference between these two sums is $Ar(1 + r)$. According to Ricardo, this difference cannot be explained by the quantity of labour spent for the production. According to the determination of the value based on embodied labour, since both branches employ 100 workers with capital A to draw the same quantity of labour from them, they must produce the same amount of value. Where then does this difference of the produced values come from? Ricardo explains it by the existence of the general (or natural) rate of profits. These general profits are grafted on the value of the fixed capital employed in the second branch in the second year. In Ricardo's theory the general rate of profits intervenes in the determination of value, which makes possible his presupposition of the profits grafted on the fixed capital. The profits become thus a constituent part of the value of commodities. It is because of this conception of profits that Ricardo is obliged to recognise the second determining factor of value, which is the difference of the proportions that the fixed capitals occupy in the invested capital (in this case 0% and 50%).

The general profits grafted on the fixed capital are thus a value of unknown origin. For this part of the produced value the determination of value only by the amount of embodied labour is in fact already 'modified', even before Ricardo tackles the 'curious effect'[17] exerted on the prices by wage increases.

Although Ricardo himself makes use of the term 'modify' in the subtitle of section four, we indicated up to now by the 'modifications of value' the fact that the value is no longer determined only by the quantity of embodied labour because of differences in the conditions of production, which corresponds to our interpretation asserting that the determination of value in Ricardo's theory does not suddenly undergo changes of principle in section four. Indeed, Ricardo regarded the determination by embodied labour as the principle of the determination of value, and although he had to recognise the 'modifications' of this principle due to the use of fixed capital, he tended to underline, to try to escape out of the difficulties, the non-gravity of the influence of these 'modifications' (cf. I/36). But Ricardo's theory of value was made by presupposing from the very outset the capitalist relations and the general rate of profits, and if the problems relating to the 'modifications of value' make their appearance not in the first sections but only in section four, it is not because the modifications are brought to the principle of the determination of value here for the first time, but only because these problems were neutralised and made invisible as it were because of the restrictive conditions set in the first sections. These are expressed in the equations given above, **ratio of embodied labour = ratio of employed labour = ratio of amounts of capitals = ratio of amounts of values**, which express the situation of this neutralisation[18].

The first paragraph of section four specifies that the question here is the variations of value caused by those in wages. But, in the first phase of the numerical example on the 'modifications of value' we have just examined, Ricardo shows only that the same quantities of labour produce different amounts of value, without mentioning any variation of value caused by the variations in wages. However, these are two distinct questions, the first being fundamental while the second is only the secondary effect of the first. Consequently, it is completely logical that Ricardo starts by turning his attention to the differences in the conditions of production, disregarding the variation in wages and examining this latter thereafter (it is also why we chose the second numerical example as object of our examination).

Below is the schematic representation of 'curious effect' by which the wage increase does not raise the price in proportion, but on the contrary lowers it (cf. I/35–6).

Branch II	First year	Second year
Before the wage increase	£5,000 → £5,500	£5,500 + £5,000
	= £10,500 → £11,550 = £6,050 + £5,500	
After the wage increase	£5,000 → £5,500	£5,500 + £5,000
	= £10,500 → £11,495 = £5,995 + £5,500	

(£5,995 = £6,050 − 55, 55 = £5,500 × 1/100)

(The rate of increase in the wages being 1%, the rate of the profit falls from 10% to 9%. The product of the first year is used as fixed capital for the production of the second year. Since the value produced at the end of the first year remains the same afterwards as before the wage increase, it should be considered that the number of workers employed (and thus quantity of embodied labour) does not undergo any change. It would follow from this that for some unknown reason the capital of the same amount will continue to employ the same number of workers in spite of the wage increase.)

The effect of the wage increase is not to raise the total value of product but to lower it from £11,550 to £11,495 (the amount of this fall is equal to the product of the value of the fixed capital and the rate of increase in the wages). The part of the capital invested as circulating capital undergoes no influence from the wage increase, and the value of the product resulting from this part remains unchanged after the wage increase, which has effect only on the rate of profits grafted on the value of fixed capital. The value of this part of the product decreases in proportion to the wage increase. It is this reduction in the profits grafted on the fixed capital which is at the origin of the 'curious effect'.

From where comes the value corresponding to the profits added on the fixed capital? And why has the rate of profits grafted on the fixed capital to change in parallel with the rate of profits coming from the labour employed with the circulating capital? All these are quite simply presupposed and left unexplained. If these profits are not explicable by the principle of the determination of value only by embodied labour, this principle itself was already fundamentally 'modified' (modified in fact, though implicitly, from section one). The 'curious effect' is thus only the secondary effect involved by these profits obtained by using fixed capital in variable ratios. Ricardo's second numerical example can be interpreted in this manner.

The degree of fall of the sum of value depends on the proportion which fixed capital occupies in the invested capital. Therefore, a capital made up only of circulating capital (?) is not subject to any influence from a wage increase. On the contrary, the capital consisting totally of fixed capital (?) undergoes the maximum influence (the value of its product falls as much as the wage increases). However, they are the two extreme cases unthinkable even theoretically. In fact, every concrete case is somewhere between these two extreme cases (it is moreover necessary to take account of the raw materials constantly disregarded by Ricardo. In the current context they could be included in 'fixed capital' (!)). The same movement of the level of wages (supposed to be general) has unequal effects on the values of commodities according to the composition of capital. It follows then that the same quantity of labour leads to values of unequal amounts, and that the values of commodities can undergo variations only because of variation in the wages without change in the quantities of labour spent on their production.

Ricardo says the same, making use of the term 'relative value'. The following passage is also the synthesis of the 'modifications of value' in the second numerical example:

> The degree of alteration in the relative value of goods, on account of a rise or fall of labour, would depend on the proportion which the fixed capital bore to the whole capital employed. All commodities which are produced by very durable machinery, or in very valuable buildings, or which require a great length of time before they can be brought to market, would fall in

> relative value, while all those which were chiefly produced by labour, or which would be speedily brought to market would rise in relative value. (I/35)

That is, a part of the value of commodities produced exactly with the same quantity of labour will depend on conditions of production other than labour, and this part of value will move inversely to the alteration in the level of wages according to the proportion of fixed capital. The same movement of wages (assumed to be general) will give rise to different changes in the value of commodities in different branches of production. This is expressed in the above quotation as variations in relative values, i.e., exchange rates between commodities. The value is here understood predominantly as relative. Originally, in the 'formulation of the determination of value by expended labour in its purest form' stated in the subtitle of section one and in this section itself at the beginning of *Principles*, the value was defined as 'the value of a commodity, or the quantity of any other commodity for which it will exchanged' (I/11) and it was regulated by 'the rule which determines how much of one [commodity] shall be given in exchange of another' (I/12). We see in the above quotation from section four only a more concrete form of the same understanding of value with the introduction into the theoretical model of concrete conditions of capitalist relations. Therefore, it may be roughly said that, at least in the theory of value in *Principles*, value is understood as relative.

1.6 Fundamental character of Ricardo's theory of value

We will draw up, in conclusion, the balance sheet of our examinations up to now on the fundamental character of the theory of value of chapter one of *Principles* in referring to the last paragraph of section six.

In sections four and five Ricardo introduces differences in the conditions of production to advance that the relative values as the rates of exchange of commodities are not given only by the quantities of labour employed for their production. And in section six, by taking account of these circumstances, he makes clear the theoretical difficulties in presupposing an 'invariable measure of value' capable of confirming unequivocally the 'real values' of all the commodities. In the last paragraph of this section, he once again disregards differences in the conditions of production between the branches, just as he had done in the first three sections, and summarises his theory of the determination of relative values of commodities solely by the quantities of labour employed for their production. One can thus consider that this paragraph summarises in its 'pure' form the determination of value by the 'quantity of labour necessary to produce commodities', by disregarding completely the influence of the variations of wages on the relative values (subject of sections four and five) which would be '6% or 7%' at most[19] and which would never exceed this threshold (I/36). Ricardo intended to settle the problems of the 'modifications of value' and devoted many pages to examining them, nevertheless he had to take the attitude of tergiversating and said that in the last analysis the variations of value caused by differences in the conditions of production, independent of the quantities of labour, are only tiny and that, roughly speaking, the univocal determination of value still remains valid. One can thus consider that rather the theoretical model disregarding this 'trifling influence' can clearly express the essentials of Ricardo's theory. Below is the text of the paragraph put at the end of section six.

> I have not said, because one commodity has so much labour bestowed upon it as will cost 1,000 *l.* and another so much as will cost 2,000 *l.* that therefore one would be of the value 1,000 *l.* and the other of the value of 2,000 *l.* but I have said that their value will be to each other as two to one, and that in those proportions they will be exchanged. It is of no importance to the truth of this doctrine, whether one of these commodities sells for 1,100 *l.* and the other for 2,200 *l.* or one for 1,500 *l.* and the other for 3,000 *l.* into that question I do not at present enquire; I affirm only, that their relative values will be governed by the relative quantities of labour bestowed on their production.
>
> (I/46–7)

In the note added at the end of this paragraph, Ricardo quotes comments on his theory made by Malthus and replies to him as follows: 'Mr. Malthus appears to think that it is a part of my doctrine, that the cost and value of a thing should be the same; it is, if he means by cost, "cost of production" including profits' (I/47)[20].

This text summarises clearly the fundamental character of the theory of embodied labour value such as is conceived by Ricardo. We have repeated that his theory of value always presupposes the capitalist relations of production and general profits. In the text quoted above too, this presupposition is maintained. The value is said to be determined by the quantity of bestowed and embodied labour. What is used here as a unit to express the quantity of labour, is not a unit of time during which the workers work in the production process (to be expressed as a continuous variable), but the cost necessary to employ these workers (or rather this 'labour', according to the expression of Ricardo) in other words the amount of circulating capital. The wages paid per worker per day being given, the amount of wages (which directly expresses the product of the number of workers employed and the number of the days of employment) is worth for Ricardo the index of the quantity of labour spent by the workers. It is because employed labour is everywhere homogeneous in Ricardo's theory, and that one working day is of a given and fixed length (the unit of the quantity of embodied labour is thus a working day). In this way, the cost for the employer of workers and the quantity of labour spent keep always a given relation between them, and one of them can express the relative quantity of the other. But for Ricardo they do not have the same weight. It is only the cost spent by the capitalist which is significant for him (capitalist and Ricardo also). And the quantity of embodied labour can have significance only in relation to this cost. That is, the theory of value of Ricardo is not of the nature of a bird's eye view observation of the capitalist economy, but it is constructed from the point of view of capitalists organising production by investing costs in view of obtaining profits. It can in this sense be characterised as a bourgeois theory.

Ricardo doesn't say in the text quoted above that the cost determines value so that the amount of cost spent in the form of wages becomes directly that of the value of the produced commodities, but he says that the relative value is fixed at a value somewhere higher than and proportional to the cost. It is because he thinks that the general profit and the value of fixed capital (which is supposed to keep everywhere the same relation to the circulating capital and to have everywhere the same durability) are to be added to the wage cost at the same rate in all the branches. However, since the added part remains always in the same proportion to the wage cost, the relative values of the commodities are given as ratio of the amounts of the invested capital for their production = ratio of the employed labour (number of workers multiplied by the number of working days) = ratio of embodied labour. This is to restore the equations given on page 20. Why do these equations become valid here again? Of course, because the theoretical framework of the determination of value has returned here to that of the first three sections of chapter one. That these equations hold means that the value of commodities is determined by the addition of the quantity of invested capital and general profits everywhere at a same rate. And, as Ricardo recognises without ambiguity when responding to Malthus in the text referred to above, if the sum of invested capital and general profits can be called the 'cost of production', the value is determined by the cost of production. This is the simplest form which is brought back to the determination of value by 'labour necessary for the production' in capitalist relations. The last sentence of section six of chapter one of *Principles* identifies the determination of value by the cost of production advanced in this paragraph with the determination of value by the 'relative quantities of labour bestowed on their production'[21].

By the way, the cost of production in Ricardo's theory, while being the determining factor of value, includes in it the general profits as a component part, so that this determination of value does not imply any interlocking between the cost of production (in particular the wages as its important item) and the value of a commodity. In other words, even if a rise in wages augments the invested capital (assumed to be made up solely of circulating capital) as one element of the cost of production, the cost of production itself will not alter because the part corresponding to the profits will decrease as much as the increase of invested capital as far as the number of workers employed does not change. This applies only to the increase in the amount of invested capital taking place with a rise in wages, but as far as the wages remain constant, this increase in capital investment means as much increase in the cost of production (i.e., rise in value). Therefore, Ricardo's theory of cost of production, while taking the latter for the factor determining value, is of a different type from that of Smith comparing the magnitude of value with the cost and the profits conformable to it. However, with regard to the fixed capital or to the total capital made up of both circulating and fixed parts, we can find in Ricardo's theory a certain remnant of Smith's conception of profits (as a category of income accruing naturally to the advanced factors of production). And, as we have already seen in detail, this view of Ricardo on profits is the fundamental reason at the origin of complicated problems in his theory of value. However, unlike Smith, Ricardo does not add profits at a 'natural' rate to the part of fixed capital without giving any account, instead he substitutes for it a rate of profits to be grafted on the part of circulating capital, for which he tries somehow to give explanation. This allowed him to avoid admitting the movement of prices in parallel with wages and hence the price rise arising with a wage rise. But, with regard to fixed capital, he left totally unexplained the reason why profits are to be added at the same rate as the profits to be grafted on the circulating capital, why the rate of profits moves in parallel for both of these parts of capital, and the provenance of the profits for the fixed capital which does not employ any labour. In this way, Ricardo's cost theory, while claiming an inverse relationship between wages and profits and negating correlatively with this claim the parallel movement of wages and prices, still shares the traditional way of thinking of the classical political economy since Smith[22]. Accordingly, he assumes without any explanation that the advanced factors of production can naturally require and obtain a certain amount of revenue to be integrated into value as its component part.

Notes

1 To the best of our knowledge, Ricardo's theory of value has been interpreted in most cases as a theory of value determined by the labour incorporated in commodities, beginning from his contemporaries like Malthus (1820, p. 261), J. Mill (1821, p. 59), McCulloch (1825a, p. 71), Torrens (1821, p. vi) via Marx (2010, p. 389), Jevons (1965 [1871], p. 165) and Marshall (1920, p. 816) until recent researchers (for example, Peach (1993), p. 160, 170). In the Japanese literature on Ricardo's economic thought carried on since the interwar period, his theory of value has also been seen for the most part and for a long time as a theory of labour value. Sato, S. (2013) presents the related Japanese researches after the War. On the other hand, Cassels (1935) advanced nearly a century ago an interpretation of Ricardo's theory of value, similar to ours, on a detailed reading of chapter one of *Principles*.

2 Cf. Peach (1993), where is used many times the term ' "pure" labour theory'. For the debates about this book of Peach, cf. also Kurz (1994), Kurz and Mongiovi (2002), Peach (2002).

3 'The value of a commodity, or the quantity of any other commodity for which it will exchange, depends on the relative quantity of labour which is necessary for its production, and not on the greater or less compensation which is paid for that labour' (I/11).

4 Smith (1976), p. 65.

5 Sraffa quotes in his note in the first paragraph of section three the text of Ricardo which had made up the first three paragraphs of the first and second editions and which was eliminated from the third edition. In reading this eliminated text, it becomes clear that the aim of section three and the following sections of the third edition was to examine the influence of the accumulation of capital on the determination of value, and that of chapter two related to the appropriation of land. This is why, in the theory of distribution of *Principles* which starts from chapter two, Ricardo takes up the rent, income derived from profits, in advance of the wages and the profits, which are 'fundamental' incomes. The ground rent, income derived from the profits, must be logically preceded by the profits as it is the case in Smith. The elimination of these paragraphs in the third edition could be explained by the fact that the structure of the theoretical development conceived originally as critique of Smith was transformed into a positive development of the theory of Ricardo himself and then he took corresponding measures of change. However, in spite of this change (elimination of a part of text), the fact remains that the theoretical construction of the third edition had been originally motivated by the critique of Smith. This critique is not only what justifies the development of the first section, but it is indeed the leitmotif of the whole of the theory of value of Ricardo including his theory of rent. In this sense, it would be necessary to include the theory of rent as an indispensable constituent part in his theory of value. Hadori had indicated the essential significance of the theory of rent for the theory of value of Ricardo in Hadori (1972). Cf. sec. 5 in chapter 5 'Chapter composition in the *Principles* and the theory of rent'.

6 On the change of contents of 'early stages of society' of Ricardo, see chapter 4 "The theory of value and the early stages of society – on the passages modified in the third edition of the *Principles*," in Hadori (1982).

7 'Almost exclusively' was 'solely' in the first and second editions. This change of letter, with the insertion of 'the almost exclusively' in the sentence concerning the determination of value put at the beginning of section two of the third edition, was often taken for the proof of loss of conviction of Ricardo, who was exposed to various criticisms after the publication of the first edition. In opposition to this point of view Hadori advances an interesting interpretation which assigns the cause of this change to the fact that Ricardo brought, in the third edition, modifications to his presupposition on the primitive state of the society and for this reason he could not advance his determination of value any more in completely disregarding 'modifications of value', problems he was going to treat later on in sections four and five. See Hadori (1982), chapter four.

8 As we can see in the quoted text, Ricardo uses, after the example of Smith, hunting and fishing as two examples of branches of production to be compared, which can suggest a primitive stage of the technique of production at a primitive stage of society. And these branches as examples remain the same until the beginning of section four. While using these examples, Ricardo speaks about something other than a lower stage of the level of technique and productivity. He argues about the structure of the production and distribution of commodities under the conditions of capitalist relations. In regard to this point, a branch of production with developed equipment of its production is not at all distinguished from hunting or fishing. It is in this sense that Ricardo says just after the passage quoted above, that 'if we look to a state of society in which greater improvements have been made, and in which

arts and commerce flourish, we shall still find that commodities vary in value conformably with this principle' (I/24).

9 In the second part of Marx (1894), "Conversion of profit into average profit", Marx analyses the mechanism allowing the capital of each branch to obtain profit at an equal rate proportionally to its amount. Question is here about the *average* profit formed by the redistribution and equalisation between the branches through relations of supply and demand on the market of the profits obtained *initially at unequal rates individually by each branch*. The *general* profit of Ricardo is of a different nature from the average profit of Marx. It seems to us that this difference comes from the theoretical framework Ricardo adopts when presupposing the general rate of profits, and from Marx' analysis of the production process of capital (process of exploitation of surplus value proper to Marx (1867), analyses completely absent in Ricardo's theory).

10 More exactly, Ricardo does not take as an object of consideration the part of the fixed capital, when he confirms the non-influence of the distribution on value, because in this case the relation between the fixed capital and the circulating capital is presupposed to be equal in all the branches. Therefore, it becomes possible to presuppose the non-influence of the existence of the part of the fixed capital on the relative value produced in each branch. Following is the text which gives evidence to such a presupposition.

> Suppose that in the early stages of society, the bows and arrows of the hunter were of equal value, and of equal duration, with the canoe and implements of the fisherman, both being the produce of the same quantity of labour. Under such circumstances the value of the deer, the produce of the hunter's day's labour, would be exactly equal to the value of the fish, the produce of the fisherman's day's labour. The comparative value of the fish and the game, would be entirely regulated by the quantity of labour realised in each; whatever might be the quantity of production, or however high or low general wages or profits might be.
> (I/26)

11 Marx (1867), pp. 205–6.

12 Cf. Torrens1821, p. vi., Hollander1904, p. 476, also Note 2 above.

13 See Marx' analysis on the theoretical structure of chapter 1 of Ricardo's *Principles* in Marx (1861–3), pp. 393–4.

14 Ricardo had presupposed, in section one, a simple commodity production without relation of classes nor means of production, carried out so to say with bare hands. In section three, he had supposed too rudimentary means of production - simple tools - to be able to consider differences in the conditions of production. Only at the beginning of section four, he introduces as object of his theory the 'fixed capital' (equipment and facilities of production) sufficiently developed so that there can exist differences in their durability. It would then seem to be possible to conclude that Ricardo's theoretical development goes in parallel with the historical process, from the primitive state to developed capitalism. Ricardo had actually developed the text of the first and second editions of *Principles* so as to allow such an interpretation. But on taking account of the text of the third edition and the changes brought to this text as a whole, it seems that he tends to suppose from the very outset of chapter one the developed capitalist relations.

15 Ricardo's letter to McCulloch of 13 June 1820, VIII/194.

16 The general rate of profit at 10% could be interpreted as meaning that the capital can usually employ a quantity of labour which is 10% larger than that which is contained in itself. But this interpretation applies at most to the circulating capital allotted to the employment of workers, but absolutely not to the fixed capital which makes its appearance in the second year in the second branch.

17 Ricardo's letter to J. Mill of 14 October 1816, VII/82.

18 Then, value may have been viewed by Ricardo from the beginning as something relative, not existing without mutual relations among commodities. The fact that he often uses the term 'relative value' in chapter one of *Principles* seems to express how he viewed the value of commodities. However, as S. Bailey had pointed out early (cf. [Bailey] (1825), pp. 238–9), Ricardo's terminology concerning value is considerably confused, it may be dangerous to make a hasty judgement based on his use of terms.

19 Cf. Stigler (1958). According to Gilbert Faccarello ('Labour Theory of Value' in Kurz and Salvadori (2015), p. 252), Ricardo could not arrive at a definitive solution of these problems up till the end of his life.

20 'the theory of value which Ricardo quite evidently regarded as axiomatic was an expense of production theory in which profits are included among the necessary costs' (Cassels (1935), pp. 518–9).

21 Ricardo, in his 'Notes on Malthus' (written from July to November 1820), after having expressed an idea similar to that of the text quoted above in response to Malthus who reproaches him for confusing the cost with the value, makes clear with concision what he understands by the cost for the capitalist, the labour necessary for the production, the labour embodied in the commodities and the relative value of commodities, as follows (the text quoted above from *Principles* seems to be the reproduction of these sentences. Cf. I/47, editor's notes 3). 'It [commodity produced with the cost of £1,000 spent for the employment of workers] will sell for the same as another commodity the labour on which also cost £1,000; that is to say, that commodities will be valuable in proportion to the quantity of labour expended on them' (II/34). 'The real value of a commodity I think means the same thing as its cost of production, and the relative cost of production of two commodities is nearly in proportion to the quantity of labour from first to last respectively bestowed upon them' (II/35). All these sentences are written from the standpoint of capitalist who invests capital as cost and sells produced commodities. Ricardo says that the relative value of commodities (ratio of exchange, measured in monetary term) is in proportion to bestowed (expended) labour. If the terms 'labour', 'expended' are put in the context of the sentences quoted above, the 'labour' means first of all the wages paid to the workers and the 'quantity of labour' the amount of the wage cost, and 'expended' only relates to the 'expense' of this cost by the capitalist. But, as we have seen in detail up to now, under particular conditions 'expended labour' can also have the meaning of 'quantity of labour spent by the workers to produce commodities'. This is shown in the last sentence quoted above which affirms that the value and the cost and the quantity of labour spent (bestowed) are proportional one to another, with only one restrictive clause concerning the quantity of labour spent which would be 'nearly in proportion to' the two other terms. It is because the quantity of labour spent is not exactly in proportion to the cost and value whenever there are differences in the conditions of production between branches of production, and because this disproportionality is negligible, however. This coincides with the theoretical structure of Ricardo's theory of value.

22 Torrens, who deployed a robust objection against Ricardo's theory of value, opposed the determination of value by endowed labour, arguing that the value of a commodity is equal to the amount of capital used for its production plus profits at a given general rate, therefore that value is determined by the amount of invested capital. But the way of thinking at the basis of this objection may not always be entirely heterogenous with that of Ricardo. Cf. [Torrens] (1818).

2 A characterisation of Ricardo's theory of value

2.1 Foreword

The present chapter aims to clarify one step further our point of view on the character of Ricardo's theory of value presented in the previous chapter, by taking into account his discussions with contemporary economists (Torrens and McCulloch in particular), recorded in his letters and manuscripts. The present chapter aims at reinforcing, under other angles of view and with other points of reference, our interpretation of Ricardo's theory of value.

In addition to the two above mentioned economists, Ricardo had, during his activities as an economist, multiple discussions with Malthus and J. Mill, and took much advantage of these discussions to develop his own points of view, so much so that it would have been impossible for him to conceive and write *Principles* without these discussions. However, our aim here is to highlight the character of his theory of value, by examining his debates, on the one hand with Torrens, who criticises Ricardo's theory (determination of the value of commodities by the sum of the present labour directly employed to produce them and of the past labour indirectly employed for its production) by proposing his own theory ('capital theory of value', in place of 'labour theory of value'), and on the other hand with McCulloch who follows, on the contrary, the labour theory of value by extending in a particular way the notion of labour.

Ricardo's long discussions with Malthus do not seem to contain points relating directly to our purpose. In contrast to the great role of J. Mill as 'school master' in Ricardo's writing of *Principles*, there are only very few substantial theoretical discussions in the letters exchanged between them, J. Mill doing practically nothing but approving of the theory of his 'student'.

As the theories of Torrens and McCulloch do not belong to the subject of this chapter, we will refer to them only insofar as is necessary to study the character of Ricardo's theory.

Torrens, known as an economist much earlier than Ricardo by publishing several economic works from the very beginning of the nineteenth century[1], began debates with Ricardo on the economic theory only in 1818, after the publication of the first edition of *Principles*. Direct discussions between them

DOI: 10.4324/9781003498322-3

and a 'memorandum on them' by Torrens (nonextant) led Ricardo to write a manuscript known as 'fragments on Torrens' (hereafter 'fragments' for short, IV/309–18) in November 1818. In his letter to McCulloch of 24 November 1818, almost at the same time as he was writing 'fragments' and right after the preparatory work for the second edition of *Principles*, Ricardo mentioned for the first time Torrens' criticisms and informed McCulloch of the sentences added in order to answer Torrens in the second edition[2]. In this letter he says: 'Major Torrens has written an article in the *Edinburgh Magazine* on my observations on value. I have not yet seen it, but expect to have it here in a few days' (VII/338). He is speaking here about Torrens (1818). That is, the two writings given above as final results written by each one of them are all that is left of the debates between them in 1818 until today in the written form[3]. In his writings after this time in connection with the 'modifications' of value, Ricardo seems always to be conscious of Torrens' criticism, but the direct debates between them ends here, except for only one 'continuation' by Torrens in chapter one of Torrens (1821), 'Wealth, Value, Price', to which Ricardo reacts only two years after in his last manuscript, '[Absolute Value and Exchangeable Value]' (IV/374–95). Ricardo thus ended his life without informing anybody of his reactions to the criticisms of his theory contained in Torrens (1821), in spite of expectations expressed by some of his friends (perhaps also by Torrens himself). One can say that the relation between Ricardo and Torrens concerning the theory of value expires at this point. We will concentrate in the following pages on the reactions of Ricardo to Torrens' criticisms. The latter's theory will be examined only insofar as is necessary for this purpose.

In addition, McCulloch published, during the three years between the publication of the first edition of *Principles* and that of the third, several articles to introduce or defend Ricardo's theory, in particular in the review in *The Scotsman* of which he was the editor, but these publications do not go beyond faithful presentation made by a faithful disciple, unworthy of special examinations. Theoretical dissensions between them would start to appear after the publication of the third edition of *Principles*. But it is only after the death of his 'Master', in McCulloch (1825b), that he develops his own theory. The intense discussions between them on the theory of value were pursued and opened a new phase over about two months until August 1823. Today, the letters addressed to Ricardo at that time are the only documents which can serve to inform us of the points of view expressed by McCulloch on this subject. Thus, we will refer exclusively to their letters included in Ricardo (Ricardo (1951–2), IX).

2.2 Origin of the problem

2.2.1 'Curious effect' and 'modifications of value' in the first edition of Principles

Following the strong advice of J. Mill, Ricardo began to write a systematic work in late 1816, and before long he became aware of the existence of a difficult and serious problem in his theory of value, put at the beginning as the basic theory to consider the problems of distribution. He wanted to construct a theory of distribution and of its evolution in the course of capital accumulation, founded on the proposition according to which the movement of wages does not have any influence on the value of commodities, determined exclusively by the 'difficulty of production' – quantity of labour necessary to produce them – in opposition to Smith's theory. In so doing, he had to recognise the 'curious effect'[4] of the rise of wages, which does not raise the value of commodities in parallel, but on the contrary lowers it. He had many difficulties in the theoretical treatment of this point, which was the main cause of the delay in his writing of *Principles*[5] (he talks about this circumstance in his letters to J. Mill and McCulloch written between December 1815 and October 1816). This 'curious effect', although in a direction contrary to the parallel movement of wages and prices of Smith, was likely to darken the prospect of showing convincingly the neutrality of wage movement with regard to value. Ricardo, honest man of theory, could not neglect taking account of it[6], and he had to try many times to reconcile it in one way or another with his fundamental proposition as indicated above. The 'modifications of value' contained in the first edition of *Principles* is the result of this hard effort.

We will examine hereafter numerical examples of the 'modifications of value' in the first edition. Doing this will clear up the character of the difficulties recognised by Ricardo before its publication.

The distinction of the whole of the invested capital between fixed capital and circulating capital is the source of the problem of the 'modifications of value', and this distinction introduces the differences in the conditions of production among the branches of production. The first of these differences concerns the ratio between these two kinds of capital (composition of capital); the second concerns the durability of fixed capital[7]. According to Ricardo, the relative values of the commodities produced in two branches with differences in these two conditions are determined first by the quantities of labour employed respectively for their production, but they are also determined, in addition, by the influence of the rise in wages (i.e., of the fall of profits). He gives explanations on these two kinds of differences successively with concrete numerical examples, which belong (according to the division in sections of the first chapter in the third edition) respectively to the fourth and the fifth section.

In the first example (I/56–8), Ricardo supposes two branches (hunting and fishing), both of which employ an equal sum of capital, £200, but of different composition, to show variations of the relative value of the commodities of these two branches with the rise of wages and the corresponding fall in profit, quantities of labour employed for their production being supposed to remain unchanged. The initial rate of profit is 10%, the durability of the fixed capital is ten years, that of the circulating capital one year. The compositions of the invested capital in each branch and the compositions of the values produced one year after will then be as follows (all the figures are in £):

hunting branch: 150 + 50 → 24,4 + 55 = 79,4

fishing branch: 50 + 150 → 8,135 + 165 = 173,135

The value of the parts obtained one year after as results of the fixed capital in each branch is estimated respectively at 24,4 and 8,135, which results from the calculation of the amount of fixed capital recovered each year following the calculation of annuities[8] adopted in the first and second editions. By adding to these figures respectively 55 and 165, resulting from the circulating capital, equal to the amount of invested capital added with 10% of profits, we obtain the sums of values produced during the first year, which are extremely different: 79,4 and 173,135. However, in each branch there must remain the parts of the fixed capital (150 and 50 respectively) still to be amortised during the following nine years. The difference between the two produced values comes largely from the difference existing in these parts. Insofar as considering this numerical example, we cannot know the theoretical treatment Ricardo would make of these parts.

Let us suppose here a rise in the wages of 6%. Then the amount of the circulating capital necessary to continue to employ the same number of workers would rise respectively from 50 to 53, and from 150 to 159, and the rate of profit would fall correlatively from 10% to 4%. The reason why the figure of 4% is obtained here is not explicit, but this figure is perhaps not the result of a hasty miscalculation of 10 – 6 = 4 made by Ricardo on the ground of the 'opposite relation between wages and profit'. Since he insists on the proposition that value remains invariable in spite of changes of wages when a constant quantity of labour is employed for production, we must think that the part of the value of products resulting from the circulating capital remains the same as before the rise of wages, i.e., 55 and 165. It would then be probable that he obtained the figure of 4 by rounding 3,7735... obtained by the division 165 ÷ 159 = 1,037735... (= 55 ÷ 53) (the rates of profit used by Ricardo in his text are all expressed in whole numbers). If such an interpretation is right, the amounts of the values resulting from circulating capital after the rise in wages (55,12 and 165,36) can be explained by the rate of profit rounded during its calculation, and the small increment (0,12 and 0,36) can be regarded as being void of any theoretical meaning (i.e., this increment does not mean change – rise – caused by the rise of wages in the amount of value), and one can thus estimate that there is no substantial change in values of 55 and 165. Consequently, the calculation of the values after the rise of 6% in the level of wages will be as follows:

hunting branch: 150 + 50 → 150 + 53(= 203) → 18,49 + 55,12 = 73,61

fishing branch: 50 + 150 → 50 + 159(= 209) → 6,613 + 165,36 = 171,523

relative value at the rate of profit of 10% 79,4: 173,135 ≒ 100: 218

at the rate of profit of 4% 73,61: 171,523 ≒ 100: 233

As indicated above, the value of each commodity falls with the fall of the rate of profit caused by the rise of wages (effect of a diminution of profit added to the fixed capital), but it is the commodity produced in the branch with a larger proportion of fixed capital which falls in its relative value. According to this numerical example in the first edition, any rise of wages causes a fall of the sum of value produced proportionally to the share the fixed capital occupies.

In the second numerical example (ibid., p. 58–60) it is shown that the difference in the durability of fixed capital is a factor causing the changes of value with the rise in wages. However, this example which, according to Ricardo, would call into question the difference in the durability of fixed capital, has as its true purpose a comparison of two branches respectively using only fixed capital or only circulating capital. In other words, circulating capital is regarded here as a kind of fixed capital of short durability, and the distinction between two capitals, which was relative from the outset and void of a clear line of demarcation, is in fact deconstructed here. Any capital becomes fixed capital (since the question is about the difference in the durability of fixed capital) and at the same time the fixed capital loses its opposition to the circulating capital and ceases to be fixed capital. There remains only one criterion to compare and distinguish any capital: durability (time necessary to recover). Hereafter we always use the terms fixed capital and circulating capital according to the terminology of Ricardo in the first edition, but substantially the first means only a capital with 100 years of durability, the second a capital with one year of durability.

Ricardo supposes the two following branches here: one branch uses an engine with a value of £20,000 and with 100 years of durability without using any circulating capital (wage labour and raw materials, supposedly a completely automatic production). This engine continues for 100 years to produce each year a certain quantity of commodities. With the rate of profit of 10%, the annually produced value is £2,000.1458333 (this is equal to the sum one receives each year for 100 years with a government bond of the current value of £20,000). Here also, the procedure of the calculation of annuity is applied. Moreover, the total sum that this engine brings to its owner during the total 100 years of its durability is £2,000.1458333 × 100 which is roughly £200,000. This sum is approximately ten times superior to that of the invested capital. As in the first numerical example, Ricardo himself does not make such a calculation. But this calculation shows that the fixed capital, while employing no labour at all, brings to its owner a very great value proportionally to the time passed until its recovery – approximately 1,6 times superior in the first case, approximately ten times superior in the second – thanks to the fact that time intervenes for its recovery. And in fact, here exists a problem much more serious than that of which Ricardo was aware and which he tackled, i.e., the problem of the 'modifications of value' caused by changes in wages). In the other branch, the invested capital is £20,000, i.e., the same amount, but this capital consists only of circulating capital. Since it is circulating capital, it is realised each year as whole products, and with the rate of profit of 10%, the annual value of the products will be £22,000.

Now suppose a rise in wages of 4.76%, which makes a capital of £20,952 necessary instead of £20,000 to continue to employ the same quantity of labour in this branch exclusively using circulating capital. The quantity of labour remaining the same, the value of the products must also remain £22,000. The rate of profit will then be £22,000 – £20,952/£20,952 = £1,048/ 20,952 = 0.050019019 ≒ 5% (if the amount of the rise of wages is 952, a fraction, it is because Ricardo handled the figure so as to lower the initial rate of profit of 10% to 5%, i.e., by half.).

In the first branch no wages are paid, but in spite of this, the rate of profit must drop also to 5% on the assumption of competition allowing every capital the free movement between branches. Then, always adopting the procedure of the calculation of annuity as it was the case when the rate of profit was 10%, the annually produced value will be £1,007.6833333 (the sum one receives each year during 100 years with a government bond of the current value of £20,000 when the rate of profit is 5%). So, it is a fall of about 50%. With a rise in wages, the value remains unchanged in the branch using only circulating capital[9], while the value of the goods produced only with fixed capital undergoes a sharp fall. Moreover, if the durability of the engine is 10 years instead of 100 years, in the same branch using only fixed capital, the annual value of the commodities will be £3,254 when the rate of profit is 10%, but it will be £2,590 when it is 5%. This is a fall of about 20%. Thus, with the shortening of the durability of fixed capital, the effect of the rise in wages to lower the value diminishes, and the fixed capital resembles more and more the circulating capital. 'In proportion as this machine were less durable, prices would be less affected by the fall of profit, and the rise of wages' (I/60).

We have examined hitherto the two numerical examples of the 'modifications of value' in the first edition[10]. In both cases, the reason Ricardo gives to explain the 'modifications' – changes in the values of the products caused by the rise or fall in wages – is the existence of fixed capital, or more exactly, the existence of differences in time necessary to recover various parts of invested capital (durability). Proportionally to the durability of capital, and the share the fixed capital occupies with great durability, with the rise in wages the value of the products of this capital does not rise, but on the contrary undergoes a relative fall, although the quantity of labour employed for the production remains unchanged (both of the two numerical examples were made up so as not to change the quantity of labour). This 'curious effect' that Ricardo was faced with during his writing of *Principles* does not in fact have its origin in the existence itself of the fixed capital, but rather is due to the diminution of profit added to the fixed capital correlative to the rise in wages. Consequently, the level of this 'effect' is in proportion to the amount of profit added to the fixed capital. The explanation of Ricardo takes only one aspect, changes of prices following after the changes of this profit caused by the rise in wages, but the reason for these changes of price to occur is that in advance of these changes very great values are grafted on the fixed capital, requiring long periods for its recovery independently of the labour employed in the production. This last aspect exists, certainly in the explanation of the 'modifications of value' of the first edition, but it is not taken up at all there as problematic.

Ricardo writes that 'it is according to the division of the whole produce of the land and labour of the country, between the three classes of landlords, capitalists, and labourers, that we are to judge of rent, profit, and wages' (I/ 64. See also the sentences at the beginning of the foreword of *Principles*, I/ 5). It is certain that he regards the profit as a part of the value of product, and that according to this concept of profit the value of product is logically precedent to the profit, but on the other hand, he presupposes a general profit at a certain rate dominating all the branches of production from the very outset of Chapter One. And while having as the purpose of his theory the movement of this profit in inverse proportion to that of the wages (because they are the two divided shares of a certain amount), Ricardo does not give any explicit explanation on this profit itself (how it can exist, how the level of its rate is determined). His theoretical development presupposes a general profit uniformly grafted on the whole of the invested capital in proportion to the duration of time of investment. All of his 'modifications of value' are also on this presupposition. Ricardo seems to accept this presupposition as clearly evident. This is the fundamental cause of the difficulties in his theory of value.

2.3 Criticism of Torrens: 'Fragments' on Torrens

In the year after the publication of the edition of *Principles*, Torrens criticises Ricardo's theory of value, but the process of debates between them is not well-known. There is no letter directly exchanged between them (or such is not found yet), and among the notes written by each one of them on this occasion there are some which are dispersed (or are not yet found). In the 'fragments', probably written from November to December 1818 (almost at the same time as his work of revision for the second edition)[11], Ricardo took account of his direct discussions with Torrens ('long conversations on this question, without convincing each other'[12]), as well as of a short note not yet found of Torrens. But Ricardo could not refer to Torrens (1818), of which he says that he had not read yet. Of the documents on their debates at that time, all that are possible to consider today are, on Ricardo's side, the 'fragments', his letters to third persons mentioning these debates[13] and part of the passages revised in the second edition[14], and, on Torrens' side, a part of Ricardo's 'fragments' ((A2) [Torrens on Ricardo], title by Sraffa, IV/314–5) and the article mentioned above. The last respective documents of the two sides show the final results, reached by each of them independently. The debates in 1818 came to an end only in making clearer the positive points of each one of them.

In the middle of (A1) [Ricardo on Torrens] (title by Sraffa, IV/309–13), Ricardo adopts the same theoretical framework as Torrens in (A2). Let us suppose two capitalists having respectively a capital of the same amount[15]. But, the proportion between fixed capital and circulating capital is very different: 10 + 90 for one capitalist and 80 + 20 for the other. (Under Torrens' influence, Ricardo classifies here exceptionally as fixed capital the whole of the capital not used for the payment of wages. But what is really classified as fixed capital in this example, is only the 'flax' used as raw material, which requires the same duration of time for its recovery as the wages as circulating capital. One can thus say that the problem of distinction between fixed capital and circulating capital according to the criterion of the time passed between the investment and recovery, a problem mentioned in the previous section, does not really exist in this example. The only criterion of distinction is whether used for the employment of labour or not.)

To Torrens' conclusion, according to which the values of commodities produced by these two capitals are equal, Ricardo gives his assent in saying that 'I answer yes' (IV/311). The quantities of labour employed in each branch are not the same: 5(10/2) + 90 = 95, 40(80/2) + 20 = 60. However, Ricardo thinks just like Torrens that these products have an equal value, because the same rate of profits is added uniformly to all the parts of each of the two capitals. Ricardo agrees with Torrens, who maintains that given the domination of a general rate of profits and the quantitative equality of the invested capital the amount of the produced values is equal, even if there are quantitative differences in labour employed. But Ricardo tries to justify in his own way the proposition that even the products of different quantities of labour have the same value. 'To which I answer that the proposition in my book requires that they should be of equal value although there be different quantities of labour employed in their production, because in this case the raw material in both manufactures is really fixed capital[16] of equal duration, but of unequal value' (ibid.).

The justification Ricardo advances is thus his arguments on the 'modifications of value' already developed in the first edition, and with which he tries to face the criticism of Torrens. We have noted in the previous section that Ricardo says in the first edition that with the same quantity of labour the value produced in a branch is larger as the proportion the fixed capital bears in the whole of the invested capital becomes larger, and the value of the products of such a branch fall in a larger proportion with the rise in wages and the correlative fall of profits. According to the example of the 'fragments', the fixed capital of the second branch being 'eight times more valuable' (ibid.), the value of its products with a larger share of fixed capital must have a relative value compared to the products of the first branch more than in proportion to the quantity of labour employed in the second branch. Consequently, 95:60 in terms of the quantity of labour becomes 1:1 in terms of relative value, which is the same result as Torrens': the value of commodities is in proportion to the quantity employed not of labour but of capital. That is the explanation Ricardo has given above.

However, the duration of time necessary to recover the raw materials classified here by Ricardo as fixed capital, is the same as that of the wages, which was not the case of the fixed capital such as defined in *Principles*. Moreover, the raw materials were completely lacking within the framework of Ricardo's distinction of the two parts of capital. If they make an appearance by chance here, it is only because he took Torrens' example for the model in his example in the 'fragments'. Ricardo's refutation consists in including the raw materials in the category of fixed capital in order to treat the problem Torrens raises as that which he had already solved in the first edition of *Principles* as a particular case of 'modifications of value'. This explanation is at the price of erasing the essential point in his definition of fixed capital (difference in the time of recovery). The raw materials are neither fixed capital, nor circulating capital which is *de facto* wages. They are unclassifiable within Ricardo's theoretical framework, unless adopting a contradictory expression such as 'circulating capital besides the wages' (it is probably the cause of the distinction of the parts of capital different from that of *Principles*, conceived temporarily by Ricardo. See note 16).

Far from making a valid refutation of the 'capital theory of value' of Torrens, according to which 'it is always the amount of capital, and never the quantity of labour, expended in production, which determines the exchangeable value of commodities'[17], Ricardo cannot but agree with it, while justifying himself with his own basis of arguments.

Ricardo tries then, from his theoretical point of view, to tackle the problem of difference between the quantity of labour and the amount of value. The question is about the difference between the two branches of production in which wage cost and raw material cost are in two different proportions. In such a case, in spite of the quantitative difference of labour employed, commodities of the same value are produced because of this difference in the conditions of production. To be clearer, Ricardo makes use of his following 'strong case' (IV/312).

He always takes as examples two branches of production with extremely different conditions of production.

The capitalist of the first branch manufactures iron by employing five workers for one year. The iron produced in this way one year after will be sold at a price, 'not only for the labour which produced it, but for as much more as the profits on the capital which employed the five days labour' (ibid.). He should have said 'five workers during one year'. Usually, Ricardo uses 'day's labour' as the unit of quantity of labour. He is mistaken here probably because of this habitual use of words.) The 'labour' of Ricardo does not (always) mean the living labour carried out in the direct process of production, but it means the wage cost paid to the workers employed by the capital, in other words the amount of circulating capital[18]. Since the whole of the capital is regarded here as made up of circulating capital, it is in the final analysis the amount of invested capital. The price of iron as product is then equal to the sum of the invested capital and the profits. In addition, these 'profits' are not presented in the form of a ratio between the amount of value used for the employment of workers and what they produce, but it is defined very vaguely and generally 'profit on capital' (naturally to be 'added to the capital' at an unspecified rate), whose source and amount are not the subject of theoretical explanation.

In the second year, the capitalist invests again the proceeds from the product of the first year entirely as circulating capital, to produce once again the same commodities with the same method of production. However, the production is now enlarged by the profits obtained in the previous year, the quantity of labour employed rises from five persons for one year to six for one year. It is an enlargement of 20% equal to the rate of profits, and during the second year the production continues on a scale homothetically widened by 20% under the same conditions in every regard. The same operation is repeated 20 times. It will be possible to express the value of the iron produced at the end of the twentieth year as the quantity of value able to employ for one year $5 \times 1{,}2^{20}$($\div$ 192) workers, according to the method of calculation used initially to express the value of capital.

As for the capitalist of the second branch, he invests the same amount of capital as in the first, and also employs five workers during one year. He makes them cultivate oak trees. They finish their work at the end of one year and their employment finishes at the same time. But, for the growth of the trees and their completion as commodities, it takes an additional 19 years, during which the process of production without intervention of human labour continues. Wood thus available at the end of 20 years without employing any labour, although it is produced only by five workers employed during one year, will be sold at a price equivalent to the value capable of employing during one year $5 \times 1{,}2^{20}$ ($\div$ 192) workers, just like in the branch producing iron, and will bring the same profit to the capitalist of the branch producing wood.

This example shows that the capital of the same amount, whatever the branch of its investment and whatever the quantity of labour it employs there, brings about the same profits during the same time (calculated at a rate made up of annual profits compounded with the number of years of investment), and so produces the same value. Here is a result in striking dissension with the principle of determination of value by the quantity of labour necessary for production. One capitalist employs approximately 192 people, the other only 5, but both will have the same values produced at the end of 20 years[19].

This 'strong case' is literally a 'strong case', which, contrary to Ricardo's intention to counteract Torrens' criticism, ends up in supporting, even more emphatically than the preceding example, the latter's theory of value (the same value produced by the same amount of invested capital for the same period, independently of the quantity of labour employed).

In the last paragraph of the 'fragments' (IV/313), Ricardo reveals still another aspect of the problem by supposing the case in which iron and wood produced in the two respective branches are used as raw materials (which must have been absent from Ricardo's theory!) in other different branches of production. With the same amounts of invested capital in these two branches, and with the same costs to get iron and wood and all the other parts of circulating capital, the values of the two kinds of produced commodities will also have to be the same. However, iron and wood are being produced by two very unequal quantities of labour, and the quantities of labour really employed for the production of these two kinds of goods, which are of the same value on the market, differ in the same degree. The preceding example had as its aim the case of the identity of the values of products in spite of quantitative differences in labour employed in the process of production. Here, the question is about another case which raises problems even more serious for Ricardo: the values of various kinds of goods produced with the same amounts of costs and under the same conditions of production (as regards the composition of capital and durability) must naturally be identical, and yet these values can be produced by labour quantitatively very different because the quantities of labour contained in the raw materials bought at the same price can differ according to the nature of the process of their production[20].

In these 'fragments', Ricardo does nothing but raise the question about how the difference in the conditions of production is the cause of the difference between the quantity of labour and the amount of value, which is only a development of the problem Torrens had raised to him to criticise him. To this Ricardo does nothing but simply repeat his principle. The last sentence of the 'fragments' is: 'This last is Major Torrens case and is in my opinion completely answered by shewing [sic] that in the production of the raw material different quantities of fixed capital were used' (IV/313). He claims, thus, that the problem can be explained completely by the difference of the composition of capital in the preceding process of production. It is only a repetition of the comment added by him to the preceding case. 'They should be of equal value although there be different quantities of labour employed in their production, because in this case the raw material in both manufactures is really fixed capital of equal duration, but of unequal value' (IV/311, i.e., the problem is already solved in *Principles*).

It becomes clear that Ricardo did not seem to have concern for the problem Torrens had raised to him and could not make any convincing refutation of his criticism, in spite of its serious theoretical connotation. But that does not make, in any way, a dissolution of the problem for Ricardo. This problem continues, on the contrary, to obsess him until the last moment of his life.

2.4 'Modifications of value' in the third edition of *Principles*

The third edition of *Principles* has naturally been improved after the second revision. At the beginning of the fourth section of Chapter One, Ricardo makes explicit the very particular assumption on which his development rested until there (revealing the device of his theoretical exposition so to say), before making the distinction of capital into the circulating part and the fixed part[21], and on the basis of this distinction he introduces the difference in the conditions in production. The logical structure of Chapter One is clarified here for the first time[22]. The illustration of the 'modifications of value' by means of concrete numerical examples rests on such a device.

In section four, two numerical examples are used to illustrate how the relative value of the produced commodities changes, correlatively with the movement of wages in branches of industry with different compositions of fixed capital and circulating capital. They are the numerical examples which all are newly introduced during the writing of the text of the third edition, and those which had existed since the first edition are not resumed there any more just as they were (in particular, the paragraphs developing the mode of amortisation of fixed capital and that of its progressive recovery according to the procedure of the calculation of annuity are all deleted). The significance of such an amendment of the numerical examples will also be a subject of our following examinations.

Initially, in the first numerical example[23] (I/33–5) are supposed to be two branches with different conditions of production (indicated below as A and B). Just as for the other examples, the period of production is one year, and the general rate of profit is 10%. In the first year, both branches employ 100 workers with annual wages of £50 for each worker. The capitals of both branches are thus made up only of circulating capital of £5,000. A cultivates corn, B produces machines. At the end of the first year, in A there is corn, in B there are machines. The corn is assumed to be sold as commodities with the value of £5,500 with a profit of 10%, on the other hand the machines remain in the branch to be used in the second year for the production of fabric, the end product of B[24]. During the second year, A repeats the same process as in the first year to produce the same quantity of corn, while B produces fabric by means of the machines produced in the first year, by employing once again 100 workers with an additional capital of £5,000. The total quantity of labour employed respectively in the two branches is 100 persons × 2 years. The sum of value produced in A for two years is simply two times more value produced in the first year, i.e., £5,500 × 2 = £11,000, but this is not the case with B. Here the object of comparison of values as commodities at the end of the second year is the value of 'goods and machine together' (I/33)[25].

Both of branches employ an equal quantity of labour, but the values produced during the two years are unequal, i.e., A<B. It is because in A the profits of the first year were 'expended and enjoyed' (I/34), whereas in B they were 'added to their capitals' (ibid.). The difference of the values produced in the two branches is equal to the amount of the profits resulting from the profits of the first year incorporated into the production of the second year in B. Thus, values in different amounts result from the same quantity of labour (i.e., the same amount of circulating capital) . Ricardo explains this difference by 'something more, to compensate for the greater length of time which must elapse before the most valuable can be brought to the market' (ibid.). That is, the cause of this difference lies in 'the different degrees of durability of their capitals', 'the time which must elapse before one set of commodities can be brought to market' (ibid.). According to what Ricardo says literally, the fourth section of chapter one was to have as its objective an explanation of the evolution of the value correlative to the movement of wages in the case of different

compositions of capital. In examining the first numerical example more closely, however, we cannot find any fixed capital defined by himself, and moreover, even before the movement of wages, 'times' necessary for recovery, unequal from one branch to another, cause the 'differences' of the values produced in the two branches.

Only in the last part of the first numerical example, does Ricardo introduce the movement of wages by raising the following problem: 'how will their relative value be affected by a rise in the value of labour?' (ibid.). The rise in wages, instead of raising the total sum of the value of the products, lowers it in proportion to the amount equal to the product of the value of the fixed capital and of the rate of profit lowered in the same proportion as the rise in wages. The proportion of the fall in value caused by the rise in wages thus depends on the share the fixed capital occupies. In this example, branch A being entirely of circulating capital, the value undergoes no change. On the other hand, in B, as the profit incorporated in the machine used in the second year (the aforementioned 'something more') falls, its value falls equally. This explanatory logic of the influence of the movement of wages on the relative value is altogether the same as that of the first edition. We should pay attention not so much to this last part, as to the great change in the explanation on the 'difference' caused by the differences in the conditions of production.

In addition to this numerical example, there is still another in the fourth section (I/37). This second example starts with the following sentence: 'Commodities which have the same quantity of labour bestowed on their production, will differ in exchangeable value, if they cannot be brought to market in the same time' (ibid.). In the two branches (named hereafter A and B) the same quantities of capital (£2,000) are invested, and both are made up only of circulating capital. In both branches the period of production is one year, the rate of profit is 10%, the wage rate is £50 (annual wages per capita). A employs 40 workers during one year to produce commodities. The value of these commodities is assumed to be £2,200. B employs initially 20 workers for the first year. There will be commodities to the value of £1,100, which will be used as a means (their nature is not made clear, they can be machines as in the previous case or means of subsistence) for the production of the following year, which will be carried out with the employment of an additional 20 workers. Then, at the end of the second year, commodities of the value of (£1,100 + £1,000) × 1.1 = £2,310 will be produced. Both of the branches employ annual labour of 40 persons (with the same amount of capital, £2,000). But, in spite of that, the produced values are different, respectively of £2,200 and £2,310. This difference is explained by the difference in the incorporated profit corresponding to the difference of time between one year, necessary for the recovery of the whole of the capital in A, and two years, necessary for the recovery of half of the capital (£1,000) in B. Here we no longer have any problem of the ratio between fixed capital and circulating capital (composition of capital), which had been raised at the starting point of the fourth section.

These numerical examples (Nos. one and two) relate to the same problem (that of the difference in time necessary before the products of capital can be brought to market), and excepting the trivial point whether the production in A is carried out during two years in two successive phases or it completes at the end of the first year, these examples are substantially identical.

> This case appears to differ from the last, but is, in fact, the same. In both cases the superior price of one commodity is owing to the greater length of time which must elapse before it can be brought to market. ... The difference in value arises in both cases from the profits being accumulated as capital, and is only a just compensation for the time that the profits were withheld[26].
>
> (ibid.)

In the fifth section, Ricardo tackles the problem of the change of relative value caused by the movement of wages in the case not of different compositions of capital, but of different durability of fixed capital and circulating capital in the branches with the same composition of capital. However, only one numerical example which occupies most of this section (I/39–42) is a very confused text, made up of some related passages of the first edition. There are inserted points foreign to the problem, as discussion on the possibility of a rise in the price of machines by the movement of wages, or differences in reasons of introduction of machines into developed countries and so-called backward countries. Moreover, Ricardo withdraws his former development halfway and advances an opposite view... All in all, one cannot regard this numerical example as an illustration by concrete figures of the possible influence on the value of commodities exerted by the difference in durability or time of recovery of capital independently of labour necessary to their production. There is no knowing about the reasons for this but, in any case, one can say that Ricardo tried to address the problem of 'time' without being able to give a clear illustration.

It follows that, in the third edition, Ricardo gives explanations on how the difference in the time of recovery of capital (fixed and circulating) led to differences in the values of commodities, not in the fifth but in fact in the fourth section. On the other hand, the problem of the 'modifications of value' caused by the differences in composition of capital, which was the subject of the fourth section explicitly announced in its title, finally disappears, the distinction between fixed capital and circulating capital being made ambiguous. In particular, although the explanation of the recovery of the value of fixed capital by the procedure of the calculation of annuity such as we saw in the first edition is withdrawn, no alternative explanation on this point is given. *De facto*, the fixed capital does not have its place within the theoretical framework of the third edition. Consequently, Ricardo does not deal at all with the problem of the specificity of the fixed capital[27], which consists in its progressive recovery through several periods of production, as well as the problem of the influence of such a specificity on the value of commodities. As a matter of fact, the aforementioned procedure of the calculation of annuity in the first edition constitutes his first and last tentative explanation of this problem[28]. In tracing the trajectory of his later thoughts, we become aware of the reinforcement of a tendency to reduce the fixed capital to a more general and vaguer concept of 'part of the capital requiring a longer period for its recovery' (and at the same time the concept of circulating capital loses its meaning). This tendency is recognised already in the explanation of the 'modifications of value' of the third edition we examined in this section. And this tendency becomes decisive in the last manuscript of Ricardo '[Absolute Value and Exchangeable Value]' where the term of fixed (and also circulating) capital is not used any more. Ricardo thus reduced all the differences in the conditions of production to that of 'time'[29] when tackling the difficulties of research of an invariable measure of value, inseparable from the problem of the 'modifications' of value. In the next and last section, we will examine the significance of this research into an invariable measure of value and its difficulties.

2.5 Fundamental character of Ricardo's theory of value: debates with McCulloch in 1823

Immediately after the publication in April of Malthus (1823), Ricardo wrote critical comments on this new work just like on Malthus (1820), three years before[30]. But, as Malthus' new work consists of the arguments 'fallacious from beginning to end' (letter to McCulloch of 3 May, IX/287), we cannot find any new advancement of Ricardo's thinking. However, this pamphlet of Malthus provoked new discussions on the measure of value, and Ricardo continued fierce controversies until the end of summer of this year with Malthus, and also with McCulloch. The debates in such a context proceeded in epistolary form, in particular with McCulloch and the last manuscripts of Ricardo '[Absolute Value and Exchangeable Value]' were written in parallel with these debates. At that time Ricardo made mention of the criticism of Torrens on several occasions, not only in his manuscripts, but also in his letters. All of these letters were those addressed to McCulloch, to whose arguments Ricardo retorts by saying that 'they are points advanced by Torrens'. In the whole of his last manuscripts, Ricardo considers the problem of choice of an appropriate measure of value in reducing all the differences in the conditions of production to those of 'time', i.e., of the period of production. The fact that Ricardo raised the problem in this way[31] shows well that he was always extremely conscious of the criticism of Torrens since 1818.

Therefore, the main subject of the epistolary discussions on the theory of value with McCulloch is the influence exerted on value by 'time' (necessary since the investment of capital until its recovery, a variable completely independent of the quantity of labour). It is since Torrens had pointed out to him in 1818 the need for taking into account the durability of circulating capital, that Ricardo has come to raise the problem of 'time', one of the 'two causes'[32] determining value. The only document available as sources on his debates with Torrens is that which is supposed to be written at the end of 1818, but Ricardo expresses on several occasions his point of view on this problem in his letters to McCulloch, not to Torrens who made him aware of it. McCulloch, having written articles of review and presentation in periodicals since the publication of the first edition of *Principles*, was a faithful follower, ready to defend and popularise Ricardo's theory, but the publication of the third edition of *Principles* revealed clear divergences between them[33], which were to become decisive in the aforementioned epistolary debates during the summer of 1823. McCulloch posed Ricardo, from an already different position, a fundamental problem for the latter's theory of value. However, either because this problem appeared to him too serious, or on the contrary because he was not able to understand its gravity, Ricardo never tried to take up again this problem raised by McCulloch in what he wrote during the short time left to him. His last debates with McCulloch, in spite of their very interesting problems for Ricardo, abruptly ended without opening any new perspective because of the incomprehension on Ricardo's part and his sudden death. As for McCulloch, he continued to develop his ideas after Ricardo's death, but these do not directly concern him.

It is in the letter to Ricardo of 11 August 1823 that McCulloch gave him a detailed development on the pending problems in answering Ricardo's request in his letter of 8 August: 'I wish also you would send me your own views on this subject in writing' (IX/330). In this letter Ricardo confesses frankly that he could do nothing about the problem, in saying: 'I cannot get over the difficulty of the wine which is kept in a cellar for three or four years' (ibid.). McCulloch's original point of view, developed in response to Ricardo's request in the letter quoted above, was roughly speaking as follows.

According to McCulloch, what determines the value of commodities is the amount of invested capital for their production. Judging only from this point, his theory can appear to be similar to Torrens' 'capital theory of value'. But McCulloch, unlike Torrens, advances a 'labour theory of value' brought to the extreme, and he gives a particular justification to his proposition above. A certain amount of capital expressed in terms of money is transformed into various elements of production. Labour is only one among them. The parts not allotted to the employment of workers are transformed into machines, raw materials, etc. However, these elements contribute just as much as labour to the production of certain products, serving to cause natural changes (physical movement, fermentation, purification etc.). There is thus no reason to regard only the human activities as labour and to admit to them the privilege of producing value. In this respect, the part of capital assigned to the employment of workers and that which buys machines are completely on the same footing. Both are equally spent to use (employ) 'labour'. If this is true, a certain amount of capital must always mobilise the same quantity of labour for a certain period. 'Time of itself produces no effect whatever; it only affords space for really efficient agents to produce effects. But whether these agents be men, or the processes which nature herself carries on in the production of commodities seems to me to be wholly immaterial provided it require *equal capitals to set them in motion*' (IX/342–3, emphasis by McCulloch). He thus introduces the proposition that a capital of the same amount always produces for a certain period the same quantity of value. The fact that an oak tree or wine has a value much larger in proportion to the quantity of human labour employed for their production, because of the long time necessary for the growth or ripening, can be explained without any difficulty according to the point of view of McCulloch. For his 'labour theory of value' with a particular concept of 'labour' which includes the whole of the natural processes contributing to the production of material goods, there cannot be naturally any problem of 'modifications of value', the fundamental source of trouble in Ricardo's theoretical thinking. 'I can see no difficulty in the case of the tree' (IX/343). According to McCulloch's concept of labour, the whole of capital is spent on employing labour, the whole of the period of production is regarded as that of labour. Consequently, the differences in the conditions of production (use of unequal quantities of labour by a capital of the equal amount during unequal times), which were the ultimate cause of the 'modifications of value' for Ricardo, are perfectly nullified.

In the face of such a theory of value with a concept of labour enlarged in a particular way, Ricardo makes his response very soon. But he does not mail the first draft of his letter and sends a second version of it on 21 August, which is exceptional for him. (This draft, published for the first time in *Works*, is supposed to be written on 15 August, immediately after the reception of McCulloch's letter). These two versions do not contain any substantial changes. There is no knowing why Ricardo held what he had written once and sent another rewritten version one week later. Considering these circumstances, we will take here mainly the first draft to examine Ricardo's reaction[34].

He characterises McCulloch's theory as follows:

> You estimate the value of the commodity not by the quantity actually worked up in the commodity but by the capital which employs it, and therefore if equal capitals are employed you have a right to say equal quantities of labour are employed, and a capital employed for two years though of precisely the same amount as one employed for one year may be said to employ more labour than a capital employed for one.
>
> (IX/355)

In the third edition, Ricardo himself had used a similar numerical example to explain the 'modifications of value'. He showed there that a capital of the same quantity, used for the production during two consecutive years, produces a greater value than that which is produced by another capital of the same amount, used during only one year. The result at which McCulloch is supposed to arrive in the quotation above is the same as Ricardo's. What matters is how to explain and estimate this result. Their divergence lies in this point. Ricardo regards as a 'modification' of the theory of value the increase in value caused by the fixing of capital in the process of production without any workers employed by the operating capital, whereas McCulloch regards as explicable with his 'labour theory of value' the value which continues growing due to the fact that the elements of production the capital continues to employ (machines for example) do not cease 'labouring'.

Both of them consider equally that the labour employed for the production determines the value of commodities. However, Ricardo, for whom only the workers employed by the capital are the source of labour, must consider the situation given above in terms of 'modifications' or 'exceptions', while McCulloch negates the existence itself of these theoretical difficulties, thanks to an extension of the concept of labour. Ricardo may be expected to give an answer which would arrive at the foundation of McCulloch's 'theory of value' and specify his points of view, but Ricardo does not touch at all on the decisive points[35], neither in the first draft nor in his letter actually mailed. Instead of making his reactions explicit, he describes on several occasions McCulloch's theory as a theory identical to Torrens'. 'But this is adopting Torrens' view and saying that commodities are valuable in proportion to the capitals employed upon them and not in proportion to the actual labour employed' (ibid.). What he says here makes us think, certainly, that the points advanced by McCulloch result in the same thing as those by Torrens (and moreover, this also applies to Ricardo himself), but there is a fundamental difference between them[36], a difference Ricardo completely neglects, purposely or unconsciously. In any case, such a reaction seems to imply that he is always extremely conscious of Torrens' criticism, and that he remains perplexed in the face of McCulloch's theoretical challenge.

Ricardo then proposes a following example to show that his difficulties are not overcome by McCulloch's theory: 'You and I are both manufacturers, you produce your commodity in two years, I mine in one, we employ equal capital. Suppose your commodity to be $2^{1/4}$ times the value of mine and that nothing occurs to interfere with the facility or difficulty of producing either commodity, but that labour rises and profits fall'. Then the relative value of the first falls and that of the last rises. In this case, the amounts of capital remain equal to one another, and the quantitative proportion of labour employed does not undergo any change. 'Nothing has altered but the rate of distribution between employer and employed, and this affects us differently – profits have fallen and there is a larger proportion of profits in your commodity than in mine – this and this only is the reason why they alter in relative value' (ibid.).

McCulloch probably thought that such a difficulty cannot arise from the point of view of his new 'labour theory of value'. The wages and the profits would also be in inverse proportion according to his theory, but, contrary to Ricardo's case, the variations in their relation would not have any influence on the values of commodities. It is also for this reason that McCulloch does not speak at all about the movement of wages. According to what he says in the letter of 11 August, he would answer this question: even if the wages rise, there will be no change in the amount of produced value and hence in the relative value, since the same amount of capital is always used for the production during the same time. McCulloch could do nothing but deny the possibility for the part of the value not coming from labour to increase or decrease according to the opposite movements of wages and profits. (It should be noted, however, that the passage of the first draft quoted above is not adopted in the text of the letter actually sent.)

Why must Ricardo always recognise the problem mentioned above in spite of the misunderstanding in the discussion with McCulloch? Ricardo said in the title of section one of Chapter One of *Principles* that the relative value of commodities 'depends on the relative quantity of labour which is necessary for its production' (I/11). In his letter to McCulloch there are following passages which can appear contradictory to the sentence quoted above. 'Value is made up of two elements, wages and profits' (IX/356). 'It is time only which makes any difference in the proportions in which profits and wages enter into the value of different commodities' (ibid.). 'Value is composed of two elements wages and profits mixed up in all imaginable proportions; ... In one [commodity] there is nothing but labour, in the other there is nothing but accumulations of capital from profits with scarcely any labour whatever' (IX/361) (the first is a commodity produced in one day only by labour – shrimps collected with bare hands at the coast for example, the second is that which is produced in a long time without use of labour – oak tree or wine for example). Ricardo presupposes here the existence of profits independent of labour and considers the sum of these two elements as the value of commodities[37]. Hence, a part of commodity value is made of profits completely independent of labour, and the variability of the share this part occupies in the whole of the value of commodities makes up the fundamental premise of the 'modifications of value' in Ricardo. As long as this premise remains intact, he could not escape from the insoluble problem which had afflicted him with so much difficulty since the beginning of the writing of *Principles:* how to understand the profits, here is the decisive problem, and any divergence on the theory of value concerns this point. McCulloch, in his letter of 24 August, responding immediately to that of Ricardo of 21 August, touches on the root of the discussed problem when he says:

> The difference principally hinges on the interpretation we are to give to the word profit. Whether is the additional value we get back in exchange for a capital we have employed in production a compensation for time, or for our forbearance in not having consumed the capital immediately, or is it a positive additional value resulting from the employment of the capital and not dependent on time?
>
> (IX/366)

In so raising the question, he chooses the last alternative and hints that Ricardo regards the profits as the first alternative.

As far as we know, among Ricardo's contemporary economists only McCulloch indicates this essential point, and only here. Ricardo himself never raised such a problem in any form. It might be that only McCulloch, in increasingly acute theoretical opposition to Ricardo, could advance a step farther and go beyond the level of only arguing on the falling or rising profits and about the relation of such movements with the wages and the value, and could realise the decisive importance of knowing how to understand the profits themselves. Whether because he did not have sufficient time to tackle the fundamental problem for his economic theory, or because he was not able to understand its importance or significance, Ricardo unfortunately did not leave any reaction to this problem, and the unilateral interrogation from McCulloch remained unanswered. In spite of their exchanges of views carried out extremely intensively until that moment, in spite of the uninterrupted correspondence with other economists (Malthus, J. Mill, Trower) during about two weeks until the beginning of September when Ricardo fell ill, finally, this letter of McCulloch did not receive any response from Ricardo. He made mention of the debate with McCulloch only once in his letter to Trower of 31 August (see note 35), without however touching on the significant point to be answered[38].

We have considered how Ricardo, until the last moments of his life, tacled the difficulties on the theory of value he could not solve. What can we say on the fundamental character of his theory of value?

In the title of section one of chapter one of *Principles* he declared that the value of commodities is determined by the quantity of labour necessary for their production, and that it is not influenced by the rise or fall in wages paid to the workers. According to this proposition, the wages are, just like profits, a share obtained by dividing an amount given independently of one another, wages and profits being thus in a relation of trade-off. This idea always remained the essential point in Ricardo's economic thinking. It is precisely for this reason that the movement of wages appears in his theory as much opposite change of profits, so that the amount of value as sum of these two elements remains constant. That would be all and there would be no problem, if every capital were spent as wages as a whole. But, in spite of Ricardo's surrealist examples, capitalist production needs necessarily some means of production, and a given part of the invested capital must be spent for these means of production. The value of this part is not resolved in wages, and hence does not bring into motion any labour. If the profits are conceived as above, this part of the invested capital should give rise to no profits. But Ricardo did not think so.

Given free competition of capital to maximise profits, every capital can be supposed to obtain an equal rate of profits according to its amount and to the period of its investment, whatever may be the branch or its composition. This is completely obvious for those who manage capital in a capitalist economy (economic agents). Ricardo, while insisting on the one hand on the concept of profits as one part of a whole along with the wages (the rent left aside), on the other he adopts just as it is a totally different concept of profits the economic agents have in capitalism, without putting them into any theoretical relation.

This is at the bottom of the difficulties which afflicted him since the preparatory phase of the first edition of *Principles*.

Ricardo certainly has the idea of value, the amount of which is determined by the labour employed in the process of production. However, the labour about which he speaks is nothing other than the wage cost (he says, 'labour rises'), and he sees the 'labour' only from the point of view of those who employ workers in spending wage cost. Hence, for him, everything which relates to the material labour workers carry on in the process of production, such as duration of a working day, intensity of work, etc., has no relevance to the theory of value, which makes it difficult for us to see how he understands the profits. Consequently, from his theory we cannot know how the level of profits themselves are determined, apart from the evolution of their level. Within Ricardo's theoretical framework labour (wages) and profits are connected only by one point, the opposite movement of their rates.

The profits in this meaning, profits added to the part of capital spent otherwise than for the employment of labour, and the profit accumulated at a compound rate according to the duration of time of investment, plays a great role in his theory of value. How is its rate determined? Why is it that the profits evolve in opposition to wages, while the source of the former remains unknown? Ricardo not only cannot answer these questions, but he cannot raise such problems (cf. his reactions to McCulloch's problems).

Ricardo's theory of value can be regarded as an odd amalgam of these two concepts of profits. The following formulation in his 'Notes on Malthus' *Principles of Political Economy*' written right before his work of revision for the third edition during the second half of 1820, seems to express briefly and clearly the fundamental character of his theory of value.

> If by cost Mr. Malthus means cost of production, he must include profits, as well as labour; ... A commodity is at its natural value, when it repays by its price, all the expenses that have been bestowed, from first to last to produce it and bring it to market. If my expression conveys the same meaning as cost of production, it is nearly what I wish it to do.
>
> (II/34– 5, see also I/47, Ricardo's note)

The essential point of Ricardo's theory of value is not that of embodied labour, but that of cost of production, according to which the value is determined by the addition of the expenditure by the capitalist for the production and of the general profits. If Ricardo cannot fundamentally criticise Torrens' and McCulloch's theories and must partially recognise the validity of their theories, it is probably because his theory had certain common points with theirs, in spite of differences in detail.

Notes

1 See 'Bibliographical Appendix' (list of the works of Torrens and their summary explanations), attached to Robbins (1958).

2 See VII/338–9 and also I/60–1, note 1. In these added sentences Ricardo speaks about the influence the 'differences in the durability of circulating capital' exert on the determination of value. Ricardo had not at all mentioned these differences in the first edition. According to what he says in this letter, these differences are in obvious relation with a point indicated by Torrens. But neither in Torrens' article mentioned in the next note (the only extant document nowadays of his criticism of Ricardo at that time), nor in the 'fragments' written by Ricardo in response to the written criticism of Torrens (nonextant), no mention is made of this point. The 'differences in durability of the circulating capital' will become a major problem relating to Ricardo's theory of value, which he will have to tackle in the form of the problem of 'time'. Considering this circumstance, this problem may have presumably its origin in a point advanced by Torrens in his oral debates with Ricardo which would have allegedly taken place in February 1818.

3 Torrens, contemporary of Ricardo, who made a criticism of considerable importance for Ricardo's theory and was personally acquainted with him. However, there is no correspondence left between them.

4 Letter to J. Mill of 14 October 1816, VII/82.

5 Terry Peach affirms, in Peach (1993), that Ricardo realised difficulties in his theory of value only after the completion of the writing of the manuscript corresponding to the first seven chapters, and that he found the 'curious effect' only after having made the distinction between the fixed capital and the circulating capital and having considered the differences in durability of the fixed capital, so that in the first version of his manuscript he had developed a 'pure' labour theory of value. According to Peach, the arguments on the problems of which Ricardo had become aware afterward were 'interpolated in the first draft chapter' (p. 168). Peach wants thus to explain the apparently incoherent construction of the first chapter of *Principles*. But the theory of value of *Principles* has a coherent structure in its own way, and it is not a marquetry of two manuscripts written according to two different points of view on value. It is just after the completion of the writing of *Proposals for an economical and secure currency* (published in 1816, IV/49–141) that Ricardo started to write the manuscript of *Principles*. And he informed of the completion of the writing of this manuscript in his letter to J. Mill quoted above in note 4. During all this period Ricardo spoke in his letters on several occasions about the difficulties he had encountered in his theory of value. Ricardo was thus quite conscious of the problems expressed in terms of 'curious effect' and tackled it from the very moment when he began to write the manuscript of *Principles*.

6 On the other hand, J. Mill does not recognise this problem itself in insisting on the validity of the principle of the determination of value. He seems to have always kept such a reaction since the time when Ricardo made him know of the difficulty encountered during his writing of *Principles*. In the letter of J. Mill of 18 November 1816, in response to that quoted in note 4 (announcement of the completion of the manuscript corresponding to the first seven chapters), he says:

> With the curious result pointed out in your letter with respect to the effects produced by the rise of wages, on the price of those commodities which are chiefly the return from fixed capital, I was very much struck; but have no doubt what so ever as to the validity of your conclusions, the proof of which I think is incontrovertible.
>
> (VII/98)

Although given at a later time, the following answer of Ricardo to McCulloch, who had reacted to this problem just like J. Mill, shows well his character as theorist:

> I am always willing to allow that some of the variations in the relative value of commodities may be referred to causes distinct from the quantity of labour necessary to produce them ... To this second cause I do not attach near so much importance as Mr. Malthus and others but I cannot wholly shut my eyes to it.
>
> (IX/178, letter to McCulloch of 19 March 1822)

7 In a note added to the second edition (I/52, note 1) for a supplementary explanation of his distinction between fixed capital and circulating capital, Ricardo says: 'A division not essential, and in which the line of demarcation cannot be accurately drawn'. And a little afterward, in a paragraph revised in the second edition, Ricardo indicates, in addition to the two points of difference, a third point which is the difference in durability existing among circulating capitals. 'It is also to be observed that the circulating capital may circulate, but be returned to its employer, in very unequal times. The wheat bought by a farmer to sow is comparatively a fixed capital to the wheat purchased by a baker to make it into loaves' (I/53, note one). The two quoted notes emphasise the fact that the distinction between fixed capital and circulating capital according to the difference in time necessary for recovery did not originally have a clear line of demarcation, and that moreover the difference in durability exists for every part of capital, whether classified as circulating or as fixed. It follows that every part of capital is fixed capital in a certain degree, and at the same time circulating capital in a certain degree compared to other parts, i.e., both at the same time. This reasoning will finally lead to the disappearance of the distinction between fixed capital and circulating capital, and the whole capital (all parts of it) is compared and distinguished according to one single criterion, which is the length of time necessary until the moment of its recovery. Ricardo expresses in this way the differences among various capitals. This can be seen most clearly in his last manuscripts on [Absolute value and Exchangeable value] (1823) where a distinction of capitals (conditions of production, branches) is adopted, which are neither fixed nor circulating anymore, according to the sole criterion which is the time necessary for the production. Considering the notes and the rewriting of the text in the second edition on the distinction between fixed capital and circulating capital, one can say that Ricardo goes along with this line at the end of the year 1818. Torrens had indicated the existence of a 'durability of circulating capital'. He pushed Ricardo to this direction. Thus, it becomes clear that the adoption by Ricardo of time as a single criterion of the conditions of production was in fact a result of his debates with Torrens. (Incidentally, when Ricardo speaks about 'time', he has in mind not the factor which measures the quantity of labour by its duration, but the duration of time necessary for the recovery of capital completely independent of the quantities of labour.)

8 The two values respectively express the sum which can be gained each year with negotiable government bond at price of £150 or £50 when the rate of profit is 10%. The current value of certain amount of money is regarded as descendent in proportion to the time which must elapse until it will be received. It is the interest rate which determines the difference between the future value and the current value. When, for example, the annual rate of interest is 10%, current 10 is equivalent to 11 in one year, and on the contrary 10 in one year is equivalent to current 9.09 (10 ÷ 1.1). The interest (or profit) is regarded here as remuneration naturally and rightly expected from money advanced during a certain time (whatever its employment may be). In the numerical example examined here, the calculation is as follows: 24.4 ÷

$1.1^1 + 24.4 \div 1.1^2 + \cdot \cdot \cdot + 24.4 \div 1.1^{10} \fallingdotseq 150$. This calculation means that by receiving the sum of £24.4 each year over 10 years, one is supposed to possess a current value equivalent to £150. Conversely, by investing £150 to buy an annuity, I will have received at the end of the 10 years a total sum of £244, which is approximately 1.6 times larger than the initial sum. Ricardo thus takes for granted the increase in value with the elapse of time, independent of labour and proportional to the interest rate, which means already a fundamental 'modification' of his theory of 'labour value'. In this numerical example, there is an increase in value of about 60% exceeding by far the framework of 6% to 7%, although there is no labour added. We will see afterward that the calculation of recovered values of fixed capital by the procedure of the calculation of annuity is completely withdrawn in the numerical examples of 'modifications of value' in the third edition.

9 Ricardo probably intended to say that the rise of wages does not have any 'effect on the prices of commodities wholly produced by labour' (I/60), but rigorously speaking, this is not the case. If the price remains unchanged, it is because the sum of £952 is added to the invested capital. If the invested capital remains the same as in the branches using exclusively fixed capitals, the employable quantity of labour will be that which corresponds to the employable quantity at the current level of wages with the capital of £20,000 ×£20,000/£20,952 ≒£19,091. And with the rate of profit of 5%, the sum of produced value must have lowered to £19,091 × 1.05 ≒£20,046. This fall is due to a synergistic effect of the reduction in the quantity of labour employed and the fall in the rate of profit. In any case, that is valid in the assumption of advance payment of the wages. Another scenario would be possible on the assumption of differed payment, i.e., the payment of the wages risen to £20,952 will be carried out with the proceeds of the goods produced by the same quantity of labour as before the rise of the wages. The proceeds are assumed to be always £22,000, the share remaining as profit will be £1,048. In this case, there will be no change in the sum of produced value and the rate of profit will be about 5% (£1,048 ÷£20,952 ≒ 0.05). This result coincides perfectly with Ricardo's line of argument.

10 In the second edition, at the end of the illustration by the second numerical example (end of the last paragraph of page 60), Ricardo adds a paragraph to indicate that the difference in the durability of the *circulating* capital has the same effect as that which we have just seen in the two numerical examples. This point should have developed to become a third numerical example (which would have discussed the third item of the differences in the conditions of production, absent in the first edition), but Ricardo renounces this, regarding it as useless. A detailed explanation of this point which is based on the same principle: 'It must be unnecessary to go into further calculations to prove this to be true, as it rests precisely on the same principle, namely, the different degree of durability of two equal capitals', (I/61, note 1). The whole of the paragraph, including the sentences quoted here, is transcribed just as it is in his letter to McCulloch of 24 November 1818, just after his work of revision for the second edition, with an explanatory sentence: 'The following observation to be printed in the next edition and which I think more fully answers Major Torrens' objection' (VII/338). In his letter to J. Mill of 28 December 1818, i.e., about one month later, he says: The variation of the exchange value is due 'only to two causes: one the more or less quantity of labour required, the other the greater or less durability of capital, the former is never superseded by the latter but is only modified by it. But, say my opposers, Torrens and Malthus, capital is always of unequal durability in different trades' (VII/377). Ricardo speaks here for the first

time about the 'two causes' one of which, 'modifying', is named 'more or less durability of the capital'. Already at that time when Ricardo had finished work for the second edition after his debates with Torrens, he had reduced the factors of modification of value to only one: the durability of capital. That is, he had noticed that the three points of difference in the conditions of production, enumerated in the text of *Principles* are brought back in fact to this one single point. This is to be kept in mind in following the process of his thinking about the 'modifications of value'.

11 In his letter to J. Mill of 12 December 1818, Ricardo says: 'I have written an answer to Torrens paper in the *Edinburgh Magazine* in defence of my doctrines of value' (VII/360).

12 Letter to McCulloch of 24 November 1818, VII/338.

13 Letter to McCulloch quoted above, letter to J. Mill of 28 December 1818, and at a little later time, letter to McCulloch of 18 December 1819.

14 See I/53 note, I/61 note, I/63 notes 1 and 2.

15 The value of capital is expressed in terms of the employable quantity of labour with this capital, in this case 100 persons × one day or one person × 100 days. This is how the classical economists, including Ricardo, express the quantity of labour, and the duration of time as a continuous quantity (infinitesimally dividable) is never used. And, the product as result of one working day is supposed to be able to employ double the quantity of labour.

16 The fixed capital, as defined here by Ricardo, is not the fixed capital distinguished from the circulating capital by a longer period necessary for its recovery (according to his own definition in *Principles*), but here this term indicates simply the parts of capital not spent for the payment of wages, i.e., not assigned to the employment of labour. Such a point of view on fixed capital is formulated as a definition in the following sentence of the 'fragments', once written but erased at once by himself. 'Every thing [sic] is fixed capital which is employed on production except that which resolves itself into wages. ... That part of my capital only can be considered as circulating which is exclusively devoted to the payment of wages' (IV/312). As Sraffa indicates ('Note on fragments on Torrens', IV/306), the distinction made here between fixed capital and circulating capital coincides accidentally with that of Marx. But this point was immediately withdrawn, and it is never adopted in the second edition of *Principles* and his later writings.

17 Torrens (1818), p. 59.

18 The use of the term 'labour' to indicate wages (wage cost), such a concept of 'labour', comes from the way of thinking not only of Ricardo, but also of the classical political economy in general. Smith, for example, speaks about wages in terms of 'labour' on several occasions in *Wealth of Nations*. 'Labour measures the value not only of that part of price which resolves itself into labour, but of that which resolves itself into rent, and of that which resolves itself into profit' (Smith (1976), pp. 67–8).

19 The quantities of labour really employed in the two branches of production producing commodities of the same value are largely different. This is the result of this example, which is in striking disagreement with the fundamental proposition of Ricardo's theory of value, according to which the value of a commodity 'depends on the relative quantity of labour which is necessary for its production, and not on the greater or less compensation which is paid for that labour' (I/11). But this result appears to be in no relation with the movement of wages, which was the cause of a 'curious effect', i.e., of the difficulties since the time when Ricardo had begun

to write the draft of the first edition of *Principles*. Unlike the debates with Malthus, who insists on the parallel movement of wages and price on the basis of an aspect of Smith's theory of value, the influence of the movement of wages on the price of commodities is not at all argued in the debates with Torrens, which are only about one single point: the compatibility of the proportionality between the value and the quantity of labour with the difference in the conditions of production.

20 This is an extremely general case. Since any production process must accept raw materials and means of production which arrive there finally after having made several times the object of transactions on the market as equivalents, while being products of quantitatively different labour, we must consider that the case examined by Ricardo in the last paragraph of the 'fragments' applies more or less to any production process. The example Ricardo uses in *Principles* in order to say that the maximum of modifications of value on the ground of differences in the conditions of production is around 6–7%, takes into account only the conditions relating to the process of production in question, and the values of fixed capitals, etc., used in this process are treated as being wholly determined by the quantities of labour directly necessary for their production. But, if Ricardo had noticed that the case in question here must be regarded as entirely general, he should have been confronted by the need of fundamental re-examinations of the explanations he had given on the 'modifications of value' in *Principles.*

21 On the problems of this distinction, see note seven of the present chapter. In the third edition, this distinction is postponed to a later phase in comparison to the first and second editions. This can be interpreted as a measure taken not to complicate unnecessarily the development of his theory of value until the third section, a development made in the *de facto* but implicit assumption of a non-existence of differences in the conditions of production in all the branches.

22 See the three paragraphs in I/32–3 (quoted in p.19 above). All the pages beginning from these passages, including the numerical examples, are text added for the third edition.

23 A numerical example of the same type is found already in the letter to McCulloch of 13 June 1820 (VIII/192–3).

24 Only in the third edition does Ricardo assume such a production with two successive phases (phase one is the production of the means of production necessary for the production of the end products, machines in this case, and phase two is the production of these end products with the use of the means of production produced in the phase one), which were completely absent in the first and second editions. Torrens, who criticised Ricardo and debated with him, supposed also a course of production in two phases in his numerical example (cf. IV/309, editor's note). Only with the difference that, in Torrens' case the product of phase one was means of subsistence for workers, but not machines. B produces its end products in two phases, and the machine, produced at the end of the first year is not intended for sale on the market as a commodity, but is reserved for phase two of the following year to be used for the production of other goods. However, this machine, as if it were commodities, is compared in its value with corn sold after phase one, and is considered as equivalent of this corn. It is as if Ricardo regards the value as being produced independently in the production process without any regard to the process of exchange. He says after the publication of the third edition in his letter to Trower of 4 July 1821, that 'You say if there were no exchange of commodities they could have no value, and I agree with you, if you mean exchangeable value. ... It is in the early stages of society, when few exchanges were made, that the value of commodities is most peculiarly

estimated by the quantity of labour necessary to produce them, as stated by Adam Smith' (IX/2).

25 In this example Ricardo does not say anything about the number of years of operation (durability) of the machine and does not speak at all about the depreciation of the machine at the end of the second year after one year of operation. Such a procedure, which consists in 'evacuating' from the process of production as a kind of joint product also the part of the machine still to be amortised as fixed capital (Torrens also applied the same method in a slightly different form in his article of 1818 quoted above. See Torrens (1818), p. 58, and also in the letter to McCulloch mentioned in note 23 above, Ricardo treats in the same manner the amortised value of the machine. See VIII/192), has the effect of not revealing the problems relating to the complicated calculation of values, likely to be made necessary by the amortisation of fixed capital (the first example is the procedure of the calculation of annuity adopted in the first edition). Even if one replaces this machine by the means of subsistence for workers produced during the first year by the same capitalist for the second year as in the example presented by Torrens in 1818 in his debates with Ricardo (see IV/309–10, 314), the essential point of explanation does not change at all. It is because the fixed capital in question here has just the same period of recovery as the wage cost, except for one difference: the capital used for its production requires, compared to the circulating capital, twice the time until its recovery, since this fixed capital is produced in advance in the same branch during one year. In any case, in this numerical example, the existence of the machine (or the raw materials, or of anything else provided that it is continuously used in the second year), part of capital remaining longer in the process of production, which is however not always fixed capital, is the cause of all the problems. In the passages of the letter quoted in note 23 in which Ricardo indicates a similar numerical example, he says:

> But the same result would take place if I employed circulating capital only and could not bring my commodity to market for two years, at the end of the two years, the commodity will not be worth only all the labour bestowed on it [in other words, the whole of the wage cost], but also the accumulated profits for the time that my capital was so employed.
>
> (VIII/192–3)

Here the distinction between circulating capital and fixed capital does not have meaning any more, only 'time' is important.

26 This passage shows clearly Ricardo's point of view on profits. The profits are for him a 'just compensation' for holding capital during a certain time in the process of production, and for abstaining from expenditure for consumption. He never clarifies how he understands the profits, except in an indirect way as in the quoted passage. Ambiguity in the concept of the profits seems to be the origin of the difficulties of his theory of value. In the letter quoted in note 23 in which he gives the explanation on the modifications of value, he justifies the increment of value by the investment of the products of the first year as capital in the following year, by an effect 'totally independent of the quantity of labour actually accumulated in the commodity brought to market' (VIII/192). As we will see below, this point will make its appearance as a serious problem in the fierce controversy with McCulloch, Ricardo's ex-follower, during the summer of 1823.

27 This is the problem known as 'transfer' of value. Ricardo mentioned twice the transfer of value of fixed capital (Cf. I/39) which, however, does not play any role in his illustration of the 'modifications of value'.

28 As regards the complete withdrawal in the third edition of the explanation of the recovery of value of fixed capital by the procedure of calculation of annuity, there is another problem to be examined from another point of view. As we have seen in note 25, according to the calculation of the recovered value of the fixed capital by this procedure, an enormous quantity of value would be produced independently of the quantity of labour employed, according to the length of time during which the capital remains fixed in the process of production. (In the first and second editions Ricardo admitted such a situation *de facto*, but he did not recognise it, and did not undertake its examination either, as a serious problem relating to the basis itself of his theory of value.) Although he touches incidentally on this problem in some of his manuscripts as 'fragments' on Torrens, [Absolute Value and Exchangeable Value], in the published text of the third edition he completely erases from the text the problem of progressive increase in the value under the effect of 'time', at the same time as he erases the procedure of the calculation of annuity (and the confusion of the development in the fifth section of chapter one contributes to this obliteration of the problem; in this section no substantial explanation is given of the 'modifications of value' caused by the 'unequal durability of capital' and by the 'unequal rapidity with which it is returned to its employer', in spite of its title implying discussions on these issues).

29 In the letter to McCulloch of 18 December 1819, reporting that Torrens showed him an article of criticism of his theory of value (referred to above), Ricardo says: 'there are many modifications which must be admitted in this doctrine, from the circumstance of the unequal times that commodities require to be brought to market' (VIII/142). In another letter to McCulloch of 2 May 1820, he says: 'There are two causes which occasion variations in the relative value of commodities; first the relative quantity of labour required to produce them, second the relative times that must elapse before the result of such labour can be brought to market. All the questions of fixed capital come under the second rule' (VIII/180). Still in another letter also to McCulloch of 13 June 1820, he says: 'All the exceptions to the general rule come under this one of time' (VIII/193). These three letters are all written during a time between the second and third editions of *Principles*. The sentences quoted here show that he wanted to reduce the fundamental causes of the 'modifications of value' to only one element, 'time'.

30 Malthus (18230) in Porta (ed.) (1992) contains criticisms on many points in *Principles* of Ricardo, who wrote in the same year detailed comments on the new work of Malthus (II/2). Results of this work reappear in some rewritten pages in the third edition of his *Principles*. The sixth section of chapter one entitled 'On an invariable measure of value', added newly for this edition, is an example. Ricardo's theory on the invariable measure of value in the third edition was thus an outcome of the debates with Malthus. And one of the main purposes of Malthus' new pamphlet indicated above was to undertake refutations against Ricardo on the basis of an aspect of Smith's theory of value. Ricardo's prompt reaction is due to this circumstance.

31 As we made a suggestion at the end of the previous section, the concept of fixed capital disappears in his last manuscripts. In the 'fragments' on Torrens, Ricardo

had for a moment hesitation in his distinction between fixed capital and circulating capital under the impact of Torrens. See IV/312 and note 16 above.

32 Ricardo uses this expression for the first time in his letter to J. Mill of 28 December 1818, just after his debates with Torrens. He will use it three times in his letters to McCulloch – of 2 May 1820, 13 June 1820 and 19 March 1822 – and once in his letter to Malthus of 9 October 1820.

33 The reviews and articles of presentation of *Principles* McCulloch published in periodicals like *The Scotsman* are listed in the bibliography at the end of O'Brien (1970). On the other hand, his debates with Ricardo start with his letter of acknowledgement for a complimentary copy of the third edition of *Principles* (of 5 June 1821) in which he announces his disagreement with him on revised pages (the new theory of machine in particular). The dissensions on the theory of value appear in Ricardo's letter of 19 March 1822, hardly one year after the publication of the third edition, in which he says:

> You go a little farther than I go in estimating the value of commodities by the quantity of labour required to produce them: you appear to admit of no exception or qualification whatever, whereas I am always willing to allow that some of the variations in the relative value of commodities may be referred to causes distinct from the quantity of labour necessary to produce them.
>
> (IX/178)

34 As indicated at the beginning of this section, the debates at the time on the theory of value began with the publication of Malthus (1823), and the main problems in the discussions between Ricardo and Malthus related to the theoretical possibility and the choice of a measure of value. In his correspondence with McCulloch in August, Ricardo always criticised the points advanced by McCulloch from the point of view of the conditions and the choice of a measure of value. But McCulloch denies any significance of a measure of value. The examinations hereafter will not touch on this side of the debates.

35 In his letter to Trower of 31 August, Ricardo makes a report on the whole of his discussions with Malthus and McCulloch. With regard to McCulloch's 'labour theory of value', he expresses a feeling of following dissension: 'McCulloch uses the word labour in a sense somewhat different from Political Economists in general' (IX/377). It is only here that Ricardo says something on McCulloch's concept of labour.

36 Aiming at examinations on Ricardo's theory, we cannot discuss in detail this group of problems. Significant points are: first, as regards to the determination of the value of commodities, Torrens rejects the element of labour in whatever meaning. He considers it completely differently from McCulloch. Secondly, in relation to the first point, Torrens makes the general profit uniformly added to the capital in all the branches the basis of his rejection of the labour theory of value and the basis of his 'capital theory of value', whereas the element of general profit does not play any role in McCulloch's theoretical structure. All in all, Ricardo does not appear to understand well the theory of Torrens, although Ricardo has just read Torrens (1821), a systematic work. Ricardo repeats the question (instead of criticism) addressed to Torrens (and to McCulloch also): 'You say that the capital of the same amount produces the same amount of value, but how you can justify that two capitals are the same amount?' Torrens prepared in his way an explanation on this point (aside from its relevance), but Ricardo does not make any mention of it.

37 Such a determination of the value of commodities can appear contradictory to the fundamental proposition put at the beginning of *Principles*, just quoted (this is a point stressed in De Leo (2017), see pp. 61–2). This theoretical contradiction is, however, only in appearance. This point can be explained by a particular theoretical makeup of Ricardo's theory of value. Moreover, in some sentences quoted here, what is put in contrast with profits is wages and labour, which are reciprocally replaceable. This is understandable by the meaning of the term 'labour' in Ricardo. For more detail on this point, see note 18, as well as '4) Method of chapter one of *Principles*– relation between the first half and the second half – ' and '6) Fundamental character of Ricardo's theory of value' of chapter one in this book.

38 Ricardo makes mention of McCulloch also in the last part of the fair copy version of his last manuscript, supposed to be written from the end of August to the beginning of September. On several occasions, he examines points of view of his contemporaries, with whom he was continuing oral and epistolary discussions in parallel. The mentions made of these economists are, so to say, also a prolongation of these discussions (including McCulloch's case). But the short fragment at the end of this fair copy version in which McCulloch's theory is examined (IV/410–2) is *de facto* a rather faithful summary of the points advanced by him in his letters of August, to which Ricardo adds only some ambiguous comments:

> The only doubt one can feel on this subject is the accuracy of the language used by Mr. McCulloch. It might be right to say that commodities were valuable in relation to each other according to their cost of production, or according to the quantity of capital employed on them for equal times, but it does not appear correct to say that their relative value depended on the quantity of capital worked up in them. (IX/411–2)

It is difficult to see clearly for what reason Ricardo finds McCulloch's language vague, but it is certain that here Ricardo does not want to reject wholly McCulloch's theory. In any case, Ricardo thus put an end to the discussions with him without being able to make clear criticisms of him. Moreover, in the aforementioned last manuscripts Ricardo also mentions Torrens, but his last estimate of the 'capital theory of value' is as ambiguous and nuanced as in McCulloch's case. After a quotation drawn from Torrens (1821), he says: 'If two equal capitals be employed for the same time the commodities produced will be of equal value. No one can doubt the truth of this proposition' (IX/393). And as a result of his examinations of this theory, Ricardo states: 'When Col. Torrens says that equal capitals will produce equal values he must then clearly define what he means by equal capitals, and he ought to add "when employed for equal times" for equal capitals do not produce equal results unless they are employed for equal times' (IX/394–5). In these two quotations Ricardo repeats the same point. And far from criticising Torrens' 'capital theory of value', he recognises its validity on the sole condition of clearing up the conditions relating to 'time'.

3 The value of money

Labour value theory and quantity theory in Ricardo's economic theory

3.1 Foreword

One of the remarkable features of Ricardo's writings was that each of them was closely related to an important political and economic problem of the time, and in many cases their dates of publication were chosen to coincide with the debating and voting on bills in Parliament. His activities as an economic polemicist had the explicit aim of intervening in debates on the issues most ardently discussed at that time, namely the currency and the Corn Laws – from the standpoint of bullionism for the former, and opposition to the laws for the latter – and of influencing the parliamentary debates on these bills.

His writings concerning currency began with his newspaper article *The Price of Gold* and some related articles (from August to November 1809), extended and developed into the tract *The High Price of Bullion, a Proof of the Depreciation of Bank Notes* (published at the beginning of 1810 in three editions, the fourth and last edition in April 1811, hereinafter *High Price* for short), and followed by *Proposals for an Economical and Secure Currency* (published in February 1816, hereinafter *Proposals* for short), in which he expounded his conception of the English currency regime after the resumption of convertibility of Bank of England notes made possible by the ending of the Napoleonic Wars. This series of his writings ends with *Plan for the Establishment of a National Bank*, the manuscript of which was written in the summer of 1823, just before his sudden death, and which was published posthumously by one of his younger brothers.

His writings concerning the latter topic began with his tract opposing the Corn Laws: *An Essay on the Influence of a Low Price of Corn on the Profits of Stock* (1815). On the strong advice of J. Mill, he systematically extended and developed this tract, the result of which was his main work: *On the Principles of Political Economy, and Taxation*. Moreover, his last, unfinished manuscript, '[Absolute Value and Exchangeable Value]', written in the summer of 1823, was the culmination of his lifelong reflection on one of the most important issues in debate at that time and raised by his main work.

The writings of Ricardo belonging to the latter series, including *Principles*, which is highly esteemed as the systematic theoretical work at the apogee of

DOI: 10.4324/9781003498322-4

English classical political economy, have continued to exercise a profound influence on the development of economics both inside and outside the English-speaking world after the death of their author, influencing the works of J. S. Mill, Marx, Marshall, Sraffa, etc. Those belonging to the former series, on the contrary, do not include any systematic theoretical work comparable with *Principles*. They are rather a set of writings of a temporary character, calling into question the contemporary English currency regime and criticising the circulation of inconvertible banknotes. Probably because of this, they have not been taken up and held in high esteem in the literature (recent publications such as Deleplace (2017), Marcuzzo and Rosselli (1991), etc., are among the small number of exceptions[1]). Along with the fact that Ricardo explicitly adopted the so-called Say's Law, his theory of money was generally simplified and taken to be a Quantity Theory, and even today it is fairly customary to regard him as a quantity theorist[2]. But the Quantity Theory of Money has a long history, beginning with Hume and Montesquieu in the mid-eighteenth century, and continuing until Freedman in recent times, and, in such a tradition, Ricardo is apt to be considered as rather a minor figure. As a result of all these circumstances, Ricardo's theory of money has rarely been taken up, and even when it has been, it has scarcely been examined in relation to his theory of value and distribution[3].

In addition, the foundation of Ricardo's economic theory is generally taken to be the theory of labour value. Also, the money that appears in the abstract theory of chapter one of *Principles* ('On value') is itself one sort of commodity, namely gold, and, as such, its value is determined in the same way as every other commodity, by the quantity of labour necessary for its production. In the quantity theory of money, conversely, the value of money is determined by its quantity in proportion to the dimension of the commodity transactions, the circulation of which it serves as the medium, and hence it is considered to be incompatible with his theory of value, and rather is contradictory to it. 'The contradiction between a quantity theory and a labour (or a cost production) theory of the value of money is obvious. ... There is no explicit attempt at reconciling the two conflicting views in Ricardo' (De Vivo (1987), p. 195, see also Sayers (1953), p. 33, Blaug (1995), p. 31). Also, Roll says that these two are in 'a clear conflict', 'a serious inconsistency' (Roll (1938), pp.,192–3).

However, the two series of writings mentioned above did not coexist without connection in the thinking of Ricardo. We believe that they are in fact closely linked. The main purpose of this chapter is to show that such a link exists between the value and quantity of money, the most important theoretical subject in his theory of money. In fact, Ricardo started to write *Principles* just after finishing *Proposals*, and his last two, unfinished works, '[Absolute value and exchangeable value]' and *Plan for the Establishment of a National Bank*, were written in parallel.

Hereinafter, we will pursue our purpose chiefly by examining *High Price* and the appendix to its fourth edition, *Proposals* and chapters 1, 13 and 27 of *Principles*.

3.2 Basic framework of Ricardo's theory of money

In chapter one ('On value') of *Principles*, money appears as a measure with invariable value ('invariable measure or standard of value') with which to judge how much of the cause of a variation in the exchange ratio between two commodities should be imputed to each of them.

> If there were any other commodity which was invariable in its value, we should be able to ascertain, by comparing the value of fish and game with this commodity, how much of the variation was to be attributed to a cause which affected the value of fish, and how much to a cause which affected the value of game.
>
> Suppose money to be that commodity.
>
> (I/27–8)

Money is therefore one sort of commodity in Ricardo's theory. But, in order to serve as money (a measure of value), its value must be relatively stable with regard to the other commodities. As commodities vested with such a property, precious metals (gold and silver) are considered the most suitable. Money is gold as a commodity, and gold has its proper value ('intrinsic value' III/52) just like any other commodity. This is Ricardo's fundamental position on the value of money, and it remained unchanged throughout the whole period during which he addressed the question of money, despite a great change (or rather evolution or clarification) in the determination of the value of commodities before and after the writing of *Principles*.

Money is a commodity and has value as a commodity, so that it is exchanged according to this value, just as the other commodities are. If the exchange between a commodity and money is conceived as such, then it is only one sort of exchange equivalent to that between any two commodities. An exchange in which one of the sides is money differs from the exchange between two sorts of commodity other than money, only insofar as money, with its invariable value, accurately expresses variations in the value of the other commodity, making it possible to ascribe these variations entirely to the non-money commodity. Therefore, the respective roles of money and other commodities in the exchange are not considered to be asymmetrical, as in the well-known dictum 'money buys commodities but commodities buy neither commodities nor money', but the exchange in which one of the sides is money is regarded simply as one instance of the exchange of two commodities. Hence, Ricardo may never have conceived an explanation of how monetary exchange becomes necessary or indispensable, because of the difficulties of direct exchange of commodities, as Adam Smith did in chapter 4 ('Of the Origin and Use of Money') of *The Wealth of Nations*, and indeed there are no passages in his writings on money that correspond to this chapter.

Ricardo's viewpoint on the commodity money is to be distinguished both from that of the quantity theorists who consider money to be a non-commodity, the value of which is determined solely in the circulation (Hume, Montesquieu), and from the mercantilist conception of money which, on the contrary, raises money to a special rank among commodities and considers it to embody the wealth to be pursued and accumulated. For Ricardo, precious metal is only one element of wealth, not at all distinct from the other commodities, insofar as it is allotted to satisfy consumption desires just like the other commodities, and its value is determined on the same footing. But, insofar as it is used for a function particular to it as money (measure of value and exchange medium), the precious metal (gold) is not an element of wealth, as it no longer satisfies consumption desires and is rather regarded as so much deduction from the wealth of a nation, as its value is high relative to its weight and size. In contrast to mercantilism (or in its wider sense the tradition of 'the monetary theory of economy' from J. Steuart to Keynes), Ricardo rejects the hoarding of money as theoretically impossible. For him, hoarding is entirely useless and irrational behaviour for a commodity possessor. Money is entirely spent, either to satisfy the desires of consumption, or on investment with a view to obtaining more of it in the future. Moreover, if the demand for money as a commodity is always equal to its quantity, its total spending made up of consumption and investment is, in principle, simultaneous with its obtainment.

In Ricardo's theory of money, the circulation of commodity money is considered within the following two frameworks[4].

The first is the existence and functioning of money without institutional premises such as state or bank, transcending them. As seen above, there is no genesis of money in Ricardo's writing, but what he discusses is the commodity money formed spontaneously during the course of commodity exchange on the market, which is fundamental in his conception of money. In this domain of circulation, only bullion of certain weight (and fineness) functions as money, and its character as commodity money appears clearly.

The second, in contrast, is the domain of each domestic economy, where money circulates as a national currency issued by the State or a bank. Insofar as gold in the form of bullion circulates among nations as the money (currency) of the world[5], and each nation is part of this world circulation (i.e., it is not completely isolated from the internationally related commodity and monetary circulation), this domestic domain of circulation necessarily has the international domain as its background, and the money circulating in a domestic area cannot be properly understood without its relation to the international circulation. Ricardo's national currency is made of the following three elements: (1) (gold) coin minted from bullion of a weight corresponding with its officially fixed mint price with deduction of a certain seigniorage; (2) banknotes convertible at sight into coins with the same face value; (3) banknotes, the issuer of which is exempt from the obligation of conversion into specie (but still officially equivalent to the quantity of gold corresponding with the convertible banknote of the same face value).

In Ricardo's time, only item (3) above was circulating. It is for (1) and (2) that the value of gold as a commodity (its 'intrinsic value') plays a role in determining the quantities actually circulating in a domestic area. On the contrary, the quantity of (3) in circulation is not regulated automatically, so to speak, by price relations or supply–demand relations. Because it is inconvertible paper, any quantity of it cannot only be absorbed in the circulation, but continues to circulate there, irrespective of the quantity of gold represented officially by the total sum of paper money in circulation, calculated on the basis of its total face value and official mint price. Inconvertible banknotes can circulate in any quantity, depending on the policy and practice of the issuing bank, but their purchasing power over commodities, including bullion, varies in inverse relation to their quantity in circulation. The bullionists[6], including Ricardo, express the purchasing power of inconvertible banknotes in terms of their purchasing power over bullion on the market (the reciprocal of its market price), which they call 'value of money'[7] (distinct from the value of gold money as a commodity). At a certain number of inconvertible banknotes in circulation, this market price coincides with the mint price. Ricardo and other bullionists adopted this conformity as the criterion to judge the appropriate quantity of inconvertible banknotes issued, and they argued that the issuing bank should use this criterion as a guide for their issuing policy. At the time, the market price of bullion was over and above its mint price, and the bullionists advanced this as the proof of over-issue (as is precisely expressed in the full title of *High Price* itself). As for the national currency which is in such a state, it appears as if the quantity of money determined its value.

Such an appearance arises not only for the national currency in an inconvertible regime, but also for its antithesis, i.e., gold in the form of bullion, 'the money of the world'. These two forms of money are opposites, because gold is itself a commodity with its 'intrinsic value', and such a commodity money serves as a medium of circulation, and also because there are no issuing bodies like states or banks in the international domain, and the money circulating there arises spontaneously from among the commodities exchanged.

In Ricardo's theory, when money serves as the medium of exchange in a domestic area it is considered tantamount to the direct transfer of cash in the direction opposite to that of commodities, i.e., to the physical exchange of paper money or coin and commodities. Certainly, Ricardo does speak of 'economy in the use of money'[8] in various passages of his writings, but he never discusses how this economy is carried out, or to what extent and in what manner it changes or diminishes the amount of money in circulation. What exists and circulates in England, thus helping to form the purchasing power of money over commodities including bullion, is made up exclusively of inconvertible banknotes issued by the Bank of England (hereafter BoE for short), all of which seems to be assumed to move directly from hand to hand between buyers and sellers. This is an economy where every settlement is made directly by cash, which is the direct opposite of Wicksell's pure credit economy. Ricardo's theory of the value and quantity of money is also founded on the premise of such a situation.

3.3 International trade and money: debate with Thornton and Malthus

As we have seen in the previous section, Ricardo's theory of money is based on gold money circulating among countries in the form of bullion. Just like commodities, money moves from countries where its quantity is relatively superfluous and its price (in the case of money, its purchasing power over commodities) is therefore low, to countries where it is relatively scarce, and its price (purchasing power) is therefore high. Thus, the proportions of money and commodities distributed throughout the world tend to be balanced. If a completely balanced distribution is attained, there will be no reason for any of them to move between countries. The world economy in Ricardo's theory seems to be conceived as one solely composed of 'civilised nations' (III/52) in Western Europe at that time, or rather of countries as enlarged or reduced mirror images of England. They form something like an agglomeration composed of fragments into which the world economy, as a homogeneous whole, has been broken down. Actually, of course, at that time England was in commercial relations with 'non-civilised' countries outside Europe. But, in the theoretical model of Ricardo, the non-European world (characterised by the production of different products from Europe or by very different productivity for similar kinds of products) is neglected, and so the world economy is not seen as a whole comprising heterogeneous components. In every country, as far as they appear in Ricardo's world economy, the same set of goods produced in the same proportions and by the same methods of production are circulating[9][10]. Otherwise, it would be impossible to speak about a balanced world distribution of precious metals or an equalisation of the value of money among these countries in equilibrium. And here there can be no distinction between exportable and non-exportable goods, everything being potentially exportable.

Precious metal as money is only one among these commodities. So, when the quantity of precious-metal money existing in one country as a proportion of its total amount all over the world is equalised with the quantities of commodities produced and exchanged in this country as a proportion of their total amount all over the world, then the proportion in which the precious-metal money is exchanged in this country against other commodities (i.e., the 'value' or 'purchasing power' of money) is also equalised with that in every other country. When the world economy is in such a state, the international distribution of precious metal is in equilibrium, and there is no longer any reason for trade as transactions of commodities and money among countries. At the beginning of *High Price*, where he explains the international distribution of precious-metal money, Ricardo writes: 'As soon as this equality was attained, all advantage arising from exportation would cease' (III/57–8).

International trade arises to recover the equilibrium state in the distribution of money among nations when it is disturbed. Regarding this viewpoint of Ricardo on the motive of international trade with transfer of money, Malthus points out perceptively in his (anonymous) review article published in the *Edinburgh Review*:

> He [Ricardo] seems to think, that when once the precious metals have been divided among the different countries of the earth, according to their relative wealth and commerce, that each having an equal necessity for the quantity actually in use, no temptation would be offered for their importation or exportation, till either a new mine, or a new bank was opened [till a country gets an additional supply of money to disturb the equilibrium state]; or till some marked change had taken place in their relative prosperity.
>
> (Malthus R. 1811a, p. 345)

This comment by Malthus appears to comprehend correctly an aspect of Ricardo's view of international trade which provoked his debate with Malthus and Thornton (all of them belonging to the same Bullionist camp recommending the resumption of convertibility to stem the depreciation of the English currency) about how to interpret the fall of the foreign exchange rate. In reality, unless an artificial barrier (embargo, etc.) is set up with international conflicts such as war, international trade continues without interruption; naturally Ricardo must have known this well. As we have seen, money – and in particular gold money in the form of bullion – is for Ricardo but one commodity among others moving from country to country, and the equilibrium international distribution of such money (as described in the quotation above from Malthus) is only one instance of the equilibrium distribution of all commodities. Moreover, the delivery of commodities in exchange for precious-metal money (i.e., exportation) is for him also only one way of carrying out international trade. Each of the other commodities is also distributed internationally in a certain state[11], and whether this distribution is in equilibrium is independent from the state of international distribution of gold. If the international distribution is in disequilibrium for some of the commodities other than gold, those commodities will leave the countries where they are relatively superfluous (i.e., cheap) and move to countries where they are relatively scarce (i.e., expensive). If, in such a situation, scarce and superfluous commodities correspond between two countries, they become objects of international trade and mutually exportable commodities, and at the same time they function as a means of payment and settlement. The commodity called money is also only one of the commodities moving between countries in this way. Ricardo does not attribute any privileged significance to monetary settlement in comparison with settlement by other commodities. On international trade in the situation of a balanced international distribution of money, he says at the beginning of *High Price*:

> While the relative situation of countries continued unaltered, they might have abundant commerce with each other, but their exports and imports

> would on the whole be equal. … exports and imports of all countries would balance each other; bills of exchange would make the necessary payments, but no money would pass, because it would have the same value in all countries.
>
> (III/53–4)

Now the progress of the debate and the points discussed in it are as follows. In the review article cited above, Malthus criticised Ricardo's viewpoint on the fall of the foreign exchange rate, to which Ricardo replied in the 'Appendix' to the fourth edition of *High Price* published two months later. Thornton had already advanced a similar view to Malthus' in Thornton (1802), and Ricardo critically examined Thornton's view in *High Price*. The central problem on which Malthus and Thornton disagree with Ricardo is whether over-issue should be considered as the sole cause of currency depreciation, or whether other additional causes should be recognised. What attracted particular attention in relation to foreign trade was the importation of corn to make up for shortfalls caused by recurring bad weather in England at that time. This debate involved the numerical data and their evaluation, namely changes in the quantity of inconvertible banknotes issued by the BoE in circulation; the evolution of harvests and corn prices in England; the evolution of corn importation and imported corn prices; and variations in the foreign exchange rate in relation to these movements. We shall not enter into the disputes about the details of these numerical data, but simply show the differences in viewpoints between Ricardo, on the one hand, and Thornton and Malthus on the other as regards international trade and the role money plays there, in order to clarify one important aspect of Ricardo's theory of money.

In a critical appraisal of Thornton's opinion, Ricardo writes:

> it appears that the temptation to export money in exchange for goods, or what is termed an unfavourable balance of trade, never arises but from a redundant currency. But Mr. Thornton, who has considered this subject very much at large, supposes that a very unfavourable balance of trade may be occasioned to this country by a bad harvest, and the consequent importation of corn; and that there may be at the same time an unwillingness in the country, to which we are indebted, to receive our goods in payment; the balance due to the foreign country must therefore be paid out of that part of our currency, consisting of coin, and that hence arises the demand for gold bullion and its increased price.
>
> (III/59–60)

Ricardo thinks on the contrary that, even if a country in need of a supplementary food supply imported corn (whether or not money is distributed in equilibrium), money would not necessarily leave this country simply because of that corn importation. The payment of money for imports is always a means of payment chosen for the benefit of a country having relatively superfluous money[12], but a country not in this situation (i.e., the value of money there not being relatively low) will not export money; it will not pay for imports with it. A country can choose what kind of commodity it gives in return for the importation, according to its own advantage. A little after the quotation above, still criticising Thornton, Ricardo continues as follows:

> If we consent to give coin in exchange for goods, it must be from choice, not necessity. We should not import more goods than we export, unless we had a redundancy of currency, which it therefore suits us to make a part of our exports. The exportation of the coin is caused by its cheapness, and is not the effect, but the cause of an unfavourable balance; we should not export it, if we did not send it to a better market, or if we had any commodity which we could export more profitably. It is a salutary remedy for a redundant currency. (III/61)

For Ricardo, imported commodities are those which exist in a country, but are more expensive because they are relatively scarce. No other reason for importation is conceivable[13]. The same can be said about exportation. In such cases there certainly exist motives to transfer commodities between countries, but if money is equivalent in both countries, there will be no motivation to use money to pay for the imports, as there would be when superfluous money circulates in the importing country, and the payment will be made with other (relatively superfluous) commodities. Ricardo has no idea of money having special significance as a means of payment compared with other commodities, i.e., having the highest liquidity so that it is necessarily preferred to any other commodity of the same value. For him, every exchange of commodities is essentially barter. And if money becomes the medium of exchange in the international domain, it is only because money moves in search of favourable conditions of exchange. Receiving precious-metal money in return for exports does not represent any greater benefit for the creditor country than if it received other commodities instead. The inflow of money is rather forced on to this country by the mechanism of equilibrium international distribution of money, when there are no relatively scarce commodities other than money in this country, and commodity prices are therefore relatively low, and the value of money is relatively high. In addition, the value of the total sum of money (money 'imported' in this way, plus that which was already there) in domestic circulation does not rise at all, and its value per unit diminishes in proportion to the increase in quantity. For Ricardo, money serves nothing other than to procure truly useful goods (virtual wealth).

3.4 The value of money in Ricardo

3.4.1 The value of metallic money in international circulation

In all the works on money that Ricardo produced during his activities as an economist, it is in the early *High Price* that the general outlines of his theory of money are most conspicuously traced, and all his subsequent writings may be said to have added to or extended points already contained in *High Price*, in relation to contemporary conditions of currency and the debates about them. In this section we will consider the value of money in Ricardo's theory, the central subject of this chapter, mainly by examining the development of his arguments in *High Price*, also referring to his later writings on money when necessary.

The starting point of *High Price* is the commodity circulation with precious-metal money as its medium, existing 'previously to the establishment of banks' (III/52). Such a setting itself and the subsequent arguments suggest a strong influence from the work of Hume[14], who is considered to have given a clear expression to the quantity theory of money in the mid-eighteenth century. But, while Hume considers precious-metal money not to be a commodity and hence not to have value in itself (cf. Hume (1752), pp. 41, 63), Ricardo declares from the outset that money gold is a commodity with its own value. 'Gold and silver, like other commodities, have an intrinsic value, which is not arbitrary, but is dependent on their scarcity, the quantity of labour bestowed in procuring them, and the value of the capital employed in the mines which produce them' (III/52)[15]. In this regard, Ricardo's theory of money must be distinguished from the Quantity Theory of Money of Hume (and Montesquieu), which excludes money from the category of commodities and deduces its value from their reciprocal quantitative relations.

At the beginning of *High Price*, Ricardo speaks of the distribution of precious metal among the countries of the world as follows:

> The precious metals employed for circulating the commodities of the world, previously to the establishment of banks, have been supposed by the most approved writers on political economy to have been divided into certain proportions among the different civilised nations of the earth, according to the state of their commerce and wealth, and therefore according to the number and frequency of the payments which they had to perform. While so divided they preserved everywhere the same value, and as each country had an equal necessity of the quantity actually in use, there could be no temptation offered to either for their importation or exportation.
>
> (III/52)

Here he explains the distribution among nations in proportion to the extent of wealth (hence of the scale of commercial trade) of precious-metal money circulating in 'civilised nations', but this distribution says nothing about the quantities of money as its result. These quantities of money in circulation in each country are determined by the total sum of money circulating all over the world. Ricardo's theory of the international distribution of precious-metal money (maybe just as in the case of Hume) has nothing to do with this total sum of money. Given the 'economy in the use of money' and the 'state of wealth and commerce', i.e., the 'number and frequency of payments', the quantity of money in circulation must be determined by the value of the money commodity itself. And, according to Ricardo's fundamental point of view seen above (money is a commodity with its own value, exchanged with other commodities on the basis of this value), the quantity of money thus determined must be distributed among each nation proportionately to its scale of transactions.

However, following the quotation above, Ricardo says that the theory of proportional distribution shows how a given total sum of money is distributed in a certain way, without implying the quantity to be distributed:

> If the quantity of gold and silver in the world employed as money were exceedingly small, or abundantly great, it would not in the least affect the proportions in which they would be divided among the different nations – the variation in their quantity would have produced no other effect than to make the commodities for which they were exchanged comparatively expensive or cheap. The smaller quantity of money would perform the functions of a circulating medium, as well as the larger.
>
> (III/53)

The quantity of precious-metal money attributed to each country can be greater or smaller according to the total sum of precious metal existing in the entire world. And the quantity allotted proportionately to each country circulates there necessarily (since in Ricardo's theory money can never be hoarded), causing the prices of commodities to vary accordingly. It is as if the quantity of money functioning here as a circulating medium was not determined by its value as a commodity, but that money entered into the circulation in any quantity was devoid of its own value, and its value was determined only by its relation to the quantity of commodities (total sum of their value) for which it served as circulating medium. Why does Ricardo, after affirming that the value of money determines the quantity of money in circulation, immediately give an opposite, quantity-theoretic explanation of the value of money on the following page? The increase and decrease in the quantity of money is nothing other than the variation in the relation between the quantity of money and the quantity of commodities. If the production of money as a commodity changes at the same pace as that of the other commodities, the quantitative relation between commodities and money cannot continue to change in a certain direction for very long, though it may be possible temporarily. If so, money as a commodity will be exchanged according to its intrinsic value. If Ricardo explains the value of money in terms of Quantity Theory in the quotation above, then it seems to be because he is aware of the specific conditions of the production of gold as a money commodity, which differ from those of other commodities, industrial products in particular[16].

In the paragraph following the above quotation, Ricardo describes the disturbance of the equilibrium international distribution of precious-metal money and its restoration by redistribution as follows:

> If in the progress towards wealth, one nation advanced more rapidly than the others, that nation would require and obtain a greater proportion of the money of the world. Its commerce, its commodities, and its payments, would increase, and the general currency of the world would be divided according to the new proportions. All countries therefore would contribute their share to this effectual demand.
>
> (III/53)

In the situation of an international equilibrium distribution of precious-metal money, if one country expands the production of commodities faster than the other countries, the equilibrium of this distribution will be disturbed, necessitating a redistribution for the recovery of equilibrium. This is because the expansion of production of commodities does not include that of the money commodity. If production in each country grows at the same rate, tracing a concentric circle, every commodity, including the money commodity, will remain in an equilibrium distribution in proportion to each country's weight in the world economy. Why then is only the production of the money commodity treated as if it remained unchanged and was left behind in the 'progress towards opulence'?

The key to this question seems to be found in the following quotation, drawn from the same context as the previous one:

> If a mine of gold were discovered in either of these countries, the currency of that country would be lowered in value in consequence of the increased quantity of the precious metals brought into circulation, and would therefore no longer be of the same value as that of other countries. Gold and silver, whether in coin or in bullion, obeying the law which regulates all other commodities, would immediately become articles of exportation; they would leave the country where they were cheap, for those countries where they were expensive.
>
> (III/54)

In contrast to the previous quotation, we have here a new supply of money gold and an increase in its quantity, although there is no increase in commercial trade in any country. The additional supply of money depends on the discovery of a gold mine 'in either of these countries', i.e., on a purely accidental factor. It does not grow in every country *pari passu* with the growth in production of other commodities. The quantity of money does not always increase according to the need for increased trade in a country. On the contrary, the production of gold may increase accidentally in a country where there is no such need. In the country where a gold mine has been discovered by chance, a quantity of newly-produced gold will be added to the gold already in existence. The gold in excess of the equilibrium distribution will become superfluous and relatively cheap (i.e., prices will inflate) in this country, and it will therefore be exported to foreign countries in search of favourable exchanges, just like other commodities. In this way, the fall in the value of gold will be exported to other countries. This exportation of gold (which involves at the same time an importation of commodities) will continue until a new equilibrium point is reached.

What is the meaning of this new equilibrium distribution of money gold among the countries? It is clear at first that the prices of commodities have again become the same in every country, so that there cannot be any exportation or importation motivated by differences in the prices of commodities. Looking at this point only, the situation appears to have returned to what it was before the equilibrium was disturbed. But the equalisation of prices everywhere is not the only result of this re-equilibration process. Prices are now higher than before all over the world, and the purchasing power of money has fallen in every country. Of course, this is because the newly-produced gold supplied accidentally in one country, irrespective of the variations in commercial activity in each country, has diffused worldwide to reduce the value of money equally everywhere. If the increase in gold production is largely a matter of accident, it may well happen, on the contrary, that in spite of an increase in commercial activities in some country or countries, there will be no new supply of gold required in them in order to maintain the equilibrium in international distribution of gold (cf. the quotation above from III/53). This will give rise to a situation contrary to that described in the quotation above. That is, in these countries, money gold will become relatively scarce, and the value (purchasing power) of gold relative to other commodities will rise (prices will fall). The exportation of commodities (importation of money) will then continue until the value of money returns to equilibrium. When a new equilibrium distribution is thus attained, prices will have fallen evenly all over the world, i.e., the value of money will have risen equally as compared to the level before the disturbance (the relative scarcity of money in some country or countries is diffused worldwide, leading to the dissolution of this relative scarcity itself). Moreover, unless a new gold mine is discovered somewhere by chance to supply gold afresh and set in motion a process similar to that described above, any force tending to reduce the purchasing power of money to the initial level will not operate.

Both of these contrary situations arise from difficulties in varying the supply of precious-metal money as a commodity *pari passu* with changes in demand for it, causing its excess or deficiency to persist. In such situations, the value of precious metal as money is apt to deviate from its value as a commodity, and these deviations can last a long time. That is to say that, even if the value of precious metal as a commodity is stable, its value as money can vary with the level of commercial transactions, resulting in the instability of the value of money and its quantity theoretic determination. From the point of view of Ricardo's 'principles of political economy', such a situation could be interpreted as an extremely special case of the deviation between the value (natural price) of a commodity and its market price. On the abstract theoretical level of chapter one of *Principles*, the deviation of the market price from the natural price is assumed to dissolve rapidly (instantaneously, in principle), so that every commodity is exchanged according to its natural price (or value), and the money appearing in this chapter as a measure of value is precisely one such commodity. But Ricardo was aware that, on a level of more concrete observation, taking into consideration the particular conditions of production of each commodity, it is not possible to apply such an assumption equally to every commodity[17].

3.4.2 Quantitative adjustment of metallic money in the domestic circulation, and instability of its value

In Section 3.4.1 we discussed international circulation. In this domain there can only be a spontaneous mechanism of quantitative adjustment of very low responsiveness, i.e., the expansion and contraction of gold mining. Here, the instability of the value of money due to maladjustment can only be left as it is. In the domestic area, on the contrary, it is national currencies issued by the State or a bank which circulate instead of bullion, and the quantities of different national currencies are regulated in different ways according to the nature of each of them, independently of the evolution of gold production.

In England, gold coin was minted from bullion of a weight corresponding to its official price, stipulated at the beginning of the eighteenth century (the mint price was £3 17s. 10½d. per ounce). The relationship between the quantity of coins issued in this way and the quantity necessary for circulation in a country can be determined by comparing the mint price of gold with its market price. If the quantity of coins actually in circulation conforms with the quantity necessary for circulation (mainly determined by the value of gold as a commodity), then the quantity of gold contained in the coin is equal to that which can be bought on the market with this coin, i.e., two different forms of gold of the same quantity are exchanged (however, in fact since the mint deducts a fraction of the gold corresponding to the seigniorage when minting bullion into coin, the gold actually contained in the coin is reduced by this amount. But here we shall ignore the question of seigniorage.).

In this case the purchasing power of coin over bullion is on a par with the quantity of gold contained in it.

In chapter 13 of *Principles* ('Taxes on gold'), Ricardo writes: 'the duration of the interval, before the market price will conform to the natural price, must depend on the nature of the commodity' (I/191). In this chapter, he discusses the case in which the quantity of production cannot be readily diminished, as in gold mining where a long time is required to reduce production so as to restore equality between the natural and market prices when the former exceeds the latter (i.e., in the case of excess supply). But a reduction in newly-produced gold alone is not sufficient to reduce the quantity of precious-metal money. Here is a difficulty particular to the quantitative adjustment of this money (downward, in this case). 'Although from its durable nature, and from the difficulty of reducing its quantity, it [metal gold] does not readily bend to variations in its market value, yet that difficulty is much increased from the circumstance of its being used as money' (I/193). Although gold used as money is produced as a commodity by gold mining, it is not definitively consumed and does not leave the economic process as other commodities do; it remains there. The quantity of such money is not diminished by reducing the new supply of gold from mines. The most this reduction can do is to restrict the increase in the quantity of money. Of course, if its relative excess reduces its purchasing power, a part of money gold may be converted into ornaments or ingredients of other industrial products, and then it may be possible to actively reduce the quantity of precious-metal money. However, the extent to which this can be done depends on the proportion of the total quantity of gold that is used as money. If an overwhelming fraction of existing gold is being used as money, its conversion into other uses (i.e., the margin of reduction in the quantity of money) will be very limited. If, on the contrary, the proportion of gold used as money is small (after Ricardo's expression, if gold has 'a very slight connexion with money' I/194), then it will be possible to reduce the quantity of money more effectively.

But, in capitalism, where economic activity generally continues to expand, it may be rare to find money, the medium of commercial activities, in a situation of excess requiring its reduction, as in the case described above. What Ricardo considered more important was that the supply of precious metal does not respond to the expansion of economic activities, so that the quantity of money becomes scarce relative to a larger quantity of commercial transactions, which destabilises the value of money irrespective of the stability of the value of gold as a commodity (its 'intrinsic value').

In *Proposals*, Ricardo advanced a plan for an 'economical and secure' currency regime. The fundamental conditions he required from a currency regime can be summed up in these two words. Before proposing a concrete regime satisfying these conditions, he shows how the value of currency becomes destabilised when an expansion in commercial transactions takes place in a country (a fictional country existing nowhere), where only precious-metal money (coin) circulates, as follows: 'If, from increasing opulence, more commodities came to be bought and sold, the first effect would be that the value of money would rise' (IV/57). Because of the relative insufficiency of the quantity of money, the market price of bullion falls below its mint price, bullion is then brought into the mint to be transformed into coin with a face value superior to the price at which it could be sold on the market. This increases the quantity of money and its value falls, i.e., the prices of commodities, including bullion, generally rise. But, since a special demand arises only for bullion to be minted, and its supply for sale on the market diminishes on the contrary, the price of bullion may be supposed to rise more (or faster) through this process than the price of other commodities, for which there is no special demand caused by the quantitative adjustment of money. In this way, the market price of bullion rises until it conforms to its mint price, and then no more benefits can be obtained from converting bullion into coin, and the process of expansion of the quantity of currency comes to an end. At that moment the prices of commodities will remain somewhat lower than they were before falling. Here, the value of money in the sense of its purchasing power over bullion will have returned to its former level, but with the rise in the value (or more exactly the market price) of bullion, the purchasing power of currency over other commodities will also have risen. In other words, although it is possible to restore the purchasing power of money over bullion (bringing the two prices back to conformity with each other) by means of an increase in the quantity of coin, the relation between money or bullion and commodities cannot return to its initial state (i.e., the fallen money prices of commodities always remain below their initial level), and in this sense the 'value of money' becomes unstable[18].

This is an illustration of the instability of the value of money on the supposition of a pure metallic money circulation in a totally fictional country, which Ricardo makes use of as a preliminary to emphasising that the issue of paper money by banks instead of an additional supply of gold from mines is indispensable for stabilising the value of currency, and that banknote circulation is better than metallic circulation, in that the former facilitates the quantitative adjustment of currency. (Incidentally, issuing banks and banknotes are also justified in the same way in *High Price*, cf. III/54–5.)

Ricardo considers it possible to remedy the instability of the 'value of money' caused by the tenacious gap described above (between the value of precious metal money as a commodity and its value as money) by the issue of convertible banknotes and the appropriate quantitative adjustment of them[19]. It was to this end that he conceived *Proposals*, the concept of which dates back to the 'Appendix' to the fourth edition of *High Price* and which took a definitive form in *Plan for the Establishment of a National Bank* (IV/276–300). But this is only applicable to the circulation of currency in the domestic area where an issuing bank can be established, and its banknotes can circulate. In the domain of international circulation beyond frontiers in the nineteenth century, where no such institutions existed or operated, money could only circulate in the form of bullion, so that the instability of the value of money seen above (varying according to the quantitative relation, determined in a way similar to the quantity theory of money) could not be remedied there[20].

3.4.3 Value of precious-metal coin and of convertible banknotes

The precious-metal coin and convertible banknotes we are going to examine in this section are issued in a particular country by the state or by a bank with some kind of relation to the state, designated by a denomination particular to that country, and able to circulate as such solely in its domestic area (as national currency). For these currencies to serve beyond national boundaries as a medium of commodity circulation, they must be restored to the form of bullion or exchanged with other national currencies on the foreign-exchange market.

When the quantity of currency in circulation exceeds the necessary level, its purchasing power over bullion falls and the market price of gold rises above its mint price. In this case, as gold has a lower value in the form of coin than in the form of bullion, coins are gradually melted down and cease to function as money. The quantity of coin in circulation diminishes, and at the same time the quantity of bullion supplied on the market increases by as much. Its market price falls and soon reaches the same level as the mint price. Then the value of coin becomes equivalent to the value of the bullion contained in it, and so the benefit from melting it down (or the loss of holding it as coin) disappears. Melting down ceases and coin circulates in the necessary quantity. In the opposite case, where the quantity in circulation is below the necessary level, the mechanism works in the contrary direction and bullion is converted into coin (minted). This raises the reduced market price of bullion, which soon conforms with the mint price, leading to the same result as above. In the case of the circulation of gold coin as money, the quantity in circulation is adjusted automatically, so to speak, to the quantity necessary for the circulation of commodities through variations in the market price of bullion. The value of gold as money and the value of gold as a commodity conform to each other. The quantity of money that brings about this conformity is the quantity necessary and sufficient for circulation.

As the quantity of money necessary for circulation is determined not only by the value of the money commodity itself, but also by the scale of the commercial transactions for which money serves as medium and by the economy in the use of money (its velocity of circulation, etc.), even if a quantity of money which was in conformity with its necessary quantity in certain conditions remains unchanged, the process of adjustment in either direction will come into operation with possible changes in the quantity necessary for circulation. Such processes will take place repeatedly with time. But as the general trend in capitalism is toward the expansion of economic activities, the quantity of money in circulation will be adjusted upwards to the necessary quantity that is expanding accordingly. An ever-increasing quantity of money will be necessary. The supply of money gold will be possible up to a certain level, by minting bullion or gold used for various purposes other than money, but it will finally require an additional supply newly-produced from gold mines. In general, however, it is very unlikely for new supplies of gold, depending on the natural allocation of rare resources, to go *pari passu* with the progress of economic activities, with the result that the commodity money generally does not circulate according to its value. Ricardo shows in *Proposals* that the quantitative adjustment by precious metal money destabilises the value of money, and he goes on to speak of the advantage of paper-money issue as follows: 'By the judicious management of the quantity, a degree of uniformity, which is by no other means attainable, is secured to the value of the circulating medium in which all payments are made' (IV/57–8). He expresses the same idea in *High Price*. The money issued by 'a bank …, such as the BoE, with the power of issuing its notes for circulating medium' (III/54) adds considerably to the sum of the currency, and so 'the same effect would follow as in the case of the mine' (III/55). But, unlike extraction from mines, the cost of issuing banknotes is minimal, and yet the quantity issued can be rapidly adjusted at will.

Historically, it has been extremely rare for currency circulation to work solely with precious-metal coin. For the most part, coin carried out its function as currency together with paper money issued from a bank. If a banknote, a mere scrap of paper, could work as money side by side with, and equivalent to, precious-metal coin, it was because both of them were guaranteed equivalence with a certain quantity of gold (they were convertible at sight into gold of a weight corresponding to the mint price). As for coin, this equivalence was maintained by the mechanism seen above. The banknote was originally a certificate of the issuing bank's obligation to pay its holder in specie. Its equivalence with coin was guaranteed by its convertibility into coin of the same face value, and on the basis of this guarantee the banknote assumed the function of money alongside coin. It is for this reason that the official mint price, which originally determined by law the relation between the face value of coin and its gold content, was applied equally to the banknote as the standard of its value as money, its face value being indicated by the same denomination as that of coin.

The circulation of banknotes therefore presupposes that of precious-metal coin, and as far as the value of banknotes in precious metal is guaranteed by convertibility, they circulate along with precious-metal coin (mixed circulation). In this case, the quantity of money in circulation in a country is made up of the sum of the quantities of coin and banknotes issued. The banknote, not being itself gold, works virtually as an additional quantity of gold backed by the guarantee of convertibility (whether and how much demand for conversion and actual conversion takes place is another question). If this sum is equal to the quantity of money necessary for circulation, determined mainly by the value of gold as a commodity, the market price of gold conforms with its mint price. If the quantity issued exceeds that necessary for circulation, the market price of gold as a sort of commodity will rise above its mint price with the rise in the prices of commodities in general. In such a situation, the holders of coin will (in spite of the prohibition by law) melt it down and sell it as bullion to make a profit equal to the difference between its market and mint prices. And holders of banknotes will convert them into coin at the bank in order to do the same thing with the coin obtained. In this way, when the quantity of money issued exceeds its necessary quantity, coin diminishes and banknotes flow back to the issuing bank. Both of these processes reduce the quantity of money, and with the general fall in prices the market price of gold will fall, so that it soon conforms with its mint price. The conformity of these two prices with each other means that, on the market, the currency actually exercises legal purchasing power over gold, and hence has as much purchasing power over the other commodities as over gold. If, on the contrary, the sum of money issued falls below its necessary quantity, the prices of commodities, including gold, fall, and, with this, the market price of gold also falls below its mint price.

In such a situation, people will buy bullion on the market and bring it to the mint in order to get coin or exchange it at the bank for banknotes at a more favourable price. The total sum of money will increase, which raises the prices of commodities, including gold. With this the market price of gold will soon conform with its mint price.

The total sum of precious-metal coin and convertible banknotes issued is, so to speak, automatically adjusted to the necessary quantity of money through the variations in the price of bullion on the market (approximately at the same pace and in the same direction as the prices of other commodities), and so the value of money (in the sense of its purchasing power over gold) is automatically stabilised. However, this stabilisation means only that the two prices of gold are in conformity with each other and money maintains its official purchasing power over gold in the market. Even if the value of money is stable in this sense, the purchasing power of money over the commodities other than bullion may become unstable when the value of gold as a commodity varies, or when the market price of bullion varies relative to that of other commodities. In other words, even if the market price of bullion remains constant (the constancy of the mint price is self-evident, with its variation deriving only from artificial price modification), there may well be variations in the prices of commodities, caused by monetary factors. There are two cases to be distinguished regarding this type of instability in the value of money (in the sense of its purchasing power over commodities other than gold).

The first case involves the variation of the value of money as a commodity, of the 'intrinsic value' of money, so to speak. This depends on the conditions of production of gold as a commodity. The production of gold largely depends on the natural allocation of rare resources and of its accidental and sporadic discovery. It is difficult for gold-mining enterprises to control the expansion of production or the reduction of production costs. And in the long run, the cost of production of gold can vary widely beyond human control. No institutional device can prevent such variations or neutralise their effects. But, on the other hand, in contrast to other industries, and agricultural production in particular, the productivity of gold mining is extremely stable in the short term, which makes gold suitable as a measure of value and money[21]. Consequently, the first case regarding the variations of the 'intrinsic value' of the money commodity can be put aside for the moment, unless we call into question extremely long-term changes such as the 'price revolution' which proceeded over centuries during the Age of Discovery.

What is more relevant is the second case of instability in the value of money. As we have seen above, the supply of gold, as the material of money, is in the short term extremely inelastic (so much so that it may be assumed to be zero) with regard to variations in demand. However, the demand for money (hence the quantity of money necessary for circulation) is considered to continue to increase in accordance with the expansion of economic activities in capitalism. As a result, the demand for monetary gold as a commodity is generally in excess of its supply[22]. And the ratio of exchange of money gold on the market against the other commodities, i.e., the purchasing power of money over them, may remain deviated in an equal degree from their value relations in favour of money (in terms of the classical theory of value and price, it is a state in which the market price remains above the natural price because of the maladjustment of the former to the latter, or in other words a state in which the price expressed in such money remains lowered). Since his debut as an economist in 1809 with the publication of *The Price of Gold* (III/15–27), Ricardo consistently stressed the stability of the value of currency in his monetary writings, highlighting the destabilisation of the value of money accompanying quantitative adjustment by means of precious-metal money, in order to emphasise the great advantage of the alternative: quantitative adjustment by means of the issue of banknotes.

As seen above, convertible banknotes can work along with gold money as their equivalent, in spite of the lack of their substantial 'intrinsic value' (although, unlike gold money, they cannot circulate beyond national boundaries). The sum of money in circulation in a country is therefore the total amount of these two kinds of national currency. When this sum exceeds or falls short of the 'quantity of money necessary for circulation', the adjustment process seen above will come into operation to eliminate the divergence between these two quantities. If, during such a process of adjustment, coin is melted down into bullion or bullion is minted into coin, this will give rise to changes in the relation between demand and supply on the bullion market. In the former case, the total amount of currency will diminish and at the same time the supply of bullion will increase. In the latter case, on the contrary, the demand for bullion (for minting) will increase at the same time as the total amount of currency. In this process of adjustment of the total amount of currency, in the former case the diminution of the quantity of money and the increase of the supply of bullion will have as their synergetic effect a fall in the market price of bullion more rapid than those of other commodities, the supply of which has no reason to increase. However, in the latter case, the increase in the quantity of money and the rise in the demand for bullion will have as their synergetic effect a rise in the market price of bullion more rapid than those of other commodities, the demand for which has no reason to increase. When the market price of bullion conforms with its mint price and the adjustment process comes to an end, the prices of other commodities will not have returned to their initial level. They will remain higher in the former case, and lower in the latter. In sum, the purchasing power of money does not completely recover from its temporary rise or fall, remaining somewhat higher or lower. Thus, the destabilisation of the value of money is unavoidable with the quantitative adjustment of precious metal money[23].

However, if we include in this process of adjustment the variations in the quantity of banknotes, we will end up with a different result. A bank issues its notes in lending them. The main method of lending by the BoE in Ricardo's time was the discounting of commercial bills. The money thus lent out will necessarily be redeemed and flow back to the issuing bank. The quantity of banknotes actually in circulation is equal to the credit balance at each moment. The issuing bank can increase or decrease its credit balance according to its lending policy[24], but this increase or decrease has no direct influence on the demand or supply of bullion on the market, so that the variation in the quantity of money caused by the bank's measures cannot give rise to a change in the price of bullion different from that of other commodities. This is because the quantitative adjustment of the issue of banknotes works as if the supply of money gold were adjusted to changes in the needs of circulation, although the banknotes themselves are not gold. The difficulties of adjustment of the production of gold extracted from mines are thus surmounted cheaply and promptly by the bank, which issues banknotes as 'virtual gold' instead of mines. If the quantitative adjustment of banknotes takes place more speedily and effectively than that of coin seen above, the instability of the value of money will be reduced in equal measure. Until now we have supposed a mixed circulation of coin and banknotes, but Ricardo aimed at a circulation consisting solely of convertible banknotes, in which coin would disappear from circulation. The conversion of banknotes would therefore involve not coin but bullion. This is his plan for monetary reform, according to which the quantitative adjustment of money will be achieved entirely by the issue of banknotes, which will totally eliminate the instability of the value of money discussed here. However, this can be said only of the currency circulating in a country and does not apply to the money of the world circulating in the form of bullion. 'A currency is in its most perfect state when it consists wholly of paper money, but of paper money of an equal value with the gold which it professes to represent' (I/361, cf. also IV/66).

About the discussions made up to now supposing a pure metallic circulation or mixed circulation of coin and paper, the only one which Ricardo considered as really existing was the worldwide circulation of precious-metal money. For him, coin and convertible banknotes in domestic circulation were something belonging to the past. Nevertheless, he discussed these forms of currency extensively. That is because the considerations about them were indispensable premises for discussing the notes of the BoE under the suspension of convertibility and their depreciation by over-issue, the central theme of his discussions about currency inspired by the debates of his time.

3.4.4 Increasing issue of inconvertible banknotes and their value

According to the Bank Restriction Act, enacted as temporary legislation in 1797 but afterwards renewed several times, the BoE was entitled to issue banknotes without being obliged to pay specie for them. The issue and circulation of inconvertible banknotes were unprecedented in the English currency regime at that time. Many worried about serious turmoil, such as rapid and substantial falls in the value of currency leading to the collapse of the currency regime itself as a result of the loss of confidence in its issuer, etc. However, contrary to these concerns, there was no such disorder immediately after the suspension of convertibility. Some time after, at the turn of the century, there was a rise in prices in England, including that of bullion, and a fall in the foreign exchange rate of the inconvertible notes of the BoE. This situation regarding English currency gave rise to a debate which was afterwards to be called the 'Bullionist Controversy'[25].

During the period when Ricardo published his writings about the problems of currency (from 1809 to 1823–4), up to the time when the resumption of cash payment was voted and officially decided in Parliament in 1819, closely following his *Proposals*, he did not cease to criticise the lax lending policy of the BoE; the over-issue of inconvertible notes; their depreciation and its evils (forced and unjust redistribution of wealth from creditor to debtor, etc.), and he continued to argue for the need to resume convertibility. In this section, we will consider his theory on the relationship between the value of money and its quantity in the context of the domestic circulation of inconvertible notes, referring mainly to *High Price*, in which he discussed most systematically the problems of currency in an inconvertible regime.

Ricardo moves to considerations of the inconvertible banknote only after having discussed the international distribution of precious-metal money. In this context he makes the following preliminary remarks:

> Such, then, appear to me to be the laws that regulate the distribution of the precious metals throughout the world, and which cause and limit their circulation from one country to another, by regulating their value in each. But before I proceed to examine on these principles the main object of my enquiry, it is necessary that I should shew what is the standard measure of value in this country, and of which, therefore, our paper currency ought to be the representative, because it can only be by a comparison to this standard that its regularity, or its depreciation, may be estimated.
>
> (III/65)

The 'main object of my enquiry' means naturally the monetary phenomena of the time, i.e., the circulation of inconvertible notes of the BoE, the rise in domestic prices and the fall in the foreign-exchange rate. The reason why the principles of international distribution of precious-metal money are discussed in detail, at the beginning of *High Price*, is that the clarification of the 'main object' must be done 'on these principles'. The precious metal distributed throughout the world functions in itself as money. The money in circulation there has its own value, and it is exchanged against commodities (buys them) on the basis of this value. For this type of money, therefore, there is no need to look for a standard outside it to indicate its value or its rise and fall. The 'standard' appearing in the quotation above is a means by which to express the value of money and its variation with its physical quantity (its weight), showing that money is equivalent to this standard through its conversion into it or exchange with it on the market (i.e., in buying it). This standard[26] works as such when the function of money is assumed by a medium which has no intrinsic value, such as paper, instead of precious metal circulating as money. But it is not because gold has definitively left its place as money, and entirely ceded its function as money to its representatives, that it becomes standard. As is evident from the quotation above, in the domain of international circulation, bullion as a commodity circulates as money irrespective of the monetary regimes reigning in each country. It is within this background context that even if gold ceases to circulate itself in a particular national monetary regime, it still functions as the standard of value with regard to the non-gold currency in circulation there. Gold functioning itself as money is the precondition for the function of gold as the 'standard' of money.

As we have seen above, money in Ricardo's theory is first of all gold itself as a material commodity, and a non-gold money which takes gold as its standard of value is understood theoretically rather as a particular form of money. In *High Price*, which is a work entirely devoted to the problems of money, the concept of 'standard' appears for the first time in the passage quoted above, where inconvertible banknotes are taken up for the first time. It is thus only in a particular aspect of Ricardo's theory of money that gold appears as a 'standard of money' distinct from the money actually in circulation. In chapter one of *Principles*, where money appears as a commodity serving as the measure of value, the 'standard' is the (invariable) standard of the value of commodities, i.e., money itself. And this 'standard' cannot be a 'standard of the value of money'.

It was naturally in the situation of circulation of inconvertible banknotes during the Bank Restriction Period that gold as the standard of money played a particularly important role. In the middle of *High Price*, Ricardo writes: 'Our circulating medium is almost wholly composed of paper, and it behoves us to guard against the depreciation of the paper currency' (III/74–5). *De facto* exclusive circulation of inconvertible banknotes was the actual state of the English domestic currency at that time. Before beginning to tackle such a state and the depreciation of currency observed therein, Ricardo accumulated, during the first half of *High Price*, scrupulous considerations about the international monetary circulation as an outer framework of the domestic circulation, and about the domestic currencies before the suspension of convertibility. His aim seems to have been to demonstrate how exceptional and abnormal is the exclusive circulation of paper money issued by the BoE exempted from the duty of conversion, and at the same time to prepare the theoretical foundation for assessing the state of inconvertible banknotes[27].

Before the suspension of cash payment in 1797, notes of the BoE and coin circulated side by side as currency (mixed circulation of gold and paper) in England. However, as we have already seen in the Section 3.4.3, banknotes originally played a supplementary role to coin and were added to it with this aim, and therefore presupposed a precious-metal circulation. We have also seen in Section 3.4.3 the mechanism through which two kinds of currency with their very different media, paper and precious metal respectively, can be treated as equivalents. The suspension of convertibility means that part of this mechanism is suspended. However, even if the conversion of banknotes ceases, inconvertible banknotes will still be regarded as equivalent to coin and treated as such, insofar as the market price of bullion does not deviate from its mint price, i.e., insofar as these inconvertible banknotes can procure on the market a quantity of gold equal to that contained in a coin with the same face value (here the question of seigniorage is set aside). But when, in addition to the suspension of convertibility, an upward deviation of the market price of bullion from its mint price (a depreciation of currency including coin) arises, these two kinds of currency, even with the same face value, will no longer be considered as equivalents. In such a situation, using coin to buy bullion on the market will amount to exchanging unequal quantities of gold at a loss. Moreover, the holder of coin, rather than using depreciated coin together with banknotes as currency to buy commodities at a loss, including bullion, could obtain an amount of currency (inconvertible banknotes) superior to the face value of the coin by melting it down to bullion, despite the legal prohibition on selling it on the market. Or, taking abroad the bullion obtained by melting coin, he could buy foreign commodities more cheaply than domestic ones, the prices of which will have risen by the depreciation of currency.

In the mixed circulation of coin and paper assumed here, the total amount of currency in domestic circulation consists of the sum of coin and inconvertible banknotes. The withdrawal of coin from domestic circulation, as seen above, in the event of currency depreciation is equivalent to a diminution of its total amount. And, at a certain point in this process of diminution, the market price of bullion will conform with its mint price because of the rise in the purchasing power of currency and the fall in the market price of bullion. Then this process will come to an end. The coin withdrawn from domestic circulation, reducing the total amount of currency, will be returned to the form of bullion and flow abroad ('will be exported', as Ricardo would say) in search of more advantageous uses (i.e., buying cheaper commodities). If there remains a certain amount of coin in circulation, the mixed circulation of coin and paper will continue as before, even with a reduced proportion of coin in the currency in circulation. But if the value of currency falls again, pushing up the market price of bullion again, the same process will come into operation anew and stop at a certain point. And if this process is repeated a number of times, coin will soon disappear totally from the circulation and only banknotes will circulate. If the depreciation of currency (inconvertible banknotes only) still continues in such a situation, there will be no more quantitative adjustment (reduction) of money and restoration of its value (in the sense of conformity of the two prices of gold with each other) as seen above. The situation Ricardo observed before his own eyes was the exclusive circulation of the inconvertible notes of the BoE, the final result of the progress to be expected after the suspension of convertibility, according to his theory. And such a state of currency and its problems were 'the main object' (III/65) of *High Price*. 'If the Bank were restricted from paying their notes in specie, and all the coin had been exported, any excess of their notes would depreciate the value of the circulating medium in proportion to the excess' (III/91).

In the quantitative adjustment of money in the context of mixed circulation of coin and convertible banknotes, as seen in the previous subsection, it was banknotes that assumed the role of stabilising the value of money and smoothing the adjustment. In contrast, in the mixed circulation in this subsection, consisting of coin and inconvertible banknotes, it is rather coin that assumes the role of quantitative adjustment. And this adjustment is one-directional; there is only the withdrawal of coin from circulation. This is because inconvertible banknotes always remain in the domestic circulation once they have been injected into it by the issuing authority, and because the issuing bank, exempted from the duty of conversion, tends to continually over-issue and depreciate its inconvertible banknotes of such a nature[28]. A mixed circulation consisting of inconvertible banknotes and coin can only subsist as long as no currency depreciation occurs. But as soon as depreciation begins, coin gradually ceases to circulate as currency, and furthermore, bullion will flow abroad. And when only inconvertible banknotes remain, there will no longer be any reaction to currency depreciation caused by over-issue, which will manifest itself as so much currency depreciation. 'We have paper money only in circulation, which is necessarily confined to ourselves. Every increase in its quantity degrades it below the value of gold and silver bullion' (III/78). And so, the currency will remain depreciated, and if the over-issue continues then it will depreciate still more. For this process to cease or be reversed and for currency to regain stability, the behaviour of the issuing bank itself must change, but such a thing can never be expected from 'a company of merchants, notoriously ignorant of the most obvious principles of political economy' (III/133)[29]. (Ricardo repeatedly criticised the BoE using similar expressions.)

> Parliament, by restricting the Bank from paying in specie, have enabled the conductors of that concern to increase or decrease at pleasure the quantity and amount of their notes; and the previously existing checks against an over-issue having been thereby removed, those conductors have acquired the power of increasing or decreasing the value of the paper currency.
> (III/75)

This leads to the actual over-issue, in danger of further aggravation. Such is the tone which made up the consequent *basso continuo* running through Ricardo's writings on the problems of currency up to the passing in 1819 of the Act for the Resumption of Cash Payments. He writes, for example: 'all checks against the over-issue of the Bank are now removed by the act of parliament' (III/78). Or again, 'There can be no limit to the depreciation which may arise from a constantly increasing quantity of paper' (ibid.).

The issue of notes by the BoE at that time was made through two channels, namely, loans to the government (mainly for financing the war with France), and discounting of bills drawn for commercial transactions. The BoE was a chartered institution of public character issuing currency, and at the same time it was a private, for-profit enterprise established as a joint stock company ('company of merchants'). Its main source of profit was the interest obtained by lending the banknotes it issued. It is therefore natural that the BoE, as a private lucrative establishment, should try to earn as much of this interest income as possible. Given a certain rate of interest, this interest income depends exclusively on the amount of loans. So long as the duty to convert its banknotes into specie is imposed on the issuing bank, the amount of issue is limited, to a certain extent, by the constraints of its gold reserve. But the exemption from cash payment removes this constraint, so that the amount of loans will constantly increase in order to expand profits. For the BoE, its notes are a very low-cost commodity for lending, producible with paper and ink, and the interest representing the profit obtained from this commodity has nothing to do with this cost. As can be seen from the quotations above, Ricardo repeatedly emphasised that when the issuing bank is put in such a situation it is always potentially apt to expand and depreciate its currency indefinitely. But the loan of money is only possible on demand. For Ricardo's argument to be valid, it is necessary to assume that the borrowers (government and merchants) will also expand the demand for loans indefinitely, at the same rate as the lender. The government finance required for waging the war, although large, cannot expand infinitely.

But, as for the discount of bills, the second channel for the issue of money, Ricardo writes in chapter 27:

> The application to the Bank of money, then, depends on the comparison between the rate of profits that may be made by the employment of it, and the rate at which they are willing to lend it. If they charge less than the market rate of interest, there is no amount of money which they might not lend – if they charge more than that rate, none but spendthrifts and prodigals would be found to borrow of them. We accordingly find, that when the market rate of interest exceeds the rate of 5 per cent, at which the Bank uniformly lend, the discount office is besieged with applicants for money; and, on the contrary, when the market rate is even temporarily under 5 per cent, the clerks of that office have no employment.
>
> (I/364)

In chapter 21, 'Effects of Accumulation on Profits and Interest', Ricardo writes about the actual state of the rate of interest on loans on the market at that time, with the 'usury laws' in force stipulating the legal upper limit of the rate of interest at 5% (I/196–7). According to him, the BoE applied the upper-limit interest rate of 5% throughout the Bank Restriction Period, but the actual rate of interest on loans from the other financial institutions was somewhat above this upper limit. In other words, the market rate of interest determined by the relation between demand for and supply of the loanable funds was over and above the legal limit, and the financial institutions (other than the BoE) which applied the market rate were conducting illegal business. Only the BoE, the issuing bank, observed the law. Ricardo argued that the rate of interest should be fixed freely on the market and not regulated by law. From his standpoint, the BoE used the usury laws of the time as a pretext for continuing loans (discount of bills) at a rate of interest below that of market[30]. In the paragraph following the sentences quoted above, he writes:

> The reason, then, why for the last twenty years [from 1797 to 1817], the Bank is said to have given so much aid to commerce, by assisting the merchants with money, is, because they have, during that whole period, lent money below the market rate of interest; below that rate at which the merchants could have borrowed elsewhere.
>
> (I/364)

Thus, 'the discount office' would be 'besieged with applicants for money'[31].

In this way, the quantity of inconvertible banknotes issued has no definite limit. It will gradually expand independently of the evolution of other economic variables. One important characteristic of this currency is that it 'is necessarily confined to ourselves' (III/78). Moreover, the inconvertible banknotes are confined not only to one particular country, but also to the circulation of that country, i.e., this currency can never go outside a domestic circulation[32]. Inconvertible paper money is of the same nature as precious-metal money circulating among nations, in that they are confined to a certain domain. These two forms of money, situated at the two opposite extremes in Ricardo's theory of money (whole world or one country with respect to the domain of circulation; precious metal or paper with respect to the medium), oddly enough have points in common in the causality determining the relationship between value and quantity. Near the end of the text of *High Price*, Ricardo writes:

> The circulation can never be over-full[33]. If it be one of gold and silver, any increase in its quantity will be spread over the world. If it be one of paper, it will diffuse itself only in the country where it is issued. Its effects on prices will then be only local and nominal, as a compensation by means of the exchange will be made to foreign purchasers.
>
> (III/91–2)

As for the precious-metal money as 'the money of the world': because of the difficulty in controlling its production and of the particularities of gold as a commodity, its quantitative adjustment is difficult (it is generally supplied in an insufficient quantity). On the other hand, inconvertible banknotes tend to be issued in a unilaterally increasing quantity because of the 'ignorance' (III/

133) and interests of the issuers (they are generally supplied in excess). The quantities of these two forms of money are *de facto* out of control. In addition, each of them remains 'enclosed' in its own domain of circulation. In such conditions, for both forms of money, the variation in quantity gives rise to a corresponding proportional change in prices. But, as precious metal is capable of international circulation as money, changes in its quantity do not affect domestic prices directly or in the same proportion. Their price effects are diffused and diluted worldwide. On the contrary, the effect of the quantitative variation of inconvertible paper money on prices is proportional to the degree of the variation but restricted to a domestic area, and has no worldwide repercussions as in the case of precious-metal money.

In the case of the domestic circulation of inconvertible paper money, the value 'inherent' in it can never determine or regulate its quantity in circulation, in whatever way. Its value varies only in accordance with the quantity issued. There is no force in the market to give rise to quantitative adjustment leading to conformity between the nominal value of the inconvertible paper money (the 'mint price' of gold) and its real value (the 'market price' of gold[34]), i.e., to a movement from value to quantity. Only a given quantity of paper money circulates, with the value determined by its quantity. This is precisely a situation akin to that described in the Quantity Theory of Money. Thus, in Ricardo's theory of money, phenomena *à la* Quantity Theory are only recognised with regard to a very limited particular state of monetary circulation (from the point of view of the bullionists, including Ricardo, it is a rather 'abnormal' state, causing 'evils' to be removed). Here gold is totally absent from the domestic circulation, either as currency or as bullion. However, this country continues to take part in world trade as a member of the 'civilised nations', without quitting the circulation of gold money. Insofar as foreign trade takes place and the inconvertible paper money of this country is thereby exchanged at a certain rate with currencies of other countries which maintain a substantial link with gold, then this country is considered to remain virtually in the mechanism of the international distribution of gold. The quantity of gold virtually allotted to this country is equal to the value obtained by dividing the total sum of inconvertible paper money in circulation in this country by the 'market price of gold' calculated from the foreign-exchange rate. This country is regarded as having virtually added this quantity of gold to the world circulation through the issue of its inconvertible banknotes, instead of by new gold production from mines (but such a virtual addition of gold was possible even with convertible banknotes, within the limits of the gold reserve). On the other hand, this virtual quantity of gold, varying with the variations of the two values that determine it (although these two are not independent of each other), does not depend on the will of the monetary authority of the country. Here again, the world money circulation, whether in purely metallic form or in the form of an 'international mixed circulation of gold and paper', always evolves spontaneously.

3.5 Afterword

Ricardo's theory of money is currently interpreted as a Quantity Theory, which is considered to be in contradiction with the labour (cost) theory of value, foundation of the principles of his economic theory (cf. De Vivo (1987), pp. 186–8). In this chapter we have tried to show, mainly through examination of his writings on monetary matters, that these views are both misunderstandings.

However, it is undeniable that some aspects of Ricardo's theory of money appear to come under Quantity Theory. A quantity of money given exogenously serves as a medium of circulation in its entirety, irrespective of its size, and the value of money (its purchasing power over commodities) is fixed in inverse relation to this quantity. If such is the Quantity Theory, a similar situation is also to be found in Ricardo's theory of money concerning the international circulation of precious metal and the domestic circulation of inconvertible paper money.

The basic framework of Ricardo's theory of money is the world circulation of precious-metal money, as in the case of Hume. But, unlike Hume, he regarded the precious-metal money in international circulation as a sort of commodity, just like others. Money therefore has its own value. But, in order for commodity money to be accepted at that value in the actual circulation, the supply of gold as a commodity must be readily adjustable in response to changes in the demand for it. The particular conditions of the production of gold render this adjustment very difficult, and for this reason the value of gold as money appears to be fixed irrespective of its conditions of production, by the extent of commodity exchanges for which money serves as a medium, i.e., by the quantitative relationship between money and commodities. But, according to Ricardo, gold is a commodity with its own value, and if its price on the market (its ratio of exchange with other commodities; its purchasing power) deviates from its value, this will trigger the forces that increase or diminish the quantity of its production, even if that is besieged with difficulties. In this sense, Ricardo's theory of money is not totally dissociated from his theory of commodity money in *Principles*; it maintains a feeble link with it, although some of its aspects appear to be akin to Quantity Theory.

Another domain in which the determination of the value of money in terms of Quantity Theory seems to be justified is the domestic circulation of inconvertible banknotes. Inconvertible paper money can be injected into circulation by the monetary authority in any quantity, according to its issuing policy, and the total sum remains in circulation. Its value per unit falls in proportion to the quantity issued. This is precisely the determination of the value of money in the Quantity Theory. The reason why such a situation takes place is that the quantitative adjustment of the domestic currency has been rendered impossible by the suspension of convertibility. Ricardo demanded the abolition of the regime of inconvertible banknotes that was destabilising the value of money and conceived a currency regime in which it is more likely to be the quantity of money that should be regulated by the relationship with its standard (gold). In his plan for monetary reform, Ricardo aimed to economise the use of gold and stabilise the value of currency by regulating the quantity in circulation, relying on the value of gold as a commodity, its ultimate anchor. This is the direct opposite to the Quantity Theory of Money. The next chapter will examine how Ricardo conceived a new monetary regime for his country.

Notes

1 One other example of earlier time is Sayers (1953), which aims 'to review as a whole the structure and the development of Ricardo's thought on monetary questions' (p. 30).

2 See for example, Sayers (1953), p. 33, Humphrey (1974), p. 7, Blaug (1995), p. 31, Arnon (2011), pp. 3–4, Smith (2013), p. 180, the article 'Gold' by Curzio and Rotondo in Kurz and Salvadori (2015), p. 175.

3 On the contrary, Deleplace (2017) seeks to integrate 'money into Ricardo's theory of value and distribution', at the same time as to prove that it 'is neither a quantity theory of money nor a commodity-theory of money' (p. 4).

4 This is most clearly visible in the development of the first half of *High Price*. In subsequent works (*Proposals*, related chapters of *Principles*), Ricardo gradually concentrates his attention on the domestic circulation of money (or currency) in England, but its world circulation surrounding the domestic one and forming its outer framework is always assumed in the background. None of Ricardo's arguments on monetary issues can be correctly understood without this context.

5 The term 'the money of the world' had been used in Steuart (1767) and has been known as such since then. Ricardo used this term twice in *High Price* (cf. III/ 53,87). He also used the expression 'the (general) currency of the world' (cf. III/ 53,57). But he does not use them in his later writings on money.

6 Name coined after publication of the Bullion Committee's report in August 1810 to designate its supporters.

7 This is the concept playing the fundamental role in Marcuzzo and Rosselli (1991) (see 'Chapter 3: The Value of Money'). But the authors seem to pay no attention to the value of money in the sense of the value of gold as a commodity functioning as money. In their theoretical framework gold in the form of bullion serves always as the 'standard of currency' (pp. 3, 49, 64) measuring the value of currency by its purchasing power over this 'standard', its price expressed in terms of this 'standard'. And the quantity of currency leading to conform this price with the mint price of the 'standard' is called 'the natural quantity of money' (pp. 3, 58, 137). See also 'Natural Quantity of Money' in Kurz and Salvadori (2015), pp. 373–4.

8 For example, in *High Price* he writes about this economy:

> the daily improvements which we are making in the art of economising the use of circulating medium, by improved methods of banking, would render the same amount of notes excessive now, which were necessary for the same amount of commerce at a former period.
>
> (III/86)

9 However, in the discussion about the comparative advantage among nations in chapter 7 of *Principles* ('On foreign trade'), Ricardo presupposes relative differences

in the conditions of production in different branches from country to country, and so a slightly different situation from the configuration of the world economy in the theory of money.

10 Therefore, the tastes for each sort of product and even the habits of consumption and life may be assumed to be alike in every nation, which recalls an important aspect of the colonialism of European nations in the non-European world since the Age of Discovery.

11 This may be unthinkable if the composition of the commodities produced, circulated and consumed differs from one country to another. To be able to talk about an international distribution for every commodity, a configuration of the world economy such as described in the first section of this chapter is indispensable.

12 Symmetrically, the quantity of money in the other country is relatively insufficient, so that the country imports money for its benefit. In this case, money is used as means of payment. Otherwise, there is no reason to do so.

13 This applies in more or less the same way to money, a sort of commodity. For Ricardo, importation is commodities (goods) brought to a country from abroad, and exportation means their movement in the opposite direction. As international trade is simply one sort of commodity exchange, these movements of commodities in opposite directions must necessarily be in equilibrium in terms of value. Consequently, since Ricardo considers money as a form of commodity, the idea of an international trade deficit or surplus, an excess in exportation or in importation and the consequent favourable or unfavourable balance of trade, are meaningless and incomprehensible expressions. 'From whatever cause an exportation of bullion, in exchange for commodities, may proceed, it is called (I think very incorrectly) an unfavourable balance of trade' (III/64). Although Ricardo employs this expression in *High Price*, it is always only as a concession to an 'ordinary usage' of the term with which he cannot agree. Such an attitude can be seen in this quotation, too.

14 Cf. Hume (1752), in particular the section 'Of the Balance of Trade'. However, in *High Price* Ricardo mentions the name of Hume only once and in a much later part.

15 At the time of *High Price*, Ricardo was not yet clear about the determination of commodity value. Here, some elements determining value – scarcity, quantity of labour, value of capital – appear side by side only in a disorderly manner. But, after *High Price*, he held the idea that the value of money is based on the value it has as a commodity and this value determines the quantity of money in circulation. 'The quantity of metal, employed as money, in effecting the payments of any particular country, using metallic money … must depend … first on its value' (Ricardo (1816), IV/55). 'Gold and silver, like all other commodities, are valuable only in proportion to the quantity of labour necessary to produce them, and bring them to market. … The quantity of money that can be employed in a country must depend on its value' (I/352, in chapter 27 'On Currency and Banks'). The idea expressed in these quotations forms the basis of Ricardo's conception about the value and quantity of money. If that were all, the matter would be very simple and would not require any investigation. However, except for the domain of international commerce, where bullion really did serve as money, a money circulation consisting solely of precious-metal money never actually existed, at least during the time of which Ricardo wrote, i.e., from the time prior to the suspension of convertibility in England up to his own time. The circulation actually involved convertible banknotes along with precious-metal money (gold coin) or inconvertible banknotes alone. The question is what becomes of Ricardo's fundamental viewpoint shown in

the quotations above, in the situation of currency circulation where precious-metal money does not circulate (exclusively).

16 Marx, in 'C. Theories of the Medium of Circulation and of Money' at the end of Chapter Two 'Money or Simple Circulation' of Marx (1859), criticises Ricardo's quantity-theoretic explanation of the value of money in *High Price* (pp. 402–3), contending that the quantity of production of gold as a money commodity is regulated in accordance with the needs of circulation, so that it carries out the function as money according to its value. This criticism by Marx is from the standpoint that gold as a money commodity can and must be treated exactly in the same way as the other commodities. However, Ricardo sought to address the difficulties of quantitative adjustment arising from the specific conditions of the production of precious metal within the framework of his commodity-money theory, of which Marx was not aware in his theory of money. These tentative efforts of Ricardo may be considered to raise problems with the commodity theory of money.

17 Below we shall examine this problem more concretely while referring to some passages of Ricardo's text. McCulloch, in his (anonymous) review article on *Proposals* (cf. McCulloch 1818, pp. 58–9), tells us about this point concisely and more clearly than Ricardo himself. He says that, according to Ricardo's theory, the value of precious metal is determined on the same principle as for other ordinary commodities, but on the condition that unlimited competition is at work in the production of precious metal, so that its production can be promptly and easily increased or diminished in accordance with the relation between supply and demand. But, in reality, he continues, the peculiarities of gold mining make this sort of quantitative adjustment difficult. And, in such a situation, the value of precious-metal money varies according to its quantity relative to the demand for it (i.e., the scale of commercial trade for which money serves as medium), so that the causality runs from the quantity of money to its value. At this time, McCulloch was, as Ricardo's 'faithful disciple', actively engaged in commenting and vulgarising his works, which is why he could make such a pertinent summary. On the other hand, in this review article, McCulloch paraphrases in detail the 'principle of limitation of quantity' which plays an important role in the explanation of the value of inconvertible banknotes and of its variation in chapter 27 of *Principles* ('On Currency and Bank'). We shall examine this in a later section.

18 It should be noted that this process of adjustment is for the case where the quantity of gold transacted as bullion in the domestic market is superior to that necessary for the adjustment, but that things will not proceed in the same manner if the quantity of bullion in the market is not sufficient for the adjustment or, in an extreme case, if there is no bullion there. Moreover, the problem of currency debated in the Bullionist Controversy in which Ricardo actively participated was the opposite to the situation he discusses here, that of excess currency and a rise in commodity prices, including the market price of bullion, and he himself was employed in elucidating these phenomena. If Ricardo analyses a phenomenon here that was alien to the actual state prevailing in his time, it may be to reconfirm the advantage of the banknote circulation he had already emphasised in *High Price*, and so to show that it is indispensable for the 'perfect' (IV/55) state of currency to be realised in the future.

19 This quantitative adjustment cannot be achieved by monetary-authority decision or policy; it happens automatically, so to say, as long as the conversion of banknotes,

the free minting of bullion and melting of coin and the freedom of their importation and exportation are assured.

20 Ricardo is thus aware of the sluggishness of the production (and hence of the supply) of precious metal used to make money, and this introduced quantity-theoretic elements into his theory of determination of the value of money based on the theory of commodity money. In other words, he was aware of the fact that it is difficult for capitalist production to control the commodity 'money' in the way that it controls other commodities (industrial products in particular). Ricardo notes that labour and houses are similar to money in this respect. Houses are closely related to the earth. Then these three items can be interpreted as money, labour and earth, three elements that are difficult to subsume under the movement of capital, but nevertheless indispensable for the working of capital, which can be related to K. Polanyi's viewpoint on the difficulties of their commodification in his *Great Transformation*, published more than a century after Ricardo. In chapter 13 of *Principles*, Ricardo has this to say about the reduction of gold production:

> The agreement of the market and natural prices of all commodities, depends at all times on the facility with which the supply can be increased or diminished. In the case of gold, houses, and labour, as well as many other things, this effect cannot, under some circumstances, be speedily produced. But it is different with those commodities which are consumed and reproduced from year to year, such as hats, shoes, corn, and cloth; they may be reduced, if necessary, and the interval cannot be long before the supply is contracted in proportion to the increased charge of producing them.
>
> (I/196)

On the other hand, chapters two ('On Rent'), three ('On the Rent of Mines') and five ('On Wages') of *Principles* can be read respectively as explaining the difficulties that capital must be faced with when trying to subsume as commodities under its movement the earth and labour, which are however indispensable for its valorisation. Incidentally, Marx, who emphasised the historical limits of capital, also put forward the difficulties of commodification of the earth and labour in the chapters on the wages and the rent of *Capital*, and made it clear that these difficulties impose constraints on the movement of capital accumulation. However, as for money, he stuck to the theory of commodity money even more radically than Ricardo, and insisted that the production and circulation of precious-metal money are not different from those of other commodities, so that money gold must be treated on an equal footing with other commodities.

21

> Though the variations in the *value* of gold or silver may be considerable, on a comparison of distant periods, yet for short spaces of time their value is tolerably fixed. It is this property, among their other excellences, which fits them better than any other commodity for the uses of money.
>
> (III/65, note. Emphasis in original)

22 The sporadic and accidental discoveries of large-scale gold mines, which took place during about a century after Ricardo's time, may have made temporary and partial changes to this situation.

23 The fundamental reason why such a thing happens is that money gold does not readily increase or decrease in response to the needs of circulation. Incidentally, we are here setting aside the connection between domestic and international circulations, and limiting our consideration solely to the problems of the former.

24 For such a discretionary action, it is naturally supposed that the monetary authority is aware of the excess or deficiency of the sum issued (more precisely, the total of the credit balance of banknotes and the amount of coin issued). But its criterion is only the relationship between the mint and market prices of gold. It is impossible to judge whether the quantity actually issued is excessive or deficient on the basis of a certain amount of money. An appropriate amount of issue is something quite unknowable. 'The issuers of paper money should regulate their issues solely by the price of bullion, and never by the quantity of their paper in circulation' (IV/64).

25 Here we will not enter into the historical details of the events leading to the suspension of convertibility, the states of currency and the developments of the debate in England at that time. On these matters, see chapters 8–10 of Feavearyear-Morgan (1963) and chapters 1–2 of Fetter (1965). On the importance of this controversy, Laidler (2000) says that 'the Bullionist Controversy did indeed provide the basis for a century or more of subsequent developments in monetary economics' (p. 27, see also Laidler (1987), p. 293).

26 This may correspond to the key-concept 'standard of currency (or money)' in Marcuzzo and Rosselli (1991) and Deleplace (2017). Cf. also note 7 above.

27 Chapter 27 of *Principles* begins with the following sentences: 'So much has already been written on currency, that of those who give their attention to such subjects, none but the prejudiced are ignorant of its true principles. I shall, therefore, take only a brief survey of the general laws which regulate its quantity and value' (I/352). This chapter 27 can be regarded as a 'summary' of the theory of currency Ricardo had expounded till then. Here, concentrating on 'the general laws which regulate its quantity and value', he briefly restates the mechanism of depreciation of the inconvertible banknote with its 'evils' and his proposals of a currency 'in its most perfect state' (I/361) that he had already explained in *High Price* and *Proposals*, while adding some new arguments.

28 In chapter 27 of *Principles*, Ricardo writes: 'Experience, however, shews that neither a State nor a Bank ever have had the unrestricted power of issuing paper money, without abusing that power' (I/356). This statement applies exactly to the BoE during the Bank Restriction Period.

29 When the Bullion Committee presented its report in June 1810, an intense debate arose over its analysis (depreciation of banknotes with over-issue as its main cause), and its conclusion (resumption of convertibility after a certain time and the restriction of paper issue to a suitable level). The most influential criticism of this report was contained in Bosanquet (1810). He sought the causes of rising prices and falling foreign exchange in factors other than monetary ones, and rejected the idea of over-issue by the BoE. Ricardo published an extensive counter-attacking pamphlet: *Reply to Mr. Bosanquet's Practical Observations on the Report of the Bullion Committee* (III/157–256), only two months after the publication of Bosanquet's tract.

30 The coexistence of different rates of interest is explained by the fact that some merchants were excluded from the service of discounts (loans) from the BoE and were therefore obliged to accept discounts at a higher rate from other financial institutions. The BoE restricted its discounts to the bills drawn or endorsed by the

merchants of sufficient credibility (mainly those who were in business to a certain extent in the London area).

31 However, according to Ricardo's logic seen above, for this to happen it is necessary that the rate of profit is over and above the rate of interest, a condition more fundamental than the difference in the rates of interest applied by different agents of discount. The face value of the bill brought to the discount office already includes the profit obtained by the sale of commodities against this bill. Insofar as a part of this profit remains in the sum of money obtained from the bank against the discounted bill, the exchange of a bill for a discount with a higher liquidity, i.e., cash, will maintain its meaning, and so the demand for discount will continue. But, for this to be the case, the rate of profit in the face value of the bill must be above a certain level. The question is whether the commercial transaction satisfying such a condition can expand indefinitely. Ricardo seems to assume such a possibility without bothering to justify it theoretically. Here, we also adopt provisionally Ricardo's position on the possibility for the discount of bills with inconvertible banknotes to lead to an indefinite increase in currency issue and its concomitant depreciation, and follow his logic on the quantity and value of currency in such a situation.

32 At the same time, it is only the issuing bank that can inject inconvertible paper into circulation; no other agents can increase or decrease at will the quantity of currency. In this case the issuing bank can regulate the quantity of currency independently of any other institutions or agents. This is a very different situation from the circulation of commodity (gold) money (free minting and melting of coin; free importation and exportation of bullion; conversion at sight of paper currency; buying of gold by the bank). In such a situation, the value of a currency depends on the quantity of it that is injected into circulation by the monetary authority. In chapter 27 of *Principles* (I/353) Ricardo proposes 'the principle of limitation of quantity' (this appellation was suggested by McCulloch, the author of the review article of *Proposals*, McCulloch (1818), and adopted by Ricardo in the second edition of *Principles* he was preparing at that time, but the original idea of this 'principle' had already been included in chapter six ('Observations on the Principles of Seignorage') of *Reply to Mr. Bosanquet's Practical Observations...* (see note 29) to explain why a paper money devoid of any value in itself can have value as money. This principle applies precisely to the currency in such a situation, and will no longer be valid if the quantity of currency depends on agents other than the issuing authority. We shall not dwell on this principle here. Ricardo has this to say about it: 'Mr. Buchanan evidently thinks that the whole currency must, necessarily, be brought down to the level of the value of the debased pieces; but, surely, by a diminution of the quantity of the currency, the whole that remains can be elevated to the value of the best pieces' (I/356). This means that the value of currency as currency can be determined and vary independently of its 'intrinsic value'. Gold money and paper money are therefore not to be distinguished, insofar as they equally pass as currency with a value free from the 'intrinsic value' of their media if their quantities are limited. Paraphrasing the well-known dictum of Keynes in *Indian Currency and Finance* (1913), it may be said that the gold of gold coin is only a medium on which to print its face value as money, and there will be no essential change if this medium is changed from gold to paper. Such a point of view may have something in common with contemporary chartalism, according to which the value of money depends on the policy of its issuing authority, irrespective of its medium. The relevance of this 'principle' in Ricardo's theory of money is stressed in Deleplace (2017), p. 10, etc.

33 In the first page (fourth paragraph) of chapter 27 of *Principles* is a sentence of similar tenor: 'A circulation can never be so abundant as to overflow' (I/352). The very succinct and concise explanation of the relation between value and quantity of currency presented in a space of less than one page just before this fourth paragraph seems to retrace the arguments developed in *High Price* written about seven years before.

34 But there can be no gold remaining in the domestic market, because it has already entirely flown out. Then there can be neither gold transactions nor a market price of gold. Nevertheless, Ricardo continues to use the 'market price of bullion' as the measure of depreciation of inconvertible banknotes in the situation of its exclusive circulation. If it is possible to talk about the 'market price of bullion' despite the absence of gold transactions and the lack of a price of gold in the domestic market, it can only be via the foreign-exchange rate with a foreign currency actually linked to a certain quantity of gold and the currency of the country.

4 Ricardo's plans for the reform of the monetary regime

Chapter 4 takes up and examines some other more concrete aspects in Ricardo's theory of money, i.e., his plans for the reform of the monetary regime intended to overcome the difficulties contained in the English monetary regime during the Bank Restriction Period (1797–1821).

In the last few pages of 'Appendix' added at the end of the last, fourth, edition of his first pamphlet *High Price* published in 1811, Ricardo showed for the first time the outline of his plan for the resumption of convertibility of the banknote, but unlike the Bullion Report published in the previous year, his plan proposed a payment in bullion instead of specie. Though his proposal could not attract attention at that time, Ricardo seized every opportunity after that to have it widely recognised. In 1819, he succeeded as a member of Parliament in getting it integrated into a bill and passed. At the same time a conception of establishing a national bank in place of the Bank of England which he did not cease criticising, dates back to this period before the enactment of Peel's Bill, prior to his last manuscript of 1823. This chapter examines the process of his thinking and his acts up to this moment.

4.1 Foreword

Of the various aspects of Ricardo's monetary theory, we tried in Chapter 3 to analyse and estimate what seemed to be the most fundamental: the relation between 'value and quantity of money'. This chapter presupposes the view advanced in Chapter 3 and takes up and examines some other more concrete aspects in his theory of money, i.e., his plans for the reform of the monetary regime intended to overcome the difficulties contained in the English monetary regime of his time (we adopt the term 'plan', just as Ricardo used for a long time to express his concept). From a different point of view, since the subject of the present chapter is the same as in Chapter 3, some points already treated may be occasionally mentioned again, but we will try to minimise the repetitions.

As is well known, Ricardo appeared as an economic polemist in 1809, in the midst of a time called the Bank Restriction Period, and he attracted attention

DOI: 10.4324/9781003498322-5

in arguing for the position to be called afterwards 'bullionism', claiming the resumption of convertibility. It was thus that the pamphlet *High Price* appeared in the following year, 1810. It met so many reactions that he produced a fourth edition in April 1811. And, in the last few pages of 'Appendix' added at the end of this last edition, he showed for the first time the outline of his plan for the reform of the monetary regime. Though this plan attracted practically no attention nor was it spoken of then, Ricardo himself attached much importance to it. Every time it was possible to make approaches to political leaders on monetary issues or in preparing publications, he made an effort to elaborate it in detail. And, in 1819 when he sat as a member of Parliament, he succeeded in getting it integrated into a bill and passed. But once his plan was implemented in outline, a difficult situation, unforeseen at the time of its conception, appeared, and Ricardo had to continue struggling with it in and outside Parliament till the end of its session just before his death (July 1823). In the summer of that year, after the close of the session, he drafted a new manuscript of 'plan' with a view to publishing it. But this manuscript was unfinished, because of his sudden death and was published in the following year by one of his younger brothers, Moses, under the title of *Plan for the Establishment of a National Bank*. In this way, Ricardo did not cease elaborating his measures for the reform of the English monetary regime, trying to realise them by every possible means, during almost the whole of his life as an economist.

The present and next chapters aim to examine the content and character of Ricardo's plan(s) for monetary reform. On each of the key steps from 1811 to 1823, we will see how Ricardo conceived, elaborated and modified his plan, taking into consideration the surrounding situation at each time (international relations including in particular war and commerce, deliberations in Parliament on bills and decisions).

Since J. Bonar published his monumental article in 1923 in commemoration of the centenary of the death of its author (Bonar (1923)), Ricardo's plan for monetary reform has usually been called the 'Ingot Plan' after the title of the article. Until his 'later years', Ricardo required the resumption of convertibility to be implemented not with specie or cash (meaning a quantum of precious metal moulded into coin) as prior to its suspension, but with bullion or ingots stamped with weight and fineness on it cast into a form of a certain size which was easy to handle with human hands – which may be described as an intermediary form between bullion and coin but the same as bullion, insofar as ingots do not circulate as currency. In this sense, to call his plan for monetary reform the Ingot Plan may not be beside the point. But, as far as referring to the materials included in *Works*, Ricardo himself used this term only once in his letter to Trower of 5 March 1822, IX/176. This letter was published for the first time in Bonar and Hollander (1899). If Bonar used the term in the title and text of Bonar (1923), it may possibly be because he knew the content of this letter well as its editor. But, except for this sole case, speaking of his project of monetary reform, Ricardo always called it simply 'plan'. Of course, a plan including the claim of payment of a banknote with bullion is virtually an Ingot Plan. In attributing to it a definite name, an idea Ricardo himself did not clearly and coherently conceive, would be fixed as his 'plan' with a particular title.

On the other hand, he came to conceive imprecisely a plan of the establishment of a national bank, not included in the plan of bullion payment of 1811, about a time when he was preparing and writing in 1815 *Proposals*, aiming at giving theoretical foundation and further development to his former plan. Before and after this period, he expressed the content of his reform of monetary regime invariably with the term 'plan'. At least after that period, this term seems to indicate either 'ingot plan' or 'plan for the establishment of a national bank', or possibly both of them at the same time. Therefore, a coherence between them or a passage from one to the other may have been out of question for him. The manuscript of 1823 came to be known as 'plan for the establishment of a national bank' only after its publication, but the original title given to it by Ricardo at the time of its drafting was simply 'PLAN, &c.'. It seems clear that in writing it he did not intend to treat a subject as different from what he used to call 'plan'. As was seen above, Ricardo's theory of money was a minor theme in the history of research on his economic theory carried on up to the present, not to mention his plan for the reform of monetary regime (one of the remarkable exceptions is Sayers (1953)).

4.2 The first version of the plan for the reform of the monetary regime added at the end of 'Appendix' to the fourth edition of *High Price*

4.2.1 Circulation of currency at the beginning of the 1810s (coin and paper), Ricardo's commentaries on A Chart *of Galton*

For examining Ricardo's plan for monetary reform, it would be necessary to confirm in advance how he recognised the actual situation of currency circulation. He says in *High Price* as follows: 'Our circulating medium is almost wholly composed of paper, and it behoves us to guard against the depreciation of the paper currency with at least as much vigilance as against that of the coins' (III/74–5). He confirms here the disappearance of coin. Indeed, in the situation of suspension of convertibility of banknotes, coins gradually went out of circulation and finally disappeared quasi-totally (for the detail of this mechanism, cf. the first pages of Section 3.4.4).

After having confirmed the situation of a quasi-exclusive circulation of paper, he says that against the depreciation of paper one must be more vigilant than against that of coin now disappeared. He explains how the depreciation of coin takes place as follows: 'If one-fifth [miscalculation of Ricardo, this should be corrected to one-sixth, cf. Sraffa's note 2] were taken off from every guinea, the market price of gold bullion would rise one-fifth above the mint price.' (III/78–9) He says therefore that the depreciation of coin, i.e., the deviation between the above two prices (rise in the former) arises from 'clipping our coins' (III/78). The coin made of precious metal is itself a lump of valuable material. If its possessor clips a part of it before delivering it to buy a commodity, he can obtain as much material of value. Thus, the precious metal coin was liable to gradual diminution of weight as it continued to circulate. Besides, even in the absence of such stealing by clipping, the coin gradually undergoes similar loss of weight caused by wear and tear during its long use. But it is practically impossible that such processes go on evenly for every piece of coin in circulation, which we daily experience with the contemporary token coins with their wear and tear or stain in a degree different from piece to piece. If the 'depreciation of coin' should be understood as in the quotation above, such circumstances should necessarily be taken into account. But Ricardo seems to suppose an even change (diminution of weight) for every piece of coins just like in the case of the depreciation of a banknote. What he says about the depreciation of coin may have been based not on what was really happening at his time, but on his abstract theoretical presupposition. In fact, just as he says himself, at the time of writing *High Price* gold coins hardly circulated, and in addition, the few pieces of coin still remaining in circulation did not undergo a depreciation (or rather deterioration) as in the above meaning.

An interesting literature in which Ricardo argues about the relation between coin and paper and about the depreciation of coin has recently been deciphered and published for the first time in Depoortère (2015), pp. 344–5. This is his commentaries on the manuscript of Galton (1813), contained in his letter of 6 December 1812, a little after the publication of *High Price*, to Leonard Horner, a younger brother of Francis Horner. In this manuscript Galton intends to show visually in the form of *A Chart* the relation between the amount of currency issued and the evolution of prices and foreign exchanges after the suspension of convertibility going back as far as to 1760, on the basis of numerous numerical data published in Mushet (1810), then master of the Royal Mint. This was a project in line with the protagonists of bullionism like F. Horner, R. Mushet, Ricardo, etc. Ricardo received and read this manuscript probably at the beginning of December, and he expresses in his letter of response an almost entire agreement with *A Chart* in saying that 'I find but very few positions with which I do not entirely agree' (Depoortère (2015), p. 344), and writes in conclusion that 'I hope that your friend will be induced to publish his chart and explanations as I think it very strikingly illustrates the theory which we are both anxious to establish' (ibid., p. 345) (it was actually published at the beginning of March of the following year (1813), and a complimentary copy was sent also to Ricardo). A brief letter of Ricardo to Galton written in the third person without signature was discovered at the same time and is published in Depoortère (2015), pp. 345–6. According to the author, only with the discovery of this letter of Ricardo did it become clear that the work on which he wrote commentaries in his letter to L. Horner was written by Galton[1].

Now, Ricardo says in his letter about the difference of opinion with the author of the manuscript as follows:

> It does not appear to me to follow as a necessary consequence that in proportion as the coins in circulation are diminished in weight by wear, they will become depreciated in value. It is possible that a currency might consist wholly of coin diminished in weight by wear, 10 or even 20 pc[t], without any effect being produced on the price of bullion. Whether the price of bullion would rise under such circumstances would depend entirely on the abundance of such coin. Coin is never depreciated but by excess of quantity. The assertion therefore at the bottom of page two though practically correct, because worn coins have always been accompanied by an excess of paper money, is not correct in theory. Coins may be deteriorated without raising the price of bullion, but the standard bullion cannot rise above the mint price unless the currency is depreciated.
>
> (ibid., p. 344)

In the passage quoted above from *High Price* Ricardo said that the coin may depreciate as it becomes lighter by clipping, but here he denies such depreciation in the same situation. Why does he make such contradictory statements?

Ricardo explains why it is 'practically correct' to say like Galton (and like himself in *High Price*) that a diminution of metal content in coin (deterioration) leads to its depreciation, i.e., the rise of market price of bullion over its mint price. The reason is that, with the depreciation of inconvertible paper over-issued simultaneously with the ongoing deterioration of coin, the coin has equally depreciated together with the paper insofar as the former makes up a homogeneous constituent part of the total currency circulating with the same face value alongside the latter. But he adds immediately that it 'is not correct in theory'. And he develops his critical comments to Galton, in affirming that a depreciation of currency can arise only with the change in its quantity in circulation, but never with the change in value of its material medium (gold or other metals for coin, paper for note).

As is evident from the context of these arguments of Ricardo, the point of view he advances here presupposes 'in theory' a situation (never existing in reality) in which the circulation is entirely filled with coin without any paper circulating. Such a supposition may be interpreted as being obtained in turning over 'in theory' to the exclusive coin circulation the quasi-exclusive inconvertible paper circulation really observed at the time of Ricardo's writing of these commentaries. And probably he applies just as it is the principle of depreciation of inconvertible paper to that of coin. Here he seems to treat coin, though in no need to be further 'converted' nor ever becoming 'inconvertible', just like the inconvertible paper. With the cost of only printing figures on a virtually valueless medium, paper notes can be issued in principle without limit or contracted at will, and once issued it must necessarily remain within the domestic circulation in its entirety as far as the issuer does not intend to recover some part of it. On the contrary, coin is issued in minting bullion which is an expensive commodity containing a certain value in itself. As far as the Mint responds passively to the demand of minting, the minting of coin (its issue) will cease of itself as soon as the coin becomes excessive and the market price of bullion exceeds that of its mint price (its change into coin incurring a loss), or insufficiency of coin will lead automatically to the reopening of minting (holding gold in the form of bullion incurring a loss). In the absence of a prohibiting law[2], the gold in the form of coin can be melted down for other uses or sent abroad (exported) for more advantageous exchange, so that it never remains enclosed in its totality within the domestic circulation but can freely pass both economic and political borders.

In this way, although both inconvertible paper and coin function equally as currency, there exists between them a large difference in nature. Ricardo's critical comments to Galton seem to be made in identifying 'in theory' the coin with the inconvertible paper at a time when practically gold coin entirely ceased its circulation. On the other hand, Ricardo critically comments on Galton's *A Chart* on the basis of his observations on the real evolution of currency. Ricardo points out the problem of calculation contained in Mushet (1810) which Galton relied on when composing *A Chart*, and also enters into technical details concerning the fabrication of coins both from gold and silver. As these details are out of the scope of the present chapter, here we refrain from their presentation. But, as the last point in Ricardo's commentaries seems to be essential to know how he recognised an aspect of the real evolution of currency up to the beginning of the 1810s (and this constitutes a presupposition for his plan of monetary reform), we will try to present and examine it.

Ricardo criticises as inappropriate the procedure of Galton in that he includes the small notes of £5, etc., issued only after the enforcement of the Bank Restriction Act of 1797 in the total of the amount of issue from the BoE together with the large notes of £10, etc.:

> The variations in the price of gold and in the foreign exchanges would I apprehend accord more exactly with the variations in the issues of the Bank of England since 1797 if in all cases we were to reject altogether the amount of notes in circulation of £5 and under, and it is quite just that they should be so rejected when we consider that the greater part of these notes have been issued as a substitute for the gold coin exported they cannot be accounted as so much added to the amount of currency.
>
> (Depoortère (2015), p. 345)

The circulation of currency of small face values, i.e., of coin and small notes, underwent an extensive influence, along with the variation in the whole quantity of money in circulation, by the suspension of convertibility at the end of the eighteenth century, and by its resumption a quarter of century afterward (two changes in opposite directions, from gold to paper and from paper to gold – for the latter change see below). Through the suspension of convertibility into specie (coin) and the export of gold brought about by the increased issue of inconvertible paper, small notes substituted themselves for gold coin, which gradually disappeared from circulation, and about ten years after the suspension of convertibility paper became virtually the exclusive medium of circulation. Therefore, the issue of small notes during this time did not mean an augmentation of the total amount of currency in domestic circulation, in calculating this amount the amount of newly issued small notes was to be subtracted. Otherwise, the amount of currency would be overestimated, so that the rise in prices (bullion price) and the fall in foreign exchange would not be correctly explained, making it difficult to comprehend the relation between the expansion of money and the evolution of these indexes. In eliminating the dually calculated part in Galton's *A Chart*, this relation can be recognised more properly, claims Ricardo.

In fact, in advance of these commentaries on Galton at the end of 1812, Ricardo, already aware of this relation of substitution between small notes and coin, had claimed not to include the former in calculating the total amount of currency. In a passage in 'Notes of the minutes of evidence' for the preparation of *Bullion Report* (Cannan (1919)), probably written after September 1810, he says as follows:

> The question is whether in judging of an excessive issue by a comparison of the present amount of notes, and the amount in 1797, the amount of small notes should be taken into consideration. If the small notes substituted have not exceeded the amount of guineas withdrawn, it is clear they should not be taken into the account.
>
> (III/371–2, 'Notes on the Bullion Report and Evidence')

In 'Appendix' to the fourth edition of *High Price* he says also: 'The increase of small notes, then, will ultimately be a substitution of one currency for another, of a paper for a metallic currency, and will not operate in the same way as an actual and permanent increase of circulation[3]' (III/114). (In relation to this point, see also the following: III/34, 37, 177, 384.)

In the latter half of the passage from *High Price* quoted above (III/74–5), Ricardo said that both paper and coin is equally depreciating, but that the problem is more serious for paper than for coin. In the case of coin, its depreciation by deterioration may be physically checked to a certain degree ('legal standard', IV/69. The pieces of gold coin become too much lighter than the legal weight – about 8g for one pound – and would probably not have circulated. If the limit is half of its legal weight, the deterioration of coin would have stopped there and would not have gone further), but in the case of paper its depreciation is in no relation to its physical alteration (deterioration), exactly identical new paper money would be continually issued only to be added indistinctively to all the paper money already in circulation, so that the danger of its depreciation would be as serious (any physical check preventing it from going beyond a certain degree as in the case of coin does not work, as there is a possibility it could progress infinitely). In another passage from *High Price* he also says:

> This depreciation in the actual value of bank-notes has been caused by the too abundant quantity which the Bank has sent into circulation. The same cause which has produced a difference of from fifteen to twenty per cent. in bank-notes when compared with gold bullion, may increase it to fifty per cent. There can be no limit to the depreciation which may arise from a constantly increasing quantity of paper.
>
> (III/78)

This may be right in an abstract theory. In his works written in the midst of the bullion controversy, Ricardo had a tendency to emphasise a little excessively or rather exaggerate the risk of depreciation of inconvertible banknotes. Here he suggests the possibility of depreciation attaining 50% or going infinitely farther. Of course, this may have been a sort of rhetoric to advance vividly the claim of bullionism for the resumption of convertibility and to arouse public opinion. In fact, all through the bank restriction period, the depreciation of paper reached its peak at the end of 1813, when the maximum value of bullion price was 5*l.* 10*s* (Feavearyear and Morgan (1963), p. 210). Since it depreciated thus to as much as about 41.3% with regard to its mint price of 3*l.* 17*s* 10½*d.*, despite a little exaggeration Ricardo's discourse cannot be regarded as a simple political demagogy.

Indeed, with a depreciation of currency progressed so far, certain parts of the community like manufacturers and merchants may have obtained enormous profits from such a situation, while the others like creditors of contracts concluded before the currency depreciation or those who lived with fixed income, would incur a serious negative influence, which could lead to destabilising social relations in the country. In the year 1811, when the depreciation of banknotes was advancing toward the above maximum, there were important moves concerning the currency in Parliament on the background of such a situation.

4.2.2 Conflict on the depreciation of banknotes ('dual prices' and legal-tendering of banknotes, King and Stanhope)

Already from the time of writing of *High Price* at the end of 1809, Ricardo had foreseen what would be brought about by the ongoing depreciation of inconvertible banknotes as follows:

> If an ounce of standard gold in guineas would sell in the market … at 4*l.* 13*s.* per oz., what shopkeeper would sell his goods at the same price either for gold or bank-notes indifferently? If the price of a coat were 3*l.* 17*s.* 10*d.* or an ounce of gold, and if at the same time an ounce of gold would sell for 4*l.* 13*s.*, is it conceivable that it would be a matter of indifference to the tailor whether he were paid in gold or in bank-notes?
>
> (III/82–3)

As a matter of hypothesis, Ricardo raises here the question whether a seller of a commodity would accept indiscriminately a gold coin or a banknote of the same face value, despite the manifest depreciation of the latter. Equally legal currency, both of them should officially be able to buy the same commodity if the same face value was tendered. But actually, the banknote of a certain face value is worth only a quantity of gold contained in a coin of inferior face value. In the above example, this means that the seller of a commodity would incur about 16% of loss in accepting payment by a banknote. In such a situation he would set a higher price for the payment by a banknote than for that by coin, or if the price has already risen in proportion to the depreciation of the banknote, he would allow a discount for the payment by coin. Therefore, Ricardo speaks here about the possibility of emergence of a 'dual prices system' or (with a little exaggeration) of a collapse of the monetary system of a country, since currency of the same face value cannot buy the same commodity or that the same commodity sells with different prices according to the sort of currency tendered (in speaking about the possibility of differentiation of treatment on the market between coin and paper, Ricardo invariably supposes a homogeneity of every piece of coin as in the case of paper, and makes no question of actual disparity between them).

But in reality, as at that time the guinea almost totally disappeared from circulation and the discriminatory treatment of currency of the same face value was forbidden by law, the public could not behave like this and officially coin and bullion were always considered to be of the same value.

> Whilst it is a criminal offence to buy guineas at a premium [to exchange it with the banknote of a higher face value], it does not seem probable that we can possess the only test which would satisfy these gentlemen [anti-bullionists disclaiming the depreciation of banknote], namely, two prices for commodities, a price in guineas, and another in Bank notes.
>
> (III/201, Reply to Mr. Bosanquet's Practical Observations on the Report of the Bullion Committee, hereinafter Reply for short)

> When it [coin] is prevented from openly rising to 15 or 18 pc^{t} (its real and intrinsic value above paper) by the terror of the law which deters all men of character from engaging in a traffic which is disreputable and illegal. Whilst the law can be enforced the currency may be depreciated 50 pc^{t}, and yet the coin and paper may preserve the same value as currency.
>
> (III/415–6, 'Observations on [Vansittart's] propositions respecting money, bullion and exchanges')

According to Sraffa, these observations were written from the end of April to the beginning of May 1811, immediately before the bill requiring the resumption of cash payment was rejected.

Even if the rise in the market price of gold and the depreciation of banknotes were evident, therefore coin and banknotes of the same face value were clearly of different value in terms of gold (the quantity of gold contained in the former is superior to that which the latter can buy on the market), the law regards both of them as equivalent and enforces a consequent treatment of them. The affirmation that the depreciation of currency goes on simultaneously and in the same degree for metallic coin and banknotes, therefore their values cannot deviate from each other, must be understood in such a context. An application of dual prices to commodity sales is considered a criminal offence. But, if people act obeying the law, in treating the two kinds of currency as equivalents, it is for fear of punishment, but whenever anyone can violate the law by escaping the punishment, premium will be given to guinea and discount applied to banknotes (in economic logic it is more rational and corresponds with the interest of agents).

Despite such a denial by law of the depreciation of banknotes and its enforcement, in 1811 a move openly claiming the discrimination between coin and banknotes appeared from within Parliament. It is the circular letter of Lord King, young aristocrat and member of the House of Lords, addressed in March to the tenants and farmers conducting agriculture on his land. In this circular, he claimed the payment of the rent due to the contracts concluded prior to the beginning of the depreciation of banknotes by the suspension of convertibility, with coin or bullion amounting to the sum initially determined, or with banknotes at a due premium (of about 15%). He affirmed this claim to be just and legal for the protection of his property rights, and at the same time proclaimed that he himself would do the same for his debts owed to others[4] (Feavearyear and Morgan (1963), p. 204–6). Ricardo did not give open consent to the action of King, but he belonged to the camp of bullionism like Ricardo and had criticised the depreciation of banknotes since King (1804). According to Bonar, such action by King motivated Ricardo to advance his plan for the reform of the monetary regime in 'Appendix' to the fourth edition of *High Price* (published in April 1811).

> In the fourth edition ... an Appendix is added which contains Ricardo's Plan. It is just possible that Lord King had again [as when Ricardo began writing *High Price* in 1809] been before him. Lord King's famous letter to leaseholders in March 1811 required them to pay their rents according to old contract. ... The idea may have been 'in the air'; the two men, though quite good friends, made no acknowledgements to each other. King applies the idea to private contracts; Ricardo to the whole system of currency.
>
> (Bonar (1923), p. 282)

As if opposing this action by King, after the rejection of the Bill of Resumption, Lord Stanhope, equally member of the House of Lords, proposed a bill enforcing the reception of the notes of the BoE as equivalents to the coins of the same face values regardless of the evolution of bullion price and foreign exchange, so as to make the banknotes *de facto* a legal tender. As a part of the deliberation on this bill, King delivered a speech in the House of Lords on 2 July, to further develop the idea of his former circular with numerical data (King (1811 [1844]), pp. 231–59). In this speech he explains his position as follows:

> In this state of things, for the defence of my property, I have thought it advisable, in the management of my private concerns, to inform my tenants holding lands under old leases, and under old leases only, that I can no longer continue to receive bank-notes at their nominal value in payment or satisfaction for such contracts.
>
> (ibid., pp. 232–3)

But, despite the arguments of the dissident members, to begin with King, the bill of Stanhope was approved on 24 July and became a law of specified duration valid until 15 March of the following year (Lord Stanhope's Act). Afterwards this Act continued until the resumption of cash payment in May 1821 as the Gold Coin Bill passed in the House of Lords on 18 December (Gilbart (1837), pp. 53–4. VI/88, editor's note 1). In view of such a move in Parliament following the rejection of the Resumption Bill, Ricardo increased the sense of crisis of further continuation of the depreciation of banknote[5]. About 12 years after that time, on 11 June 1823, in a parliamentary speech responding to the criticism of Western about the results of the Resumption Act (Peel's Act) passed in May 1819, he mentioned anew the conflict between King and Stanhope from the standpoint of supporting the former (cf. V/316). This was the only one occasion for him to talk publicly about the dispute between them.

On 27 July, three days after the passing of Stanhope's Act in Parliament, Ricardo sent a letter, a direct petition, to Spencer Perceval, Prime Minister and Chancellor of Exchequer at that time, in order to inform him of the serious crisis and to appeal to him to implement a measure for preventing the further depreciation (VI/43–4). Violent changes in the prices and contents of contracts were foreseen soon after the expiration of the law enforcing the fulfilment of contracts according to the prices stipulated prior to the depreciation, not recognising the depreciation of banknotes. From the moment when the Act was approved, the public was under 'all its terrors' (VI/45). The proposal Ricardo made to Perceval was a provisional measure aiming at 'secur[ing] the public against any depreciation of the currency beyond that to which it has already reached' in order to release them from these terrors, and was not a radical one (like an immediate dissolution of the depreciation or resumption of cash payment). Concretely it was to oblige the BoE

> to sell gold bullion, for their own notes, to any purchaser that shall apply for a quantity not less than 5 ounces [correspondent to a little less than 24 pounds], at the rate of £4. 15 p^r oz. for standard bullion [i.e., at the current price of bullion], and whatever the bullion so delivered by the Bank may

> arise from, whether from foreign coin, or from light guineas, let it be freely exportable at the will of the purchaser.
>
> (VI/43–4)

This proposal follows, with minor modifications with respect to the way of setting the minimal sum and the selling price of bullion, Ricardo's 'plan' put forward for the first time in 'Appendix' to the fourth edition of *High Price*, of obliging the BoE to sell bullion for its notes above a certain minimal sum. If the depreciation of banknotes goes further and the market price of bullion rises over the above price, bullion will be bought more advantageously at the window of the BoE than on the market. Since the BoE will then be obliged to sell bullion at a loss under the market price, it will avoid such a state of affairs (further progress of depreciation by over-issue). In this way, further depreciation can be checked.

But Ricardo's direct petition resulted in an indirect response sent a week later from a secretary confirming the reception of his letter including the proposal (VI/46). Ricardo took his proposal to be 'politely declined' (VI/70) and tried again with a similar proposal in sending a letter on 11 December of the same year to George Tierney, leader of the Whigs and ex-member of Bullion Committee (VI/67–71). In this way he persistently continued action for implementing his plan. In Subsection 4.2.3, we will examine the contents of the plan for the reform of monetary regime Ricardo put forward for the first time in the last few pages of 'Appendix', to think about how it was conceived, its character and its aims.

4.2.3 First version of the Plan added at the end of 'Appendix' and its outcome

The fourth edition including 'Appendix' was published at the beginning of April 1811, about one month before the 'Resolutions' prepared by F. Horner, president of the Bullion Committee, on the basis of 'Bullion Report' (Horner (1811), pp. 5–8) were proposed to the House of Commons on 6 May and rejected a few days after. This 'Appendix', supplemented to this edition containing the first sketch of the plan for the reform of the monetary regime, can be considered to have been written and published just at that moment with a view to intervening in the then ongoing deliberation in Parliament. At the same time, this fourth edition including 'Appendix' seems to be a summary review of the fierce controversy over the Report Ricardo attempted from his point of view nearly a year after it had been proposed to the House of Commons on 8 June 1810. Toward March of the following year the main points of discussion were already available, and it was high time to review the whole of the debate. The first sketch of the above plan occupies such a place, it may be regarded as a nodal point in the debate from 1809. Ricardo seems to have proposed this plan with a view to giving a better form to the conclusions of the bullionists for their realisation at a moment when the main arguments in the debate were already available, and the political decision in

Parliament was imminent. In such a context, this plan of Ricardo, who consistently made public his support for the 'Bullion Report', had to become an alternative containing some modifications to its conclusions. For him the above arguments can be reduced to two points, each of which he successively introduces and examines as follows.

The first argument against the 'Report' is: the gold reserve of the BoE from 1810 to 1811 amounted to £3,000,000 at legal mint price, corresponding to about one seventh of more than £20,000,000, the total amount of banknotes issued during the same period (Feavearyear and Morgan 1963), to resume cash payment with such a low level of reserve a large accumulation of additional reserve would be required and 'the Bank would be exposed to considerable difficulty' (III/123). In order to avoid such a difficulty, the 'Report' did not propose an immediate resumption but allowed for two years before beginning it, recognising the necessity of 'a diminution of 15 per cent in the amount of the Bank circulation' in order to lower to the mint price 'the average price of gold' (ibid.) now risen to 4*l.* 10*s.* Despite the worries of the anti-bullionists, the bullionists including Ricardo claimed that in two years 'after such a reduction in the amount of bank notes, the value of the remainder would be so raised, that it would not be the interest of any person to demand specie at the Bank in exchange for notes, because no profit could be made by the exportation of bullion' (III/124). In other words, despite the resumption of convertibility, the recovery of the value of currency would make a great amount of gold reserve unnecessary. This is one of the important points in his plan, which Ricardo subsequently had to affirm repeatedly.

The second argument against the 'Report' is a worry about the necessity of a great amount of gold reserve for the resumption, even if recognising the above claim of the bullionists. 'What security would the Bank have that caprice or ill-will might not render the practice general of discontinuing the use of small notes altogether, and demanding guineas of the Bank in lieu of them?' (ibid.). As already seen, at that time the guinea, the gold coin in circulation from the time before 1797, had almost disappeared and the small notes of £1, £2 were largely circulating in place of guineas. Will not the resumption of cash payment reverse this situation back to that observed before its suspension? If such happens, a great amount of gold coin will be required regardless of the depreciation of banknotes. The plan Ricardo is to reveal subsequently was conceived precisely to avoid such a situation.

On these various grounds (irrespective of their validity), the anti-bullionists point out difficulties the BoE may face to oppose the resumption. The concrete contents of the plan are derived from such a context.

> It must be confessed, that whether these apprehensions are likely or not likely to be realised, the Bank could not but make some provision for the worst that might happen; and though it is a situation in which their own

> indiscretion has involved them, it would be desirable, if possible, to protect them against the consequences of it.
>
> (III/124)

The apprehensions may become actual because of the mismanagements of the directors of the BoE, and in such cases the difficulties will not be worth relief. But, at the same time as being an enterprise in pursuit of its own private interest, the BoE was an entity of public character, the bankruptcy of which would have entailed enormous damage to the public not limited to its stakeholders. Ricardo had acknowledged such a contradictory character of the BoE or rather distrusted a 'company of merchants' early on (cf. III/133).

Now, after these preliminary remarks Ricardo begins his positive 'suggestions' (cf. III/99, editor's note 1) capable of responding to the opposition to the conclusions of the 'Report', which are evidently addressed to the bullionist authors and MPs to call them to get together around these 'suggestions' in order to contain the opposition. At first, he speaks rather timidly of these 'suggestions' as 'more gentle means' than the recommendations in the 'Report' possibly apt to involve some embarrassment (difficulties or disorders) seen above. But, on the other hand, Ricardo anticipates with self-confidence that everyone who agrees with the avoidance of depreciation of currency will agree with his 'suggestions'.

> If the same benefits to the public, – the same security against the depreciation of the currency, can be obtained by more gentle means, it is to be hoped that all parties, who agree in principle [i.e., the bullionists], will concur in the expediency of adopting them. Let the Bank of England be required by Parliament to pay (if demanded) all notes above 20*l.*– and no other, at their option, either in specie, in gold standard bars, or in foreign coin (allowance being made for the difference in its purity) at the English mint value of gold bullion, viz. 3*l.* 17*s.* 10½*d.* per oz., such payments to commence at the period recommended by the Committee.
>
> (III/124)

This is the gist of Ricardo's new 'suggestions' to be habitually called 'Ingot Plan' in later times. Its characteristics are: (1) Setting of the minimal sum of £20 (far superior to the sums used for ordinary income circulation) for the banknotes to be accepted in gold payment; (2) Free choice of the forms of gold to be delivered in exchange for banknote (except for gold in manufactured products); (3) The obligation of gold payment begins in two years according to the legal mint price. It is only the third among the three points which follows faithfully the conclusions of the 'Report', which supposes as something natural the specie convertibility without setting a minimal sum.

The first and second points are measures for preventing the resumption of convertibility from recalling coin again to circulation as before the suspension. 'Notes above 20*l.*' may not mean that only the banknotes of a face value superior to 20*l.* can be accepted, but a number of small notes amounting in total to at least 20*l.* can also be accepted. And the free choice of the forms of gold to be paid (or 'sold') for banknotes is a 'privilege' (III/125) given not to those who demand payment in gold but to the BoE obliged to pay in gold. This means that the payment of banknotes to begin in two years was, strictly speaking, not a resumption of cash payment as it had existed prior to the Bank Restriction Period. It is in this sense that the BoE would consent for a while ('for three or four years'(ibid.)) to a 'privilege' of being exempted from the 'obligation' it assumed before 1797. Of course, for the anti-bullionists or directors of the BoE, this would not at all be a privilege, but rather a compulsory measure imposed upon it.

Ricardo advances these 'more gentle means' modestly not yet as a definitive, but only as a provisional measure to be tried for a certain time, but it is to 'be continued as a permanent measure' 'if found advantageous' (ibid.). He calls this 'plan' only toward the end of a long paragraph in III/125. In the space of a little more than three pages from this paragraph to the end of the 'Appendix', he explains the aims of the 'plan' (summarised above in three points) as well as how it was conceived. In the following we will try some examinations of these points.

Since the BoE responds passively to the demand for payment (sells gold at the mint price), or to say the same from the opposite side, since the banknote maintains a purchasing power over gold, fixed by the mint price, its value remains constant, and it never depreciates. 'The currency could never be depreciated below its standard price' (ibid.). In fixing the minimal sum for payment at £20 and paying in bullion[6], it becomes possible to prevent the withdrawal of small notes from circulation and the return of the guinea to circulation. It is bullion which can be obtained from the BoE in exchange for banknotes. Bullion can be sold as a commodity in the domestic market, but the sum of banknotes obtained in this way is equal to the sum of banknotes paid for obtaining the bullion now to be sold (since the market price coincides with the mint price), which renders meaningless such a transaction. Or, in order to make use of it as currency, bullion must be coined in Mint. Even if there is no seigniorage, the process of minting requires some time ('some weeks or months', ibid.), which means a loss amounting to the interest calculated for this lapse of time. This will make the public refrain from gathering small notes to bring them to the BoE for the purpose of getting bullion in order to mint it into coin. On the other hand, the bullion can work as means of international purchase or payment, but such a use of bullion is profitable only when the over-issued currency is in depreciation and the commodity prices abroad in terms of bullion are lower than in the domestic market, so that in the absence of currency depreciation bullion export can bring about no profit. Hence, in such times, purchase of bullion (payment of banknotes) at the window of the BoE for the purpose of export should be considered non-existent. In such conditions, even if the BoE is obliged to sell gold passively, there will be no necessity to hold a great quantity of reserve gold in its coffers in whatever form. In this way, from every point of view, despite the guarantee of equivalence between banknotes and gold, neither in circulation nor in bank coffer gold will be hardly necessary, as long as the value of currency remains stable.

In this way, the stability in the value of currency itself reduces the necessity of gold reserves, in this sense rendering the currency system economical. Toward the end of 'Appendix' Ricardo employs the term 'plan' for the first time.

After having thus shown that the plan he suggests can reduce to the minimum the socially wasteful expenses accompanied with the reserve of expensive precious metals and the circulation of precious metal coins, as well as it can stabilise the value of currency, Ricardo tells the provenance of his plan with such advantages as follows:

> The plan here proposed appears to me to unite all the advantages of every system of banking which has been hitherto adopted in Europe. It is in some of its features similar to the banks of deposit of Amsterdam and Hamburgh [sic]. In those establishments bullion is always to be purchased from the Bank at a fixed invariable price. The same thing is proposed for the Bank of England.
>
> (III/126)

The Bank of Amsterdam and the Bank of Hamburg, presented here by Ricardo as the prototype of his plan, were established respectively in 1609 and 1619, well-known European banks with about 200 years of history, far longer than that of the BoE. During this long history the organisation and business categories of these banks probably underwent several changes. It is difficult to know what aspects of their businesses of what time Ricardo takes as 'reference' for his plan, but it is their character as 'banks of deposit' that he regards 'similar' to the bank in his plan.

According to one of a very few specialised studies available on the Bank of Amsterdam, it was engaged neither in discounting of commercial bills nor in issue of banknotes (Hashimoto (2013), p. 35). But the 'certificate of deposit' issued to the depositor in exchange for bullion deposit could 'circulate from hand to hand like paper money', was beginning to acquire *de facto* function as currency (Nakatani (2006), pp. 31–2). And such a currency as deposit certificate was at any time exchangeable with a fixed quantity of bullion in the form of 'withdrawal of deposit'. In this sense, as far as the confidence in the capacity of payment of the bank did not lessen, its 'value as currency' was perfectly stable (however, it is not clear what social classes used this 'currency' for what purposes, how its face values were set, how far it circulated). But on the other hand, the 'security' of such a 'currency' was guaranteed by a 100% payment reserve, in this sense it was extremely 'uneconomical' as Ricardo himself recognises. 'But in the foreign banks of deposit, they have actually in their coffers, as much bullion, as there are credits for bank money in their books; accordingly there is an inactive capital as great as the whole amount of the commercial circulation' (III/126). For Ricardo it would be equal to incurring a tremendous waste. In addition, in a 100% reserve system, it is impossible to enlarge at will the quantity of money in accordance with the need of commercial transactions. In his plan Ricardo intends to issue and supply a currency with stable value in any quantity required by the commercial transactions, while getting rid of such waste. The bank reserve is reduced to the minimum in the following way:

> In our Bank, however, there would be an amount of bank money, under the name of bank-notes, as great as the demands of commerce could require, at the same time there would not be more inactive capital in the bank coffers than that fund which the Bank should think it necessary to keep in bullion, to answer those demands which might occasionally be made on them.
>
> (ibid.)

The above discussion is on the 'sale' of standard metal by the issuing bank for assuring the stability of the value of currency. It is thus possible to check the over-issue of banknotes and the fall in the value of currency, but to stabilise the value of currency it is equally necessary to check unstable movements in the contrary direction. Ricardo's plan includes also the 'purchase' of standard metal by the issuing bank (delivery of banknotes in exchange for gold, in fact issue of banknote[7]). The BoE bought actual gold in some cases, but this was mainly its active operation aiming at preparing the reserve necessary for conversion of its banknotes (therefore a certain amount of purchase as target was determined in advance). In contrast, the purchase of gold Ricardo includes in a part of his plan is a passive (and unlimited) trade of gold with the aim of checking the upward destabilisation of the value of currency. These two purchases are of very different character. Here Ricardo takes the Bank of Hamburg[8] as the precedent. 'In imitation of the Bank of Hamburgh, who purchase silver at a fixed price, it would be necessary for the Bank to fix a price *very little below* the mint price, at which they would at all times purchase, with their notes, such gold bullion as might be offered to them' (ibid.).

If, when the market price of bullion falls below its mint price and it becomes more advantageous to make it mint and use as coin than to sell it as it is (i.e., the currency in circulation is insufficient), the BoE did not issue additional banknotes in buying gold, bullion would be brought into the Mint to be converted into coin and circulate as currency. But, for coinage, in addition to the payment of seigniorage, the interest due for the period of coinage (loss of potential benefit) must be taken into account as an additional cost. Then, even if the price set by the BoE is inferior to the mint price, when the loss due to it is less than the seigniorage imposed by the Mint, it will be more advantageous to receive banknotes immediately at the window of the BoE in exchange for gold. Therefore, the purchase of gold at a price fixed by the calculation Ricardo proposes here is a measure conceived by him, inspired by the example of the Bank of Hamburg, for the purpose of preventing the coinage of gold and the circulation of coin, relying exclusively on banknotes for the increase of currency.

In setting the purchasing price of gold a little lower than the mint price, the bank can obtain a certain profit by the difference with the mint price for its sale (charge for issuing instead of seigniorage as charge for minting), but such a price setting was rather for the purpose of stabilising the value of currency than for obtaining profit. It will be when the market price of bullion falls below the mint price (i.e., the currency falls short of its necessary quantity), that the public will sell gold to the bank at a price a little below the mint price. On the contrary, it will be when the market price of bullion rises above the mint price (i.e., the currency exceeds its necessary quantity), that they will buy gold from the bank at the mint price. The variation in the price of gold will be thus enclosed within this narrow range between these two prices and the value of currency stabilised as much ('The variations in the price of bullion, ... would be confined within the prices at which the Bank bought bullion, and the mint price at which they sold it' (III/127)). In any case, Ricardo introduced in his plan a free and unlimited bilateral transaction of bullion between the bank and public and its free movement across the border.

By the way, in 'Notes on Bentham[9]' (written from 25 December 1810 to 11 January 1811, only one or two months earlier than the drafting of 'Appendix' to the fourth edition of *High Price*), Ricardo says as follows:

> The Bank of England is certainly not *quite* so secure as a bank of deposit such as at Amsterdam and Hamburgh, – but is infinitely more useful in making the whole capital of a country available. Paper in England performs the office of the precious metals, – and the precious metals are exported for those commodities which can be usefully and advantageously employed. In Holland and Hamburgh the advantages of the Banks is [sic] 1°. in the use of paper instead of metals which has been admirably described by this author [Bentham], and 2dly. in having a uniform measure of value subject to no debasement or deterioration.
>
> (III/288, 'Notes on Bentham's "Sur les prix"', emphasis in original)

Ricardo gives here the advantage and disadvantage among the representative banks in Europe. First, in point of being 'secure', the BoE, issuing inconvertible notes, is inferior to both Banks of Amsterdam and Hamburg 'having a uniform measure of value'. This is of course because, while the value of the paper of the former being unstable, the metal conserved in the latter, never coined and released in circulation (hence undergoing neither 'debasement' nor 'deterioration') maintains constantly a uniform value of its paper (in circulation as 'deposit certificate'). On the contrary, in point of being 'useful', the BoE is far more advantageous. It is because, while the banks on the continent as 'deposit banks' leave idle a huge amount of deposit in precious metals in their coffers, the BoE, generalising the banknote circulation and holding an extremely small amount of metal reserve in exemption from convertibility, and so economising to a maximum the precious metal for use as money, contributes thus to the promotion of the wealth of the nation. The BoE, as is depicted here, is not that Ricardo thinks as it 'should be' but as it really was at that time.

In view of 'Notes on Bentham' written immediately before the plan was proposed, the comparison made here between the banks of contrasting characters may have served as a reference for this plan. As seen above, Ricardo's plan is made up in adopting respective advantages from both of these types of banks. The monetary regime during the Bank Restriction Period, which he did not cease criticising in *High Price*, was certainly very insecure, but at the same time it was in a certain sense (only for the BoE) extremely 'useful' (or 'economical') (in the quotation above, Ricardo quite exceptionally praises the contemporary state of English currency). Since it was possible to increase the issue of money at will very cheaply with paper and ink, the business of the BoE at that time was more economical than any other. As it is particularly manifest in the example of small notes, it may be that the aspect of being 'economical' in Ricardo's conception of an ideal currency was intended to succeed to such a (positive though unexpected) result of the Bank Restriction Period as it was, i.e., the generalised paper circulation, in expelling the coin from circulation. His plan may be said to have been inspired also from the state of currency during the bank restriction period. However, the benefit from this economy was naturally not to be monopolised by a private company as it was then, but to be allocated to the public, and his plan was provided with the institutional guarantee for that purpose.

Now, for finishing the presentation of his plan, Ricardo speaks of a perfect banking system as of something feasible:

> The perfection of banking is to enable a country by means of a paper currency (always retaining its standard value) to carry on its circulation with the least possible quantity of coin or bullion. This is what this plan would effect.
>
> (III/126–7)

The last sentence sounds as though anticipating the proposals to be made still five years afterward and the slogan in chapter 27 of *Principles* another year later (IV/66, I/361).

Anyway, Ricardo says that the quantity of such a currency is constantly regulated to a perfectly right level. 'The amount of the circulation would be adjusted to the wants of commerce with the greatest precision; and if the Bank were for a moment so indiscreet as to overcharge the circulation, the check which the public would possess would speedily admonish them of their error' (III/127). As the adjustment of the quantity of currency is carried on automatically by the public admonishing against an inappropriate quantity of currency (mainly by buying and selling gold, actually meaning the withdrawal and additional issue of banknotes), there is no need for the issuer to constantly watch certain indexes to intervene actively at any necessary moment with discretionary measures. Only if a proper institutional framework is in order, it suffices for the issuing bank to behave passively.

We have introduced an outline of the plan for reform of the monetary regime Ricardo made public for the first time at the beginning of April 1811 and made some examination of it. In proposing to the bullionist members of Parliament, in particular those belonging to the Bullion Committee, his proper project diverging in some points from the concluding recommendations of the 'Report', he may have intended to persuade them to incorporate his plan into the Bill to be drafted soon. The Bill was composed by F. Horner, chair of the Committee, and proposed to the House of Commons on 6 May. On the same day he delivered a speech explaining and defending the Bill, but it was finally rejected. In the 16 articles of the 'Resolutions' prepared by him along the lines of the 'Report', Ricardo's plan outlined at the end of 'Appendix' was not taken into consideration at all, the 'Resolutions' stated only a resumption of cash payment to be implemented in two years (see Horner (1811), p. 8). Considering the provisional ending of the bullion controversy with the rejection of this Bill, Ricardo's plan did neither draw attention, nor become subject of discussion. Except that a few of his friends spoke a little about it, it remained forgotten for a time[10]. But Ricardo himself continued during the whole of the rest of his lifetime to try to realise his plan relying on every means possible.

4.3 From the rejection of the Resumption Bill to the writing of *Proposals*

4.3.1 Ricardo's action after the passage of Stanhope's Act: blockage of currency depreciation and its progressive dissolution

Three days after the passing of Stanhope's Act, Ricardo addressed on 27 July 1811 a 'direct petition' to Perceval to recommend a measure for checking further depreciation of the currency, but it ended in failure (see supra). But he did not lose hope and tried again: on 11 December of the same year, just in the middle between the passing of Stanhope's Act as a legislation of specified duration and its expiration on 15 March of the following year, he addressed a letter to Tierney to propose to him similar measures. The tenor of these two letters is virtually the same, but in the latter one Ricardo explains his proposals somewhat more in detail. Moreover, since here we see some points a little different from those contained in the plan in 'Appendix' and some new measures, we will briefly introduce and examine them.

Ricardo proposes here to carry out the conclusions of the 'Bullion Report' 'by more gentle means', just in 'Appendix', and to try them at first for a limited time, admitting that the 'Report' had already been rejected. In this letter addressed to a political leader, though the contents of the plan of bullion payment are explained in less detail as in 'Appendix', in contrast he details the preliminaries to its ultimate execution.

He claims as before that the BoE should be obliged to pay its banknotes above a certain minimal sum with bullion at a certain price, but here he sets a new minimal limit and a new 'sales' price of bullion. This is conformable to the aim of a letter to recommend to a political leader a measure to be implemented immediately, if possible.

He says that bullion will be sold in exchange for banknotes to 'any purchaser of not less than 50, 100, or 200 ounces' (VI/67–8). The three numbers are given only as examples, meaning no more than the necessity of setting a minimal quantity of bullion to be sold around these amounts. Since the current market price of bullion was a little more than £4 per ounce at that time, this minimal quantity would correspond approximately to a sum from £200 to £800. Thus, in choosing any of these sums, the minimal limit would amount to more than ten times higher than that given in 'Appendix' (£20). In thus raising the threshold, the demand of bullion payment would become correspondingly more difficult and consequently the total amount of bullion sold by the BoE would decrease. This may be interpreted as a certain concession from Ricardo's part to the counter-argument of the anti-bullionists worrying about the necessity for a great amount of gold reserve for cash or bullion payment. And it is only big traders, etc., who can demand transactions of such large amounts or be in need of them, and their demand for bullion is for the purpose of its export (payment for imported commodities). Therefore, such bullion payments have no direct relation with the small domestic circulation. Among the differences from 'Appendix', no less important than this is the change in the way of expressing the minimal amount from pound, unit of the face value of currency, to ounce, unit of the weight of bullion. If the BoE should pay the banknotes of any sum above a certain minimum with bullion, it will be a practically impossible procedure, dividing the mass of bullion into a weight corresponding to the sum of the banknote tendered at its window according to a determinate price of bullion. In order to avoid such technical difficulties, the BoE should have relied on the 'sale' of ingot (or some sorts of ingots, if necessary) of a certain weight amounting to a certain round number of pounds prepared in advance for bullion payment at a determinate price (which in turn can be a number with fractions without major inconvenience)[11]. The payment in bullion may be apparently similar to a cash payment with a certain number of minted gold coins, though bullion used in payment may not be handled like coins, 20 ounces being a gold bar of about 600g with a dimension of about $30\,cm^3$, 60 ounces being a gold bar of about 1.8kg with a dimension of about $90\,cm^3$.

In the 'Bullion Report' the cash payment was to be resumed in two years for every amount of banknote at the legal mint price of 3*l.* 17*s.* 10½*d.*, and equally in 'Appendix' the bullion payment was to begin at old par for the banknote of an amount above £20 when the bullion price would have fallen to the mint price. But in the letter to Tierney, equally in setting the minimal limit as above, the bullion payment was to begin as early as possible (immediately if possible) 'at a fixed price somewhere about the present market price' (VI/68).

If the Resumption Bill had been approved and the depreciation of currency would surely not go further, it would have been possible to wait two years for the fall of bullion price to the mint price before resuming the bullion payment. But now that the Bill was rejected, and in addition an Act enforcing an equal treatment between depreciated banknotes and coin, i.e., the virtual treatment of the former as legal tender was in force, an unlimited depreciation of currency was to be feared (in fact it continued depreciating) so that it had to be checked as soon as possible, thought Ricardo. For this it was indispensable to 'secure the public against any further depreciation of Bank notes' (ibid.).

But, while being effectual in preventing the further depreciation of currency, this was not for raising the value of currency to the mint price. This was therefore a provisional measure for gaining time for thinking out a more fundamental measure and deciding on it. 'It would afford leisure too for the consideration of such further measures as might be necessary, without pledging Parliament to any particular course of proceeding' (ibid.). Hence here is not the end, and so the next step was prepared. Ricardo's next proposal is as follows: continue the above measure for half a year and if then the rise in the price of bullion is surely stopped, reset the selling price of bullion lower than that applied during the foregoing six month by six to nine pence and continue this for one month, and after that successively bring down the selling price of bullion every month at the same pace until it finally coincides with the mint price (VI/69).

The monthly rate of bringing down the selling price of bullion was roughly calculated by Ricardo considering the two opposite restraints: it was neither to be so slow as to require too long a time to arrive at the destination, nor so fast as to cause the public anxiety. He foresaw three or four years before reaching the target price. When in this way the banknote would become finally equivalent to the standard metal, i.e., the same quantity of commodities would be bought either with gold coin or with banknotes, the demand for gold (bullion or coin) at the window of the BoE would virtually cease, even if institutionally guaranteed. In such a situation an exclusive circulation of paper as was seen in 1811 would be possible, without any worry about depreciation. This was what Ricardo aimed at.

> If the public were secured against depreciation by possessing the power of exchanging their notes for bullion at the mint value [price] of gold, I should prefer a circulation, such as ours, consisting wholly of paper, to any other, even as a permanent measure, as being more economical and possessing other obvious advantages.
>
> (ibid.)

To this letter Tierney himself responded on the following day in expressing his gratitude for the proposal and intention of examining it (VI/71). But there seems to have been no clear reply. Thus, again in this second action of trying to make approaches to a political leader, Ricardo could not attain his aim. After that for some time Ricardo did not speak or take action about the currency issue, he resumed it more than three and a half years afterward, in summer 1815 (immediately after the defeat of Napoleon's army at the Battle of Waterloo).

In any case, after the letter to Tierney in which Ricardo showed for the first time the plan of beginning bullion payment with the current high price superior to the mint price to bring it down step by step, he never mentioned this plan in his publications or letters, until he brought it forward again in spring 1819, when in Parliament the resumption of cash payment began to be required (evidence in the House of Commons on 4 March (V/382), evidence in the House of Lords on 26 March (V/439–40)), and this plan was adopted in Peel's Act approved in the same year (V/7–8).

4.3.2 Critique of the BoE and the concept of the establishment of an alternative institution

Ricardo was consistent in criticising and opposing the BoE from the very beginning of his appearance in the bullion controversy. But his plan for the reform of the monetary regime we have seen above was for regulating or enforcing with legislative measures the businesses of the BoE as the issuing bank, without bringing its existence into question. But, in summer of 1815, when he was asked by Pascoe Grenfell, a member of the House of Commons, to write a pamphlet criticising the businesses of the BoE for profits and their way of distribution (to be published in the following year as *Proposals*), Ricardo had occasion to read massive data materials offered by him, and as a result his view on the BoE underwent a substantial change. He came to think it right to propose 'Government to be the issuers, and to derive the advantages from the substitution of paper for metallic money' (Ricardo's letter to Say of 24 December 1814, VI/165). In his letter to Malthus of 10 September 1815 , soon after he began writing the pamphlet, he shows a large change in his thinking as follows:

> I think the Bank an unnecessary establishment getting rich by those profits which fairly belong to the public. I cannot help considering the issuing of paper money as a privilege which belongs exclusively to the state. I regard it as a sort of seigniorage, and I am convinced, if the principles of currency were rightly understood, that Commissioners might be appointed independent of all ministerial controul [sic] who should be the sole issuers of paper money, by which I think a profit of from two to three millions might be secured to the public. … They might invest the 11 million [sic] which is the average of public deposits in Exchequer Bills, a part of which might be sold whenever occasion required. This, of course (at least all of it) could not be effected till the expiration of the Bank Charter in 1833, but it is never too soon to give due consideration to important principles, which might be recognised tho' not yet acted on. In looking over the papers which have

> from time to time been laid before Parliament I think it might clearly be proved that the profits of the Bank have been enormous, I should think they must have a hoard nearly equal to their Capital. By their Charter they are bound to make an annual division of their profits, and to lay a statement of their accounts before the Proprietors, but they appear to set all law at defiance. I always enjoy any attack upon the Bank and if I had sufficient courage I would be a party to it.
>
> (VI/268–9)

Here we can find some of the important points to be developed in the manuscript he was to draft in 1823, eight years after this letter ('Plan, &c.', entitled 'Plan for the Establishment of a National Bank' when it was posthumously published in 1824). He affirms here for the first time that the right to issue money belongs solely to the state, so the BoE, obtaining extraordinary unjust profits, is unnecessary and hence should be liquidated. In the same way as in the later manuscript, the issue should be assumed by the Commissioners, acting independently of the government solely for the public benefit. Though not sufficiently explained, the Commissioners can also make 'open market operations' consisting of purchase and sale of government security for the purpose of increasing or decreasing the quantity of issued currency. On the other hand, the idea of dichotomic division of the businesses of the BoE into issue and banking is not yet shown here, which is to be the starting point of the plan in the manuscript of 1823.

Here Ricardo's blame and attack against the BoE are concentrated on the huge profits it is obtaining and accumulating in its coffers which it does not make public, setting 'all law at defiance', but are not extended to the excessive issue of inconvertible banknotes and the accompanying depreciation of currency, which he had emphasised for a long time. This is probably because he then focused his attention on what he recognised anew 'in looking over the papers which have from time to time been laid before Parliament', which resulted in a radical policy of the liquidation of the BoE, which he had never thought of until some time before this letter. The request from Grenfell of writing a pamphlet, his offer of massive material, and hitting it off in the repeated dialogues with Ricardo, all seem to have motivated him to conceive a national issuing organ in place of the BoE.

But, in talking about the establishment of a national bank to replace the BoE, he recognises at the same time that there is no possibility of realising such a plan as long as the present Bank Charter remains valid until 1833. What he is speaking about here is a conception in principle about an issuer of currency to be established in the future. He says in a letter sent to Malthus in the following month that 'my views respecting the Bank are entirely prospective' (dated from 17 October, VI/304). Thus, for the moment there could be no question of subsistence of the BoE. On this point he says in section VI 'The public services of the Bank excessively overpaid – Remedy proposed' of *Proposals* that 'the charter of the Bank was renewed in 1800 for

21 years, from its expiration in 1812; consequently, it will not now terminate till 1833' (IV/88). Such a renewal of the charter was the result of a 'bargain' (IV/83) between the government and the BoE in return for repeated loans to the former in extremely favourable conditions. On every subsequent occasion talking about the same subject, Ricardo always mentioned that the establishment of an institution alternative to the BoE was not realisable for the time being (cf. the last paragraph of *Proposals* (IV/114), 'Plan, &c.' of 23 (IV/285)). In this way, although the plan of bullion payment and the plan for the establishment of a national bank were both Ricardo's plans aiming at reforming the monetary regime, the conditions for their realisation, as well as their time perspectives, were widely different, so that these two were not in an alternative relation nor in a relation of incompatibility. Ricardo did not pass from the former to the latter, but for the moment he made effort to realise the former, supposing the BoE, and was waiting for the occasion to pursue the realisation of the latter in absorbing and incorporating the former. However, after 1815 Ricardo always continued rethinking his plans in changing situations in bringing modifications and additions to both of them. We are going to continue considerations on their contents and meaning.

4.3.3 Request from Grenfell and Ricardo's drafting of the manuscript

On 1 August Pascoe Grenfell addressed a letter to Ricardo in which he required him to write 'a Short Pamphlet' (VI/242) on the profits of the BoE and its treatment by the BoE. Another letter Grenfell subsequently addressed to Ricardo on the following 25 August clearly shows that the latter was going to begin writing it in accepting the request of the former, but the reply Ricardo may have sent to Grenfell in the meantime is not included in *Works*. In any case, dissatisfied for a long time with the behaviour of the BoE, Ricardo seems to have accepted the request from Grenfell. Because it was the time when the War was ending with England's victory, Ricardo may have seized Grenfell's request as a good opportunity to develop further his plan of bullion payment that he had briefly sketched more than four years before in 'Appendix' to the fourth edition of *High Price*. This plan had afterwards fallen into oblivion, but Ricardo may have intended to revive it now.

In his letter of 1 August Grenfell asked him 'to undertake, in the course of the approaching autumn – or rather I would say – before the next Bank Court in September or October – to write a Short Pamphlet on the Subject to which I have lately called the attention of Parliament' (VI/242). What he asked him to write was a pamphlet defending the right of the stockholders in view of the next general meeting of stockholders (Bank Court) to be held in the following month or two months later[12]. In requesting this pamphlet Grenfell wanted it to criticise the BoE, which, although obtaining a huge amount of profits from the transactions with the government (loan of money and underwriting and management of government bond), was not sufficiently returning these profits to the stockholders as dividends. Therefore, while Grenfell and Ricardo agreed with respect to the need for criticising the management of the BoE, in the original purpose of the request a still larger intent of a reform of monetary regime itself was not included. Despite the frequent exchange of information and opinion with Grenfell about the pamphlet, till the end of the drafting of the manuscript, Ricardo spoke nothing to the requester about his intention of including as its first main theme the plan of bullion payment and its theoretical foundation, or about the contents of the plan itself (see infra). After Ricardo accepted the writing, Grenfell told him in his letters that he was going to send him materials like parliamentary documents for writing the pamphlet, which conformed to the aim of his request, and Ricardo quoted many data and facts presumably drawn from these materials in *Proposals*, in particular in the last part of it.

In the first half of *Proposals* (from section I to IV), Ricardo explains succinctly the fundamental points of his theory of money, and subsequently develops his plan of bullion payment conceived more than four years before, but he discusses how to check the profit seeking activities of the BoE only in the latter half (from section V to VII), a subject requested to be treated by Grenfell. And the subject Ricardo added afterwards for himself is noted also in the title as if it were the main theme of the pamphlet.

He began negotiation for publishing it with Murray from the beginning of 1816, and the pamphlet appeared on 6 February. Though not in time for the opening of the parliamentary session on 1 February, it was one week earlier than the motion Grenfell proposed to the House of Commons. It sold beyond expectation, the second edition was published at the end of February, the third in March. These were substantially the same as the first edition (cf. 'note' by Sraffa, IV/47–8).

4.3.4 Malthus' objection and Ricardo's response: variations in the value of gold as the standard of money

Ricardo sent the manuscript of *Proposals* to Malthus at the beginning of October to ask his opinion on it, to which the latter replied in his letter of 15 October and advised publishing it but pointing out some problems of style and composition. At the same time, on only one point concerning the first part of this manuscript containing the plan of bullion payment, Malthus makes a counter-argument as follows:

> With regard to the matter I agree almost entirely with you, except that I do not think you have considered all the variations to which such a currency as you propose must be subject, particularly the great variation that is likely to arise from a sudden demand for bullion operating upon the scanty supply which is likely to take place upon your plan. If Mr. Vansittart [anti-bullionist, current Chancellor of Exchequer] wanted suddenly to send four millions [sic] [pounds] in specie to Spain, as he did one year [probably from 1813 to 1814], I cannot help thinking that it would occasion upon your

> system a most distressing diminution of currency. If you recollect, we found upon calculation that the value of gold in this country at some periods during the Peninsular war [a phase in Napoleonic War, from 1807 to 1814] was ten and fifteen per cent higher than at Amsterdam and Hamburgh; and I feel no doubt that, without very extraordinary stores in the Banks, the variations in the value of the precious metals would always be found the greatest, (from sudden demand) in those countries in which a paper currency was most universal. I have no doubt that the precious metals during the last ten years experienced less variation, (with regard to commodities) in France than in this country.
>
> (VI/298–9)

Here Malthus points out first that in the plan Ricardo does not take into account all the possible variations a currency can undergo. The only one he considers is the variations, in particular the fall (i.e., 'depreciation') to which the 'value of money', in the sense of the purchasing power of a currency over the bullion on the market, becomes liable under the inconvertible regime. Malthus, as a bullionist like Ricardo, well understands this point, and cannot have any argument against it. When the 'value of money' in this sense varies, the price of bullion on the market and the prices of commodities in general vary in the same direction and in the same degree, i.e., only the relative value of the currency to both the bullion and the other commodities varies, the relative value between the bullion and the other commodities remaining the same. But, in addition to this, Malthus points out that the 'value of money' can vary in other sense. It is the variation of the value of gold as a commodity. In this case, since the money of which the value varies means bullion itself as a sort of commodity, the variations in the value of money manifest themselves as the same variations both in the price of bullion in terms of currency and in the relative price between the bullion and the commodities in general[13]. In this case, therefore, as long as there is no simultaneous expansion or contraction in the quantity of currency, there will be no change in the prices of commodities in general, and the relation between currency and commodities in general remains unchanged.

When Malthus affirms that Ricardo does not think of the variations in the 'value of money' in this latter sense, he supposes in particular its rise. If the 'value of money' in this sense rises, only the price of bullion rises, while the prices of commodities in general in terms of currency remain the same. According to the bullionist theory, including that of Ricardo, this is a situation which can be interpreted as one of the excess of currency, though there is no change in its quantity, and the issuer will be required to contract this quantity to bring down the bullion price to the mint price. When the depreciation of currency will thus be solved, there will be a general fall in the prices of commodities compared with the situation prior to such a change in the 'value of money'. Malthus calls this a 'most distressing diminution of currency'. On the contrary, what changes with the depreciation of currency Ricardo exclusively keeps in view, is both the price of bullion and that of commodities in general in the same direction and in the same degree. And, according to him, when the depreciation will be dissolved equally through a contraction of currency, every relation will have returned back to the state equal to the one prior to the occurrence of change, hence such a situation as Malthus worries about cannot appear (the prices of commodities will certainly fall, but they only fall to the initial level prior to the rise). Malthus emphasises that Ricardo does not think about the cases of a general fall in prices brought about by a contraction of currency.

Malthus says that Ricardo's plan contains possibilities of such a worrying situation to appear, because it requires an exclusion of metal currency from the circulation, as well as minimisation of metal reserve in the issuing bank, i.e., an expulsion of precious metal in relation to domestic circulation. The paper currency can circulate only in the domestic area. The precious metal money becomes indispensable for the unbalanced unilateral external payments, whether from commercial needs or not. When such payments will be needed and in great amount, a tension between demand and supply of gold will raise its value (or more correctly 'market price') and possibly lead to a rapid fall in general prices, as seen above. In order to avoid such a risk, a sufficient gold reserve ('very extraordinary stores') should be held in the country, so as to avoid the surge in the value of gold in releasing it in emergency to secure the stability of currency system. But Ricardo's plan has no protection against such risks.

This criticism by Malthus is directed at Ricardo's plan, which was still something ideal existing only in his thinking (or on paper), but in the latter half of the above quotation he tries to prove the validity of his criticism in citing a case England had really experienced in the immediate past. Such a way of reasoning was possible because, altogether irrespective of Ricardo's plan, in England at that time the circulation of gold coin was virtually equal to null and the gold reserve of the BoE was also at a level of about £2,000,000 (Feavearyear and Morgan (1963), p. 228), the lowest of all throughout the Bank Restriction Period except for February 1797 when the BoE suspended convertibility (hence inferior to £4,000,000, the amount of remittance to Spain implemented immediately before, given by Malthus as an example of sudden demand for gold), such a real situation was in certain points common to the supposition adopted in Ricardo's plan (of course at the cost of depreciation of the inconvertible banknotes). But in fact, the BoE never tried to bring down the price of bullion in contracting the currency in circulation. Hence, if the value of gold was 'ten and fifteen per cent higher than at Amsterdam and Hamburgh' as Malthus wrote, it was because the rise in the price of bullion caused by the rise in the value of gold itself was superimposed on the parallel rise in the price of bullion and the prices of commodities in general caused by the over-issue of currency.

Ricardo thought that the maintenance of the value of currency in the sense of its purchasing power over bullion on the market would simultaneously contribute to keep various economic relations stable. And it would be possible to contain the instability of the monetary system within the range of variations in the conditions of production of gold. The bullionists generally considered these variations most of the time very slow and mild, hence theoretically negligible. Here Malthus also does not bring into question the case of change in the value of gold by variation in the conditions of its production. The question for him is about the large changes in international relations in a short time, typically war and its consequences. In this regard, Ricardo's plan may be said to be conceived concentrating mainly on domestic relations, leaving aside external ones.

Now, to Malthus' letter with his critical comments on the manuscript of *Proposals*, Ricardo sent a letter of reply two days later on 17 October. The response Ricardo gave there seems to consist in incomprehension about Malthus' criticism and in switching the subject from the points in question. Perhaps because of this, unsatisfied with Ricardo's reaction of Ricardo, afterwards Malthus cast on him the same criticism or question on every possible occasion, and for the reason of a somewhat mysterious response from Ricardo the 'debate' between them further continued intermittently for several months, and it was finally 'settled' when Ricardo frankly recognised Malthus' claim (in an altogether different context) as long as four years later[14].

In the letter of 25 December 1815 addressed to Trower, Ricardo virtually recognises Malthus' contentions about the questions he had raised since 15 October, as follows:

> The bullionists, and I among the number, considered gold and silver as less variable commodities than they really are, and the effect of war on the prices of these metals were certainly very much underrated by them. The fall in the price of bullion on the peace in 1814, and its rise again on the renewal of the war on Bonaparte's entry into Paris are remarkable facts, and should never be neglected in any future discussion on this subject. But granting all this it does not affect the theory of the bullionists.
>
> (VI/344)

In accordance with the theory of currency of the 'bullionists' contained in the 'Bullion Report', Ricardo had repeated since *High Price* that the price of bullion under the regime of inconvertible banknotes varies up and down according to the rise and fall of its issue, and the level of this issue is judged 'proper' when this price coincides with the legal mint price. This proper level of the quantity of its issue is determined in its turn by the total amount of domestic transactions and by the value of money (gold as its standard), and this level varies proportionately to the former and inversely to the latter. The cause of variation in the price of bullion mentioned in the above quotation is the events suddenly happening in political and military affairs, and if they do not cause large changes in the former, it must be considered that the variations in the latter gave rise to the changes in the price of bullion. The fall in the price of bullion on the peace in 1814 means that the currency has relatively risen in its value, i.e., that its quantity has relatively fallen without any change in its issued amount, because of a rise of the proper level of its circulation, hence that the value of bullion has fallen. And on the contrary, the rise in the price of bullion on the return of war in the following year means a rise in its value. In this way, in contrast to the direct response to Malthus, Ricardo frankly recognises the variation in the value of gold itself as the 'standard of money' pointed out by Malthus since his letter in mid-October and the accompanying variation in the 'value of money', in this letter addressed to Trower, a third party, on the following day without explicitly mentioning the exchanges with Malthus[15]. In addition, here he is thinking over this point as a problem contained in the theory of the bullionists, including himself.

But finally, he ends up with the sentence that 'granting all this it does not affect the theory of the bullionists', which may be a little bluff. This theory is no doubt composed in supposing invariant the value of gold or silver, but it is equally certain that this supposition does not always apply in certain situations. While recognising this, Ricardo does not mention as before the doubts Malthus casts on the maximal economising of gold reserve and the necessity of hoarding gold to cope with the variation in the value of gold. In a letter addressed a littler later on 30 December to J. Mill, he always claims the relative (but almost absolute in his theory) invariability of the value of precious metals as an indispensable presupposition for the whole of his theory, in saying that 'this invariability of the value of the precious metals, but from particular causes relating to themselves only, such as supply and demand, is the sheet anchor on which all my propositions are built' (VI/348). The variation in the value of gold he recognised in the letter to Trower was only temporary and accidental, not negligible in analysing situations in the short term, but they were to be left aside as before on the abstract level relative to the principles of his theory.

In the letter to Malthus of 21 September 1819, Ricardo says that the value of money gold as a commodity is liable to variations, though in a context different from the bullion problem.

Ricardo had made no clear answer on the question of change in the value of money as a commodity raised and persistently repeated by Malthus, except having betrayed it to Trower, but here he recognises quite frankly the claim of Malthus. 'You know I agree with you that money is a more variable commodity than is generally imagined, and therefore I think that many of the variations in the price of commodities may be fairly attributed to an alteration in the value of money' (VIII/73). But this is not in the context of the bullion controversy concerning the variations of the value of currency, but in relation to an important point in *Principles of political economy* in the writing of which Malthus seems to have been absorbed at that time. The money of which Ricardo is speaking here is gold itself, and the 'value of money' is the value of gold as a commodity, expressed not by the purchasing power of money as a non-commodity over gold as its standard, but by the proportions of exchange of money with all the other commodities (its purchasing power over them).

At that time Ricardo was quite content with the current state of currency after the Royal Assent on 2 July of the Resumption Act (Peel's Bill). But after some time, with the appearance of a situation he did in no way expect then, he was faced with the problem of variations in the value of gold as a commodity, he was going to repeat the position stated in this letter to Malthus.

We have now arrived at a step for examining the contents of *Proposals*.

4.4 Ricardo's Plan for reform of the monetary regime in *Proposals*

4.4.1 Structure of the pamphlet and the 'General principles of the laws of currency'

The pamphlet was published by Ricardo with a long full title *Proposals for an economical and secure currency; with observations on the profits of the Bank of England, as they regard the public and the proprietors of Bank stock*, between 1 and 13 February 1816, the date when Grenfell presented to Parliament his 'motion on certain Transactions between the Public and the Bank of England' (IV/51, Sraffa's note). This pamphlet seems to have been taken up to the present as a document proposing a currency regime Ricardo considered ideal. In view of its origin, it was rather the theme of the latter half apparently somewhat receding to the background that was to occupy a central place. But, when a request from Grenfell for him to write a document criticising and attacking the profits of the BoE and their unjust treatment by it, Ricardo intended to appeal anew to the public (to Parliament in particular) his plan for the reform of the monetary regime that he had made public more than four years before but already forgotten almost entirely, in seizing as a good opportunity this period of time when the war was ending and the resumption of convertibility was in prospect. But of course, quite agreeing with the request from Grenfell, Ricardo was never negligent of it while putting it off to the later part.

Indeed, in working on this part he became much better acquainted with the real state of management of the BoE, and because of this some new important elements were added to the plan for the reform of the monetary regime he had conceived much earlier. He says in 'Introduction' as follows: 'It cannot, I think, be doubted, that all the services, which the Bank perform for the public, could be performed, by public servants and in public offices established for that purpose, at a reduction or saving of expense of nearly half a million per annum' (IV/52–3). He therefore says straight that the BoE is superfluous. And as *Proposals* sold well against the expectation of Ricardo (see his letter to Murray of 16 January 1816), the second edition was in print already on 23 February. If *Proposals* could enjoy such a favourable reception from the public, it was probably not by virtue of the first part describing an abstract theory on money not easily accessible to the general public and the plan still remaining an idea, but because of the latter part which may have widely attracted attention with its onslaught on the BoE giving concrete examples, including much numerical data.

Now, the first part is composed of four sections, and it is in the final fourth section that the concrete contents of Ricardo's plan are presented. In the preceding three sections, in order to give theoretical foundations to the plan, 'some of the general principles which are found to constitute the laws of currency' (IV/51) are explained. Along with *High Price*, these sections give a certain systematic description to Ricardo's theory of money. But, while *High Price* finally explained the present state of currency in order to criticise the BoE as its prime cause, beginning with the explanation of the principles of currency, the first three sections (particularly the first one) of *Proposals* aim at justifying the plan of bullion payment to be advanced in the last section in returning to the principles of monetary theory. For this reason, the first three sections are devoted mainly to abstract theoretical arguments rather than to the descriptions on the current concrete situation and to the critique of the policy of issue of the BoE.

Ricardo says that a 'currency in its perfect state' he is aiming at require the following three conditions: 'a currency may be considered as perfect, of which the standard is invariable, which always conforms to that standard, and in the use of which the utmost economy is practised' (IV/55).

The first condition ('the standard is invariable') means an invariability of the value (or market price) of gold (or silver) as standard, but a commodity with constant and invariable value cannot be found anywhere, the precious metals, though considered relatively invariant, are no exception to this. Hence, 'while the precious metals continue to be the standard of our currency, money must necessarily undergo the same variations in value as those metals' (ibid.). The stability of the value of money (meaning not its purchasing power over the precious metal as its standard, but its purchasing power over commodities in general) is confined within an unsurmountable limit drawn by the instability of the value of the standard itself.

The stability of the value of money, difficult to attain only with coin, is secured by the introduction of banknotes. This is an argument Ricardo has usually employed since *High Price*. 'This inconvenience is wholly got rid of, by the issue of paper money; for, in that case, there will be no additional demand for bullion; consequently, its value will continue unaltered; and the new paper money, as well as the old, will conform to that value' (IV/57). In conforming the market price of bullion to its mint price by means of supplying (convertible) paper from the bank as a virtual substitute for bullion, the value of bullion will not rise. Therefore, the currency (composed of coin and paper) has now recovered equivalence to bullion, and also its purchasing power over commodities in general (its value) has restored to the initial state, i.e., the price of commodities has returned back to its initial level. 'Besides, then, all the other advantages attending the use of paper money; by the judicious management of the quantity, a degree of uniformity, which is by no other means attainable, is secured to the value of the circulating medium in which all payments are made' (VI/57–8).

The invariability of the value of money is thus secured by the paper currency, which is at the same time the substitution for coin made of gold, an expensive commodity, of cheap paper money made of paper, meeting the 'utmost economy' (IV/55) in the use of the standard. In the example above the currency is to be partly replaced with paper, but it is possible to abolish entirely the use of gold coin 'by the judicious management of the quantity', and then the 'utmost economy' will be achieved. In this way, the three sections (in fact the first section) end with the conclusion that the 'economical and secure currency' consists in a paper currency with guarantee of its equivalence to the standard. 'The advantage of a paper circulation, when established on correct principles, is that this additional quantity can be supplied without occasioning any variation in the value of the whole currency, either as compared with bullion or with any other commodity; whereas, with a system of metallic currency, this additional quantity cannot be so readily supplied, and when it is finally supplied, the whole of the currency, as well as bullion, has acquired an increased value' (IV/58).

4.4.2 Plan for bullion payments, relation with the 'Appendix', its integration into the second edition of **Principles**

In section IV of *Proposals*, entitled 'An expedient to bring the English currency as near as possible to perfection', is presented a concrete 'plan' (IV/69) for realising in England the 'perfect currency' introduced throughout the first three sections. In this sense section IV is not only the central part of the first half of *Proposals,* but also the centre of the whole of this pamphlet. The plan itself had been already made public nearly five years before, but it found almost no reaction and remained neglected by political leaders in spite of Ricardo's repeated actions, almost wholly forgotten except by Ricardo himself. After having made public the plan for the first time, he never mentioned *High Price* or its 'Appendix' in his letters and publications (in particular in *Proposals* and *Principles*). Probably these were considered by their author himself as 'throw-away' temporary pamphlets on current topics and so as 'finished'. Therefore, in section IV of *Proposals*, Ricardo had to depict his plan for the reform of the monetary regime as an entirely new one with no precedent. For this reason, when comparing the 'first version' of 1811 and the 'second version' five years later, a reader can naturally find a number of repetitions. As the former has already gone through detailed examinations in Subsection 4.2.3 of the present chapter, here will be taken up a few points particular to the 'second version' comparing it with the 'first version', in order to characterise more accurately Ricardo's plan through these two 'versions' of it.

Incidentally, as is well known, the central part of this section IV (IV/66–70) is reproduced as a long quotation in chapter 27 'On currency and banks' in the second version of *Principles* (I/356–61). This is a measure taken following the advice of McCulloch, who published a review article of *Proposals* in *Edinburgh Review* in December 1818 ([McCulloch, J.R.] (1818)), at a time when

Ricardo was preparing the publication of the second edition of *Principles*. The inclusion in *Principles* of the essential part of the 'second version' may be said to have been a measure for making the plan known widely to the public. In fact, it is undeniable that *Proposals* has been read and examined much less frequently than *Principles*, so that his plan would have been much less known than it is now, if Ricardo had not presented it also in *Principles* following McCulloch's advice. In his letter addressed to McCulloch some time after the publication of his review article, on 7 April 1819, at the same time as reporting to him that thanks to his review *Proposals* was newly attracting attention among members of Parliament (the third edition had appeared in March, three years after the second), he says as follows: 'my plan might have slumbered, or have been forgotten, if you had not rescued it from oblivion, and said more in its favour than I had been able to do' (VIII/20). These sentences of his seem to endorse the fact that the large reaction *Proposals* had just after its publication three years earlier (a reprint was needed in less than a month) was not due to the plan in the first part, and also that the wide attention to the second part including onslaughts against the BoE was only temporary.

The core part in *Proposals* incorporated into a part of *Principles* constitutes an exceptionally long quotation, likely to give an impression of a somewhat extraordinary 'foreign matter'. Probably because of this, this long quotation may have been either read separately from the body of the text, or else totally neglected. Anyway, it seems to have been rarely read in connection with the adjacent sentences which it breaks in on. But Ricardo seems to have inserted it in a certain context considering the logical consequences in *Principles*. If such a reading is possible, a different view on the concept of his plan for the reform of the monetary regime would become possible. But the discussion on this point will be reserved to Section 4.5 of this chapter.

Now, Ricardo makes quite clear what is the target of the plan presented in section IV at its opening: 'in the next session of parliament, the subject of currency is again to be discussed; and, probably, a time will then be fixed for the resumption of cash payments, which will oblige the Bank to limit the quantity of their paper till it conforms to the value of bullion' (IV/65). Just like the plan in 'Appendix' published in April 1811, the plan here proposed is also brought forward as a concrete political measure in view of the deliberation on a possible resumption bill and its vote in Parliament which were to begin soon. Ricardo foresaw the execution of the plan through regulating the acts of the BoE. His plan of bullion payment was conceived thus as executable in a relatively short time in the existing banking institution.

Though the suspension of convertibility was accompanied with many evils, Ricardo did not propose a simple return to the state prior to its suspension. He would succeed in the cessation of the circulation of precious metal coin and the consequent domination of paper circulation, both arisen during the period of the suspension of convertibility, as an 'economical currency regime'. 'A well-regulated paper currency is so great an improvement in commerce, that I should greatly regret, if prejudice should induce us to return to a system of less utility' (IV/65). For Ricardo the advantage of the paper currency was too evident, and to deny it or act against it was due only to 'prejudice'. And 'to return to a system of less utility' is to call back again the precious metal coin into circulation, which means that the BoE withdraws small notes actually in circulation in place of the precious metal coin, to use anew the coin as money by paying it for banknotes or by new coinage. The weight of gold coin of one pound minted according to the mint price was a little less than eight grams, so that for its practical use as currency the maximum of its face value would be two pounds. Indeed, there has been no historical fact of long continual issue of coins of a face value superior to £2 (cf. www.coinsgb.com/index.html, visited on 24 September 2024.) That is, the small notes of £5 and under, rapidly penetrated in circulation replacing gold coin during the Bank Restriction Period, corresponded in their face values to the gold coin, so that these two kinds of currency were in an alternative (or competing) relation. For this reason, as it was indispensable not to allow the reflux of gold coin into circulation to realise Ricardo's plan, the treatment of such small notes was an extremely important problem for him.

Ricardo's plan consisted in paying bullion instead of coin for banknotes and was aimed among others at preventing gold coin from passing directly from the BoE to the public. But those who are paid in bullion can bring it to the Mint to transform into coin. Indeed, Ricardo says that the execution of his plan does not exclude the working of the Mint (cf. IV/67). But it is because the currency in general including coin is in depreciation, that the public bring banknotes to the BoE to exchange for bullion. To change bullion into coin in such a situation is to incur losses voluntarily, hence such an act can be supposed to be impossible. When, therefore, the currency is in depreciation, the public can neither obtain coin directly from the BoE, nor transform the bullion received from the BoE into coin at the Mint. If the coin minted in the Mint can enter into circulation as currency, it is when the market price of bullion is equal to or below its mint price, i.e., when the currency is not depreciated. It is because, in such situations, the public can get benefits from changing the bullion in their possession into currency (banknotes or coin) for use as money.

Then, the public will have to make a choice of bringing the bullion in their possession to the BoE to sell it for banknotes, or of bringing it to the Mint to make coins. Here arises a mutual relation of competition between the the BoE and the Mint. Even if the face values of the currency obtained with the same weight of bullion (i.e., the selling – or buying – price of bullion) are equal, the banknotes can be handed on immediately at the window, while a certain time is required for producing coins, giving rise to a loss equivalent to the interest for that interval, putting aside the seigniorage. This gives to the BoE a more favourable position in competition. But in addition to this, Ricardo proposes a measure for containing the coinage of bullion also in the setting of the buying price of bullion by the BoE, in saying that 'the price ought to be so fixed as to make it the interest of the seller of gold rather to sell it to the Bank than to carry it to the mint to be coined' (IV/66, note). He proposes to set this price, a little higher than that set by the Mint, so as to induce to the BoE the sellers of bullion. If this plan works as expected, there will be no possibility of new coinage and its circulation in addition to a very small quantity of coins still remaining in the country.

The selling (paying) price of bullion is, on the contrary, set at the mint price. Hence, if the value of currency ever varies up or down, the BoE can benefit from the difference between the selling and buying prices, but actually, since such transactions themselves constrain the variations in the value of banknotes within a narrow range of this difference between the two prices, 'these transactions in bullion would be very few in number' (IV/67). In this way, though the BoE is officially obliged to make unlimited payments of bullion for banknotes, actually a very small amount of reserve of bullion will suffice for this purpose. With an extreme economy in precious metal with respect to both currency circulation and reserve, the currency system will become very 'economical'. In addition to these measures, in order to reduce the necessary payment in bullion, here also as in the plan advanced in 1811, Ricardo sets a minimal sum of banknotes for the BoE to accept the payment. The BoE can refuse the demand for payment for a sum under this minimum. This can be interpreted as a measure aiming at preventing the reflux to the BoE of the small notes inferior to this minimal sum to retain them in circulation. It is clear that such a minimal sum was set for the purpose of blocking the exchange for bullion of the money in income circulation used for the general consumption spending, and so to confine the bullion payment exclusively to the money used for the transactions among dealers (moreover, between the English and foreign dealers, bullion is used in international commerce). In thus limiting the bullion payment only to the transactions of great scale, it will be possible 'not to give too much trouble to the Bank' (IV/66), since it has then to conduct business only with a far smaller number of dealers than the general consumers.

The market price of bullion at the time of publication of *Proposals* was, according to Table 1 at the end of Tooke (1838) (ibid., 276), already tending to fall somewhat, but still at the level of 4*l.* 13*s.* 6*d.* pence per ounce, i.e., superior to the legal mint price by about 20%. Ricardo foresaw the execution of bullion payment at the mint price, but if it had been executed immediately in such a situation, a serious confusion (run on the BoE for payment and a sudden fall in reserves, and possibly resuspension of payment) would have happened. But in the plan shown in *Proposals* there is no clear indication about when to resume the payment as he had done in 1811 (see supra), but Ricardo had never forgotten it: in 1819, three years later, with the opening of the session of that year when Parliament actually began to proceed to the resumption, he proposed again the same procedure, which was to be adopted in the Bill (a subject to be discussed later).

The coupling of selling and buying of bullion in Ricardo's plan was conceived as a measure to resolve the divergence between the value of currency and the value of bullion, and in so doing to stabilise the former as much as the latter.

For this the bullion must be able to move freely across national borders. This is a measure necessary to prevent the value of bullion from deviating from its international level. In this way, the value of currency will be kept equivalent to the international value of bullion as a commodity and its standard, which will secure the maximal stability in its value as far as possible under a system adopting gold as the standard of money. 'The most perfect liberty should be given, at the same time, to export or import every description of bullion' (IV/67). At the same time, Ricardo predicts that, as far as such a system operates, both the mutual conversion between bullion and currency and their import and export will almost cease although they are perfectly free. That is, under such a gold standard regime, the actual gold transaction will become almost unnecessary. Thus, in Ricardo's plan a 'secure currency' is necessarily an 'economical currency'. For him, the execution of this plan will not require a great amount of gold reserve.

But, in reality, he had to face 'the alarm of the Bank Directors at the thoughts of providing coin for that purpose [resumption of cash payment]'. And 'they have officially declared that not less than 30 millions would be necessary, besides the usual reserve' (letter to McCulloch of 7 April 1819, VIII/21). According to them, therefore, a reserve should be accumulated over and above the total amount of the banknotes currently in circulation. In addition, at the moment when Ricardo was writing this letter, the resumption of cash payment was not yet officially decided. The preparatory process had only begun: in Parliament the committees were nominated in both Houses and the hearing of evidence was going on. The words and deeds of the directors of the BoE appeared to him to be based on an entire 'ignorance' and 'prejudice', were the height of folly describable only as 'impossible to describe' (VIII/20) and he would be 'puzzled to account for' (VIII/1).

But 'irrational' deeds of the public based on such an 'alarm' were repeated many times in history. Ricardo calls them 'extraordinary occasions' happening 'when a general panic seizes the country, and when everyone is desirous of possessing the precious metals as the most convenient mode of realising or concealing his property', and 'against such panics, Banks have no security, *on any system*; from their very nature they are subject to them, as at no time can there be in a Bank, or in a country, so much specie or bullion as the monied individuals of such country have a right to demand' (IV/68, emphasis in original). Insofar as not being backed up by virtually 100% precious metal reserve like the 'deposit banks' in Amsterdam and Hamburg mentioned sometimes by Ricardo and Malthus, the banking system necessarily conditioned on a 'confidence' (Thornton) in the issuing bank is keeping in it constantly the potential danger of falling into failure as a result of a run arising from such panics. But for Ricardo who sees panics as above, there can be no devices to prevent them. If a panic happens, it is not because of the defects in the currency system, but because of the behaviour of the public triggering a panic.

When mentioning the panics in proposing the plan for a maximal economisation of the use of precious metal, he bears in mind above all the events in February 1797.

> A panic of this kind was the cause of the crisis in 1797 … . Neither the Bank nor government were at that time to blame; it was the contagion of the unfounded fears of the timid part of the community, which occasioned the run on the Bank. … If the Bank had continued paying in cash, probably the panic would have subsided before their coin had been exhausted.
>
> (IV/68)

Therefore, to be blamed is the public, upset without reason moving around in search of precious metal, to which nothing can be done. In the letter addressed to Trower on 26 May 1819, two days after Peel's Bill for resumption of cash payment was actually approved in Parliament, in reporting it to him, Ricardo says that 'the alarm that prevailed in the City is incomprehensible' and he attributes this 'alarm' to the agitation by the agents of the BoE, who might have fallen themselves into a similar psychological state (VIII/32). From his standpoint, faced with such a situation, one could only blame or look on with contempt at it as incorrigible behaviour of a certain sort of people.

Above is what happened before he wrote *Proposals*. In the process of the execution of Peel's Bill of 1819 (Resumption Act) enacted under an important influence of this pamphlet, the directors of the BoE really embarked on the actions such as Ricardo described in his letter to McCulloch of 7 April (see supra) when the Bill had not yet taken its definitive clear form. And, together with the treatment of small notes, this was to put serious obstacles in the way of realising the plan of bullion payment. It became impossible for him only to look upon it as 'incorrigible folly'.

4.4.3 Monopolisation of profits by the BoE, its abolition and transfer of the issuing power to the State

Now, the sections from V to VII of *Proposals* are devoted to the critique and attack against the management of the BoE, as was requested by Grenfell, in the last slight space of which Ricardo briefly presents an idea of transferring the issuing power of paper to the state. This is open to the idea Ricardo is to develop afterwards in his manuscript entitled 'Plan, &c.' (IV/276–300) drafted in the summer 1823, and it is worth paying attention that it is already present in this pamphlet written during the last four months of 1815. Of course, it does not appear here abruptly. We will turn our attention also to the fact that the idea is presented in this place and to the link between the first and second parts of this pamphlet.

At the opening of section VII, the turning point between sections VI and VII and central part of the latter half of *Proposals*, he says on the subjects of these two sections (i.e., of the latter half) as follows:

> I have hitherto been considering the profits of the Bank, as they regard the public, and have endeavoured to shew that they have greatly exceeded what a just consideration for *their* rights and interests could warrant. I propose now to consider them in relation to the interests of the proprietors of Bank stock, for which purpose I shall endeavour to state a basis on which the profits of the Bank may be calculated, with a view to ascertain what the accumulated savings of the Bank now are. If we knew accurately the expences of the Bank, and the amount of cash and bullion which they may at different times have had in their hands, we should have the means of making a calculation on this subject, which would be a very near approximation to the truth.
>
> (IV/96, emphasis in original)

Therefore, he is going to show with concrete numerical data and calculations how much profit the BoE earns mainly from the transactions with government, and how much of which is returned as dividends to the stockholders as its proprietors. The numerical data and the other materials, bases for accomplishing such tasks, were massively offered by Grenfell, and they appear to have been widely made use of in 'Appendix' extending to as many as 20 pages in the latter half of *Proposals*. Such tasks had to be carried out by Ricardo, a free writer out of office, because the BoE did not make public most information about the state of its management. He criticises the BoE in pointing out its concealing tendencies as follows:

> The publication of accounts, besides being necessary as a check against the *corrupt* administration of the Directors, is also necessary to give assurance to the proprietors, that their affairs are *ably* administered. Since 1797, no statement has been made of the condition of the Bank; and, even in that year, it was made to Parliament, on a particular exigence, and not to the proprietors of Bank stock.
>
> (IV/111, emphasis in original)

From the great amount of loan to the government for financing the war, which continued during the period of suspension of convertibility after 1797, the BoE obtained a huge income of interest. It was paid in the end from nothing other than a charge on the public, hence an enormous benefit of such a nature should have been correctly made public. Moreover, such a benefit of the BoE, a joint-stock company, should have naturally been allotted to the stockholders, its proprietors, it should have paid dividends satisfactory to them in detailing the breakdown of profits. The directors of the BoE are negligent of their duties to both the public and its stakeholders, and in violation of the rights and interests of both of them it has continued to accumulate huge funds 'silently'. The latter half of *Proposals* aimed at disclosing and bringing to light such a real state of the BoE in showing concrete figures and at appealing its unjustness to the stockholders, to Parliament and to the general public. At the same time, Ricardo himself seems to have come to recognise anew such 'too bad' real state of the BoE in carrying on these works. Incidentally, both Ricardo and Grenfell were its stockholders, i.e., stakeholders so to speak. The latter asked the former to write a pamphlet disclosing the real state of the BoE in his letter of 1 August 1815, originally as a campaign document for accusing the managers of the BoE and demanding a dividend increase at its general meeting of stockholders to be held on 21 September. Therefore, what Grenfell had in mind then appears to have been a pamphlet for agitation, relatively short and simple and focusing on the above subject, to be prepared in a month or so from the request to its actual publication. But in fact, Ricardo was going to write a document endowed with both a far longer range and theoretical considerations on his own theory of money, including naturally contents responding to the request of Grenfell.

A Table is printed in section VII (V/101), showing the annual evolution of the profits and dividends of the BoE from 1797 to 1814. According to it, the rate of dividends during the last ten years in the nineteenth century remains continually at the same level after it was brought down from 12% in 1806 to 10% in the following year, notwithstanding the residual profits after the payment of dividends has doubled on the other hand. Maybe this Table is also based on the data offered by Grenfell, who thinks the appropriate rate of dividends should be about 20% to 25%, more than twice as high as the actual rate (his letter to Ricardo of 24 September 1815, immediately after he himself had attended the general meeting of stockholders, proposed a motion for dividend increase and it was rejected). Ricardo for his part considers at that moment (in 1815) 19% as its appropriate rate according to his own calculation. He shares anyway the same opinion with Grenfell that 10% is too low.

> It will appear on an examination of the accounts in the Appendix for the subsequent years, that the profits of the Bank for every year, since 1801, have exceeded the annual dividend paid to the proprietors, and that in 1815, the surplus for that year only must have amounted to 1,066,625*l.* so that the Bank could have paid a dividend for that year of nineteen per cent, instead of ten per cent.
>
> (IV/103–4)

Not publishing the state of its management, the BoE is accumulating lots of funds 'hitherto withheld from the proprietors' (ibid.). 'During 18 years the directors have been silently enjoying their lucrative trade, and may now possibly think that the same course is best adapted to the interests of the Bank' (IV/113–4). This is the BoE that is tacitly continuing to accumulate funds, making tremendous benefits from collusive transactions with the government, while invading the rights and interests of both the general public and the stockholders in concealing information. Confirming such a recognition, Ricardo concludes *Proposals* with words bringing into question the further existence itself of the BoE.

In this ultimate part Ricardo adds a new reason for which the BoE is required now to publish the state of its management. This publication is certainly useful for containing the tyranny of the BoE, however it is not more than a best measure feasible for a moment, not likely to dissolve the burden actually imposed on the public by the profits gained by the BoE. For this it is indispensable that the public 'deprive them of the most profitable part of their trade' (IV/114), i.e., to abolish 'the policy of permitting a company of merchants to enjoy all the advantages which attend the supplying of a great country with paper money'. But 'the Bank are secure of their charter for seventeen years to come', 'against this danger, however, the Bank is secure till 1833'. And in conclusion Ricardo says once again that 'therefore on every ground publicity is expedient' (ibid.).

By virtue of the 'charter' still remaining valid as long as 17 years to come, the BoE is, for a considerable time, guaranteed a subsistence as an exclusive issuing bank in the central part of commerce in England. The most which can be done in supposing the subsistence of the BoE as it is will be to protect the interests of the public and of its stockholders (squeezing of its profits and a transparent dividend policy) in implementing the plan presented in the first half of *Proposals* and publishing the necessary information. For the moment it would be out of question to 'deprive them [the BoE] of the most profitable part of their trade', i.e., the power of issuing paper and to transfer it to the state. It is only possible at present to draft a rough sketch as a possibility in a distant future. But, even if such was the case, Ricardo nevertheless gave a sketch of this kind at the end of *Proposals.* probably under a firm conviction that finally the BoE should not be allowed to exist.

In the following Ricardo presents concretely a 'means' 'by which so considerable an advantage might be obtained for the state, independently of all control of ministers'. To issue paper money is to create a currency equivalent to gold as its standard from paper as its medium devoid of value. Therefore, the value of paper as money is wholly due to the seigniorage belonging to its issuer as its earning. This earning, incomparably larger that the seigniorage for precious metal coin, should be received by the public but not by a private banking company.

> Seigniorage [sic] in all countries belongs to the state, and with the security of convertibility as proposed in the former part of this work, and the appointment of commissioners responsible to parliament only, the state, by becoming the sole issuer of paper money, in town as well as in the country, might secure a net revenue to the public of no less than two millions sterling. (IV/114)

The idea that in place of the BoE the state should issue paper (naturally presupposing a non-renewal of its 'charter' and the cessation of its function as issuing bank), was already stated in the letter to Malthus of 10 September 1815 when Ricardo was writing the manuscript of *Proposals* (cf. Subsection

4.3.2). The reason why the power of issuing paper belongs only to the state, the organ assuming the paper issue, its position, the dimension of the benefit obtained by the state in issuing paper, on all these points there is no change from what was said in the above letter. And the two versions are also the same in the absence of an idea of dividing into issuing and banking departments the organ to replace the BoE. The important difference of the second from the first version is that the plan of bullion payment proposed 'in the former part of this work' is integrated here as a part of the proposal of an issuing organ substituting for the BoE. That is, Ricardo thought that, if there is a change in the issuing organ, the plan of bullion payment will remain valid as it was originally conceived. He probably did not think of alternative plans.

Another important difference is that this idea is stated not in a private letter, but in a publication. The text in the letter is very similar to the sentences quoted above from *Proposals*. This may be because Ricardo continued thinking about a new issuing organ as substitute for the BoE from the time when he began to write the manuscript, if the concluding pages of *Proposals* were written a considerable time later than the letter to Malthus. In any case, the idea of abolition of the BoE as issuing bank was not only a temporary idea but seems to have taken a fairly clear shape toward that time[16].

The way of presenting briefly an idea (or plan) at the end of a publication is the same as for the plan of bullion payment in 'Appendix' to the fourth edition of *High Price*. And in like manner as at that time, the new plan (though too succinct to be called a plan) may have been noticed at all, neither at the time of publication of the first and second editions of *Proposals* in 1816, nor when the plan in the first part of this pamphlet was taken up for the first time in Parliament in 1819. McCulloch, largely contributed to the diffusion of this pamphlet in publishing its review in the issue of December 1818 of *Edinburgh Review*, did not pay attention to this last paragraph, though he had paid attention to the last part of 'Appendix' in his review on it published in August 1811 in the same magazine. And, except for an unremarkable description in the middle of chapter 27 of *Principles*, the sentences occupying not more than half a page at the end of the last paragraph remained the only ones in which Ricardo made public during his lifetime his conception of an issuing organ substituting for the BoE.

4.5 End of the War and approach of the resumption of cash payment (*Principles* and Ricardo's Plan, evidence before the Parliamentary Committees)

4.5.1 Currency 'in its most perfect state' in the first and second editions of Principles

McCulloch, in his letter to Ricardo of 6 December 1818, probably immediately after having finished the manuscript of the review of *Proposals*, advises him as follows: 'I think you ought to extend the preliminary part of your Chapter on Currency and banks – You might in the space of three or four pages engross into it the substance of the first part of your most excellent pamphlet on "an economical currency"' (VII/353). At that time Ricardo had already finished preparation for the second edition of *Principles*, and he had already sent to Murray a list of corrections for the new edition (his letter of 23 November, VII/331). But, in adopting this advice from McCulloch at the beginning of December, he sent anew a letter (not included in *Works*) with concrete indications for inserting a passage excerpted from *Proposals* in chapter 27 (25 in the first edition. Hereinafter chapter 27 after *Works*). It may have been from such a circumstance that Ricardo asked Murray to insert the passage in question in using a copy of *Proposals* probably Murray had at hand instead of making himself a new addition to the manuscript of chapter 27. And in his letter, McCulloch did not say anything about what part (IV/66–70) to insert where (I/356–61), which was decided entirely on the judgement of Ricardo. Such a measure was taken naturally because chapter 27 in *Principles* is closely related to the subject of *Proposals*. But at the same time these two works are very different in their character. And the writing of chapter 27 of *Principles* treating a subject akin to that of *Proposals* was probably about one year after he had finished writing the latter. Taking into account such points, here we will examine how the common subject is treated in chapter 27 of *Principles* published about one year later than *Proposals*, and the meaning of inclusion in the second edition of a long quotation from the latter.

In the first edition of *Principles*, Ricardo begins in I/361 a brief sketch of an 'ideal' currency regime he conceives on the basis of the theoretical analyses on the determination of the value of currency and its variation (I/352–5). It is precisely at this logical junction that he inserts the long quotation from *Proposals* in the second edition. The opening of the paragraph ('a currency is in its most perfect state when it consists wholly of paper money, but of paper money of an equal value with the gold which it professes to represent' (I/361)) corresponds with the first sentence in the quotation from *Proposals* (IV/66, I/356–7), and in the quotation Ricardo's 'plan' (IV/69, I/360) of bullion payment is explained in the space of the following four pages. And, with the negation of the choice between 'either in gold coin or bullion' in the text of *Principles* immediately before the quotation, the payment of bank-note is unified in bullion payment. But in the text of *Principles*, Ricardo does not use the term 'plan' implicating a concrete program of action. Therefore, in the first edition of *Principles* no concrete explanation is to be found on how to execute the convertibility though its necessity is affirmed, except for a following brief comment on the above quoted sentence on the 'most perfect state' of a currency:

> The use of paper instead of gold, substitutes the cheapest in place of the most expensive medium, and enables the country, without loss to any individual, to exchange all the gold which it before used for this purpose, for

> raw materials, utensils and food; by the use of which, both its wealth and its enjoyments are increased.
>
> (I/361)

This short paragraph of less than five lines, which, in the second edition of *Principles*, follows immediately the long quotation from *Proposals*, can be regarded as an extremely compressed abstract version of what Ricardo had already explained in detail and concretely in *Proposals*. This simplified version may be said to imply the basic points in Ricardo's plan of bullion payment, such as regulation of the value of currency by means of bullion payment, and substitution of paper money for coin. But this can be said only for those who know what Ricardo had already said in *Proposals*. Considering that this pamphlet (in particular the first part of it) may have been already forgotten by many of the readers when the first edition of *Principles* was published in the following year, they may not have seen how Ricardo thought about the use of cash payment and its consequences in *Principles*. In including in the second edition the long quotation from *Proposals* following the advice of McCulloch, he restored to its original form what he had once compressed.

The sketch of an 'ideal' monetary regime, following the paragraph in which he affirmed the necessity of convertibility in the first edition of *Principles* (I/356), does not end only with this short paragraph. In some paragraphs next to this short one, he raises the problem of whether the issuer of money should be 'a Bank' (not called by name but it is evident from the context that it means the BoE) or 'the Government' (or the State) and indicates briefly the reason why it should be the latter and how to put it into execution.

> In a national point of view, it is of no importance whether the issuers of this well-regulated paper money be the Government or a Bank, it will, on the whole, be equally productive of riches, whether it be issued by one or by the other; but it is not so with respect to the interest of individuals. In a country where the market rate of interest is 7 per cent, and where the State requires for a particular expense 70,000*l*. per annum, it is a question of importance to the individuals of that country, whether they must be taxed to pay this 70,000*l*. per annum, or whether they could raise it without taxes.
>
> (I/361)

After having explained briefly the measure to be taken for stabilising most economically the value of paper currency in the immediately preceding paragraph (but in the second edition, after having explained this clearly as 'plan' in inserting a quotation from *Proposals*), Ricardo raises such a problem in relation to this explanation. It is evident that the large amount of cost to be financed by the State mentioned here means the war expenditure the Government was actually procuring by borrowing from the BoE for the long-lasting war with France. And it is also evident that he is bearing in mind here the experience during war time, that the payment of interest due to such a large amount of loan was yielding enormous profits to the BoE, and that because of this the public was assuming a heavy burden in paying taxes. It was precisely against this background that Ricardo claimed in the closing paragraph of *Proposals* that the issuing organ should be placed under the State or Government ('the public would have a direct interest that the issuers should be the State, and not a company of merchants or bankers' (I/362)).

But in these paragraphs in *Principles*, Ricardo mentions neither that it is the BoE which is profiting from the tax burden born by the public, nor that by virtue of the Bank Charter delivered from the State the BoE secured for a long time its existence so that for the moment there is no possibility of replacing it. However, one or two years before writing *Principles*, Ricardo was continually thinking about reform of the monetary regime, bringing into question also the further existence of the BoE itself (cf. Subsection 4.3.2). This must not be forgotten in reading these paragraphs. The following hypothetical counter-argument against placing the issuing organ under the Government was in fact the position Ricardo himself had taken in opposing Say's proposal in his letter to Say of 24 December 1814:

> The danger, however, is, that this power would be more likely to be abused, if in the hands of Government, than if in the hands of a banking company. A company would, it is said, be more under the control of law, and although it might be their interest to extend their issues beyond the bounds of discretion, they would be limited and checked by the power which individuals would have of calling for bullion or specie. It is argued that the same check would not be long respected, if Government had the privilege of issuing money; that they would be too apt to consider present convenience, rather than future security, and might, therefore, on the alleged grounds of expediency, be too much inclined to remove the checks, by which the amount of their issues was controlled.
>
> (ibid.)

But, in the process of preparing to write *Proposals*, Ricardo became aware of the real state of management of the BoE and came to conceive an issuing organ placed under the State in its place, to dispel such worries. At the same time, he proposes institutional devices preventing this new issuing organ from falling into such corrupt practices like the BoE (check on the collusion and adherence between the issuer and lenders, above all 'ministers' as heads of the departments in Government). The conception of an issuing organ alternative to the BoE he shows in such a context is not different from what he had already shown in his letter to Malthus of 10 September 1815 and on the last page of *Proposals*. 'In a free country, with an enlightened legislature, the power of issuing paper money, under the requisite checks of convertibility at the will of the holder, might be safely lodged in the hands of commissioners appointed for that special purpose, and they might be made totally independent of the control of ministers' (ibid.). These commissioners assuming the paper issue are nominated by Parliament and 'responsible only to parliament' (I/362–3).

What Ricardo discusses after the long quotation from *Proposals* is nothing other than a reaffirmation of the idea about the paper issue by the State sketched in the last page of *Proposals* written, presumably, about one year earlier. In reading this reaffirmation as following the quotation from *Proposals*, it will become more understandable, than in reading only the text of the first edition of *Principles*, that Ricardo's plan of bullion payment was, according to its character, to be continuously extended to what was to become called afterwards 'Plan for the Establishment of a National Bank'[17]. However, he does not intend to show in this place of *Principles* his 'plan', but to show only what a currency in its 'most perfect state' should generally be like. Therefore, it was not his aim there to enter into the details of concrete measures to be taken for actually realising it.

4.5.2 Evidence on the resumption of cash payments before the Secret Committees and Plan of bullion payment

As the war with France ended with the Treaty of Paris at the end of 1815 and the threat of invasion by the French army disappeared, the English government had no more need of financing the great amount of war expenditure. And at the same time the main grounds on which the anti-bullionists had opposed the resumption of convertibility in May 1811 disappeared. In a growing mood for abolishing the Bank Restriction Act of 1797 with a view to resuming convertibility, *Proposals* by Ricardo was written and published as proposals for putting this into execution. Though enacted as a legislation of specified duration, the Act was still in force by the measure of prolongation taken by Parliament, but as it did not prohibit executing convertibility, the BoE tried to resume it partially, considering the state of its gold reserve, limiting the banknotes to be converted to those issued before a certain date. The first trial was implemented in December 1816, but as the current market price of bullion was below its mint price, so that the conversion of banknotes into specie meant a loss at that time, there was almost no demand for conversion. A similar announcement was repeated early in 1817, but the situation did not change. In this way, the execution of conversion remaining suspended, the amount of specie hoarded in the coffers of the BoE extended to near £12,000,000. Afterwards, though the price of bullion was above the mint price by 2% to 3%, when the BoE declared again the opening of a similarly limited conversion in September of the same year, this time a large amount of demand arose. This was of course because of the benefit obtained from melting and exporting the coin delivered in exchange for banknotes (cf. Cannan (1919), p. xxxi). For this reason, the gold reserve in the BoE rapidly diminished. In view of such a situation, Vansittart, Chancellor of Exchequer at that time, though watching for the chance of resumption of convertibility, was obliged to propose in May 1818 a bill for extending the restriction further. And the subsequent high price of bullion and fall in gold reserve still continued. But, when at the beginning of the parliamentary session in 1819 he proposed a motion to nominate committees in both of the Houses to examine the expediency of further extending the suspension, these committees were set up at the beginning of February (Sraffa, 'Notes on the evidence on the resumption of cash payments', V/350). As the time limit of the extension was fixed on 5 July 1819 by the act of postponement of resumption of cash payment enacted in the previous year (ibid.), the Committees in both Houses began activities aiming at settling the issue before this time.

With J. Mill's strong advice and actions behind the scenes, it was just at that time that Ricardo took a seat in the House of Commons (on 26 February). He must have regarded this as a good opportunity to realise convertibility through his activities in Parliament in line with the 'plan' he had nourished for such a long time. As if coordinating the timing of the parliamentary session with Ricardo as a new member, the second edition of *Principles*, including the main part of 'plan' (cf. Subsection 4.5.1) was published on 27 February. The third edition of *Proposals* was also published in March, for the first time in about three years, 'rescued from oblivion' (letter to McCulloch of 7 April 1819, VIII/20) by McCulloch who published a favourable review on it in the *Edinburgh Review* in December 1818. These events which successively occurred in a short space of time, seem to have contributed to make known widely Ricardo's point of view (particularly in Parliament) and to heighten his renown as an economist and monetary theorist, hence to strengthen his position as a 'novice' member in Parliament. Two days after he had attended the session for the first time as a member of Parliament, he reported to Trower the atmosphere as follows:

> The inquiry into the state of our currency, and exchanges, is proceeding in both houses very satisfactorily. I have had many conversations with several of the Committees of both Houses – with Lord Grenville, Marquis of Lansdown[e], Lord King, Mr. Huskisson, Mr. F. Lewis, Mr. Grenfell and others. All have a very perfect knowledge of the subject, and all agree that the progress of the public in comprehending the question has been very great. The Bank Directors themselves have improved, and they are far behind every other person. I confidently rely on measures being taken to place our currency in a satisfactory state. I am told that I shall be examined. (VIII/19)

In these words we can see vividly how favourably Ricardo was received at once by the members, with whom he was in friendly relations for a long time. We can also read from these words that his opinion was known to these colleague members and obtained a certain support from them. In such an ambiance he convinced himself of an early adoption of 'measures to place our currency in a satisfactory state', i.e., his 'plan'. Though he himself was not a member of the

Committee already set up, when he sat in Parliament, it may have been already decided that he was to be examined before the Committees in the following month. This evidence before the Committees of both Houses was to become his first activity as a member of Parliament.

The examination of Ricardo before the committee was implemented twice in the House of Commons on 4 and 19 March, and twice in the House of Lords on 24 and 26 March. The subject of the examination in both Houses were officially announced as 'the expediency of the Bank resuming cash payments' (V/371, 416). As in the 'Bullion Report' of 1810 and the debates over it in and out of Parliament, both bullionists and anti-bullionists (including the directors of the BoE) understood at that time generally the resumption of convertibility as a resumption of exchange of banknotes for cash (coin) just like that practiced before its suspension. In this sense, it is questionable how far the fundamental point in Ricardo's plan of bullion payment was understood. In the above quotation he writes about the favourable estimation and understanding of his theory by his colleagues, but they may have taken Ricardo's theory and proposal only according to their own view on money. It is however certain that, on the other hand, by virtue of his important writings and the review of them[18] successively published at that time, his theory and proposal exercised a considerable influence on the examinations of the parliamentary committees and the subsequent deliberation.

The examinations in both Houses and his evidence are, on the whole, something like a catechism between the members of the committees imbued with 'most useful instruction' from his writings and their author. In spite of this, however, it seems that, with nearly 300 questions and answers exchanged during the four days in total, the record of the evidence shows some problems likely to arise when the plan Ricardo bore in mind was submitted to an official discussion before the committees, with a view to actually implementing it. In the following we will review briefly some of these problems relevant to the present discussion. But the dates of examination containing each of questions and answers will not be indicated, and related items will be taken up at random according to the nature of the problems, regardless of their dates or question numbers.

To pay banknotes not with coin but with bullion, moreover to accept such a payment only with regard to banknotes equal to and above a certain amount, were the essential points of the plan of bullion payment. To the question of the advantages expected from the former, Ricardo answers as follows:

> First, it would exempt the Bank from providing a Quantity of Gold necessary to replace all the smaller Notes which are now circulated in London and the Country. Secondly, it would obtain for the Bank, and therefore for the Nation, all the Advantages which a Capital equal to the Amount of all the small Notes would produce.
>
> (V/422)

The most important advantage and aim of the system of bullion payment is to maintain as is the circulation of small notes expanded for the first time during the Bank Restriction Period, so as not to allow coin to circulate again. 'The Object of my Plan would be most completely effected by there being no Gold Coin in Circulation' (V/424). For Ricardo himself, the advantage of paper circulation was evident in the sense that the use of paper instead of coin serves to economise the expensive money material, and also that paper is free from every inconvenience arising when handling many pieces of coin. In spite of this, it was not always certain whether it would be possible to substitute paper for coin, it 'must depend entirely on the Preference of the Public for metallic Circulation' (V/423). For Ricardo, the 'irrational' behaviour in the use of money the public was accustomed to was beyond his comprehension, so that in order to execute a plan, the advantage of which seemed to him as if 'mathematically demonstrated', he could not but fight against such a 'prejudice'. The members of the committee 'had to contend with public prejudice, and perhaps too with prepossessions which they themselves felt in favour of coin' (letter to McCulloch of 8 May 1819, VIII/27). The attachment to coin was deeply felt not only among the common people, but also among the members of the parliamentary committees deliberating on the monetary regime. But any consideration about such a point was not contained in Ricardo's plan. This was soon to place serious obstacles in the way of execution of the plan[19] (see infra).

Now, the other essential point in the plan of bullion payment was the setting of a minimal amount to the sum of banknotes to be paid. To the question obviously anticipating a certain answer: 'do you mean that the Bank should be obliged to pay each Note on Demand in Coin or Bullion, at its Option; or would you limit the Obligation to Notes of a certain Amount, and to what Amount?' (V/422), Ricardo responds as follows:

> I would limit the Obligation on the Part of the Bank to Notes of £50, £60, or £100 Value, or to a Number of smaller Notes amounting in the Whole to such a Sum. The Object which I have in view, is to regulate the Value of Currency, by having an effectual Controul [sic] over its Quantity. I have no Preference for any Sums I have stated, provided they may not be too small. (ibid.)

It was for the purpose of attaining the stabilisation of the value of currency economically, in avoiding both the circulation of coin and the massive accumulation of coin in the coffers of the BoE as reserves for cash payment, that the payment of banknotes had to be in bullion, not in coin. The holders of banknotes, supposed to behave rationally in the economic sense of the term, demand from the issuing bank exchange for gold at its legal mint price for one of the following two reasons: when paper is depreciating and the market price of bullion is above its mint price, it is more advantageous to obtain gold at the window of the bank in the form of bullion or coin than to buy bullion with banknotes on the market, or because, in selling the gold thus obtained, they can get a benefit equal to the difference between its market price and mint price. But actually, if everyone crowds in upon the window of the bank, transactions in the bullion market will cease, so that the arbitrage supposed above will become impossible. And, even if coin could be obtained in exchange for banknotes, it would not be used as it is as currency in the country, then it would be (illegally) melted down to bullion with a higher price. But actually, since it was impossible to use this bullion for any advantageous domestic transactions (to sell it on the market or to use it as currency), it would be sent (exported) to a foreign country where it could buy commodities (including foreign currencies) in more advantageous conditions.

Therefore, whether the payment of banknote is in coin or in bullion, the gold obtained from the bank should be considered to be wholly reduced to bullion and used for transactions with foreign countries. Of course, a part of this gold will be used as a raw material for the manufacturing industry, but also in this case it will be first reduced to bullion form. Thus, insofar as it is not intended to get precious metal money in exchange for paper notes simply from 'a mere caprice' or 'prejudice', the payment in coin would be meaningless. Even if the banknotes are paid in coin when paper is in depreciation (and it is only then that the banknote returns to the window of the bank), coin will only be melted down to bullion. Or the demand for cash payment will cease if the public fear the punishment for committing an illegal act. In any case, the demand for bullion actually arising in the condition of currency depreciation is wholly for foreign trade, except for demand for gold for manufacturing. In parliamentary evidence Ricardo says in this respect as follows: 'all our transactions in bullion would be confined to our foreign trade, and to the uses for our own manufactures, that is exactly the amount of our trade in bullion at this moment' (V/415). That is, otherwise than for these two purposes there are no bullion transactions.

And to satisfy these demands (i.e., payment of banknotes with bullion by the BoE) is at the same time to recover the currency issued in excess, hence to stabilise its value in resolving its depreciation. Such a demand for bullion comes wholly from foreign traders engaged in large scale transactions, and the amounts of such demand will be limited to those far superior to household expenditure. If Ricardo set a certain minimal limit of a considerably large amount for bullion payment, it was for the purpose of confining the object of payment to the banknotes used for industrial (or commercial) circulation in order to exclude small transactions at the bank window.

Now, at the moment when the plan of bullion payment was adopted in outline in the Bill and was to be executed, two practical problems arose: when to begin its execution, and how to set the price of payment at its beginning when the bullion price was still above the mint price. In the plan presented in *Proposals*, Ricardo took a position of beginning the bullion payment a few months later, in a proximate future, with the mint price. Also in the evidence based on this plan, he stated the same position when asked his opinion on this point in the first question on the first day of examination before the committee in the House of Lords (cf. V/415–7). He said then that, though the resumption of payment could be commenced on 5 July (i.e., three to four months later), on the expiring date of the last extended Act of Suspension, in view of the current price of bullion superior to its mint price by 'Four per Cent', the resumption 'must be attended with some little Inconvenience' (V/416) of 'Four per Cent' fall in the price of commodities caused by so much contraction of the total quantity of currency in circulation. However, when at the beginning of the examination on the second day one of the members questioned him:

> Are you of Opinion that it would be more advantageous to require the Bank to commence this System by Payment of its Notes in Bullion at the Mint Price, or that any Facility would be given to the Plan, by the Adoption of a graduated Scale, by which they should pay at first at the present Market Price, and at Prices successively reduced at stated Periods, until they came down to the Mint Price?
>
> (V/439)

In his answer he chose, naturally, the latter. It is evident that this questioner knew in advance Ricardo's opinion and was going to draw from him an expected answer.

In fact, Ricardo had proposed such a way of bringing down the price of bullion by 'a graduated scale' on 11 December 1811, more than eight years before, in his letter to Tierney (cf. Subsection 4.3.1). But after that he did never mention this idea neither in his letters nor in his publications. If also he did never mention it orally, it must have been only two persons, Ricardo and Tierney, who knew (if they remembered) such an idea prior to this questioning. After having answered almost echoing the questioner, Ricardo says as follows: 'by far the most important Consideration with me is, preventing the Currency being depreciated, as compared with Bullion, below the present Rate of Depreciation, and by adopting the graduated Scale you would have complete Security upon that Point' (ibid.). Since this claim of Ricardo preventing the further aggravation of the depreciation of banknotes before dissolving it and conforming the market price of bullion to its mint price, was precisely what he had stated at first in explaining his idea to Tierney in a letter addressed to him many years before (cf. VI/68), it would be difficult to think that such a question and answer occurred to Ricardo and to the questioner independently of the letter to Tierney (they were surely in agreement beforehand). But Tierney should not have been this questioner, since he was a member in the House of Commons like Ricardo. Then it may be inferred that someone in the committee of the House of Lords had made an arrangement with Ricardo (and also probably Tierney) in advance to fabricate the dialogue seen above. This is a rather extreme example, but there exist a number of similar cases in Ricardo's examination before the committees in both Houses in March 1819. Anyway, this idea of his was adopted in the Bill to be approved two months later and was restored about eight years after it had been conceived for the first time.

The gold reserve of the BoE in February 1819 is estimated at 4.2 million pounds, while the quantity of banknotes in circulation at 25.1 (Feavearyear and Morgan (1963), p. 229). According to Ricardo, during the period prior to the suspension of cash payments in February 1797, 'four millions was about the sum which the Bank considered as fair cash' (IV/99). After 1790 till the suspension, the total amount of the banknotes of the BoE was constantly around 10 million pounds, and its cash reserve before 1795 was far above 4 million, 'considered as fair cash' (though falling in the meantime from about 8 million to about 5 million). From the beginning of 1796, while there was no great change in the total amount of issue, the reserve fell to the level between 2 and 3 million to attain its minimum of 1.1 million in February 1797 when the suspension began (cf. Feavearyear and Morgan (1963), p. 227–8, Table in these pages). Calculating from these figures, the story would be that the minimal limit of the secure rate of reserve for the BoE was about 40%, and when it fell to about 10% it decided to suspend cash payments. On the contrary, calculating from the above figures, we can see that the rate of reserve at the end of the 1810s, when the resumption of cash payment was on the agenda, was less than 20%. This is a level nearer to that at which the BoE had suspended the payment than to one it considered as secure. The directors of the Bank could have never thought the resumption possible with such a level of gold reserve. But since the BoE at that time was not obliged to pay banknotes in cash or in bullion, in principle it had no need of gold reserves. If, in spite of this, it kept the reserve rate at a certain (though not sufficiently high) level while expanding note issue, it was preparing against the resumption of payment which was to come necessarily at some time. And when this resumption appeared near, the directors of the BoE were captured with 'alarm' 'at the thoughts of providing coin for that purpose' (Ricardo's letter to McCulloch of 7 April (see supra), VIII/20–1).

In this way it had become a subject, among others, in the examination before the committees what actions, impossible to check with legislative measures, the BoE would take when the outline of Ricardo's plan would be adopted in an act and executed. Here again it was as if the members of the committee had substantially the same opinion with the examinee, and they wanted to draw from him positive answers, or at most some supplements to the questions. As is clear from the figures given above, the worries about the possible reactions of the BoE were about an excessive contraction of banknotes and an excessive hoarding of gold reserves. Both of them, each through different channels, were expected to bring about a general fall in prices far exceeding the level of about 4%, described by Ricardo as 'some little Inconvenience' (V/416).

On the first point. Question: 'If the Bank should for their own Security think proper to make a further Reduction of their Notes to the Amount of Three Millions, between this Time and the Month of July next, what Effect would this have upon the Prices of Commodities?' Answer:

> I think a greater Effect would be produced on the Prices of Bullion, on the Currency and on the Prices of Commodities, than what is necessary to bring Bullion down to the Mint Price. Both Bullion and Commodities might probably fall 8 or 10 per Cent. No such Fall could take place if the Mint were open, or the Bank were obliged to buy Bullion at £3 17*s.* 6*d.* The Bank could not then reduce the Circulation Three Millions.
>
> (V/452–3)

It is as if this question foresaw the actions the BoE would really take afterwards, and also it is as if Ricardo's answer anticipated the negative results of these actions. The figures of 8% and 10% correspond to the proportion the amount of three million pounds occupied in the total amount of banknotes in circulation at that time. A fall in prices nearly equal to these figures did not take place till July of that year, but it became actual with the price evolutions two years later. The device to prevent such an excessive rise in the value of currency was already prepared in the plan as a purchase of bullion (new issue of paper) at a price a little inferior to its mint price, as well as free minting in the Mint (new issue of coin). Ricardo set this purchasing price at 3*l.* 17*s.* 6*d.*, lower than the mint price by 4½*d.* (at the rate of about 0.5%). If this measure was carried out, the value of currency should not have risen beyond the level of 4% foreseen by Ricardo.

On the second point. Question:

> Supposing the Bank not to think that they could engage with Safety to pay their Notes in Bullion at any specified Period, according to the present Market Price, without previously making a considerable Purchase of Gold, would not such Purchase have a Tendency to increase the Price of Bullion?
>
> (V/453)

Answer: 'I think it would have such a Tendency; but I should not admit this Plea [of the BoE], for I should think it not founded on a Knowledge of the true Principles of Currency, the Purchase of any great Quantity of Gold being wholly unnecessary' (ibid.). Here again, as in the previous question, at that moment the worrying situation which would appear after the passing of Resumption Act seems to have been foreseen. With his usual blame on the BoE of 'ignorance of the true principles of currency', Ricardo wants to reject resolutely such an act of 'purchase of great quantity of gold'. But it was not possible to really prevent it with his power.

The evolution of the situation after May 1819 appeared to be a theoretical and political victory for Ricardo, but with time some worries contained in his parliamentary evidence came true, which was to force him continual hard struggles during the few years of the rest of his lifetime. This makes up 'act two' of the story on his plans for the reform of monetary regime, the subject of chapter five.

Notes

1 As for the relation between these two letters and their significance, as well as for the circumstance which led Ricardo to write commentaries together with the other two bullionists and the analysis of these commentaries, see the related passages in Depoortère (2015).

2 The law in force at that time forbidding the melting of coin with a view to reducing it to bullion to be exported abroad, was intended to enclose the coin as currency, just like the banknote, within the sphere of domestic circulation once it was issued. If this law was really implemented, it might have been possible to consider, as Ricardo did, the issued quantity of coin and the variation of its value as comparable to those of the banknote (but even in such a case, unlike paper, the quantity of issue of coin can neither be increased nor diminished at the will of the issuer as Ricardo himself repeatedly emphasised). But equally as he readily recognised, the ineffectiveness of this law was so to say an open secret, it was a loophole-ridden law.

3 Ricardo adds here a note to indicate that: 'An increase of bank-notes under 5*l.* should be considered as a substitute for the coins exported, rather than an actual increase of circulation, is often and justly maintained by those who oppose the reasoning of the Bullion Report' (ibid.). We know thus that the last point in the commentaries on Galton was only a repetition of what a considerable number of participants in the bullionist controversy, including Ricardo himself (particularly the anti-bullionists who had interests in underestimating as much as possible the expansion of currency), already recognised.

4 But at that time coin had already entirely left circulation, most of which had been melted down and sent abroad or concealed for future use. Hence, coin or bullion, hardly any gold remained in the country. In such a situation King's claim was factually for payment with banknotes at a due premium corresponding to its depreciation, if not for extorting with force the concealed coin.

5 On the occasion of the publication of Ricardo's reply in 'Appendix' to the fourth edition of *High Price* published in April to his anonymous review in the *Edinburgh Review* of February 1811 ([Malthus] (1811a)), Malthus sent a letter for the first time to Ricardo on 16 June, after the rejection of the Resumption Bill, to give his name as the author of the above review, and told him of his position as a bullionist in saying that 'we are *mainly* on the same side of the question' (VI/21, emphasis in original). In his anonymous review published in the same *Review* in the following August entitled 'Review of the Controversy respecting the High Price of Bullion', he estimates positively the action of King and criticises Stanhope's Act, affirming that the only possible solution to the problem is the resumption of cash payments ([Malthus] (1811b), pp. 364–9). Prior to the publication of this review, Malthus sent a letter to Ricardo on 26 July, two days after the passing of Stanhope's Act, to make him know that 'if I should write again in the review, I will certainly mention your plan [Ricardo had sketched in the above 'Appendix'] with the approbation which I think it deserves' (VI/41). It was on the following day that Ricardo took action to make approaches to a political leader. This may be said to be a joint action between them coordinated with the political agenda of the moment.

6 In the above quotation from III/124, the BoE was said to be able to pay at its discretion 'either in specie, in gold standard bars, or in foreign coin' or in certain cases probably mixing all or some of them. This is in fact to reduce the gold in every possible form to bullion, distinguishable only by fineness and weight. Thus, the payment in any form of gold is nothing other than payment in bullion.

7 In the regions where the Bank of Amsterdam and the Bank of Hamburg belonged, the standard metal was silver, not gold as in England at that time. But, by simply substituting gold for silver, the practices in both regions could apply to England.

8 The source of information on the Bank of Hamburg for Ricardo is noted in III/175 (*Reply*, Chapter II. Sec. I 'Exchange with Hamburgh').

9 For the analysis of this manuscript and a comparative study between the theories of money and banking of Ricardo and Bentham, see Deleplace and Sigot (2012).

10 In such a situation, Malthus exceptionally paid attention to the plan of Ricardo (cf. note 5 above). In his review published soon after (anonymously) in the *Edinburgh Review* ([Malthus] (1811b)), the gist of Ricardo's plan is briefly and faithfully reproduced in a positive tone (ibid., pp. 469–70). However, concerning one of the main points in Ricardo's plan directed to minimising the precious metal reserve in the issuing bank in abolishing metal currency circulation, Malthus was to persistently repeat critical comments in their epistolary exchange in later years (cf. Subsection 4.3.4).

11 Indeed, it was only in 'Appendix' when the plan was sketched for the first time that the minimum limit of bullion payment was expressed in terms of a currency unit. After the letter to Tierney, Ricardo indicated such a minimal limit on several occasions, but except for his evidence before the Secret Committees of both Houses in March 1819 immediately after his entry into Parliament (V/409), he indicated it always in terms of weight of bullion (20 ounces in *Proposals* (IV/66), 60 ounces in Peel's Act enacted in 1819 (V/366–7), again 60 ounces in 'parliamentary speech in February 1821' (V/75), and finally 100 ounces in his last manuscript of 1823 'Plan, &c.' (IV/288)).

12 In fact, it was held on 21 September. Grenfell, himself a stockholder, attended the general meeting, put queries to the directors about the real state of the management of BoE, proposed a motion requiring an enhancement of the dividends, but it was rejected. On the same day he sent a letter to Ricardo to make him a report of the meeting (VI/278). The following general meeting was held on 21 December, and this time Ricardo, equally a stockholder of the company, attended it and made a speech criticising the state of management of the BoE, but it was ignored without any reaction from directors and many other attendant stockholders (cf. his letter to Trower of 25 December, VI/343).

13 'The Money-Standard-Equation' (MSE), advanced in Chapter 4 'The two causes of change in the value of money' in Deleplace (2017), is also to determine the variations in the value of money with 'the rate of change in the value of the standard minus the rate of change in the price of the standard' (p. 145). The 'standard' is here bullion as the standard of money. Apart from the relation between MSE and Malthus' above contention, Takenaga (2018) examines the debatable point in MSE, the practical possibility of addition or subtraction between these two elements of different nature.

14 Except for possible direct oral discussions, this debate was conducted entirely in their correspondence (not 'in print'). The related letters of them subsequent to the two mentioned above are the following: Malthus→Ricardo, 30/10/1815. R→M, 24/12/1815. R→Trower, 25/12/1815. M→R, 09/02/1816. R→M, 23/02/1816. R→M, 21/9/1819. Including the first two, we have in total eight letters, among which only one is addressed to Trower, a third party to the debate, which will be explained below.

15 Apart from the letter to Trower, in citing an example of the immediate past, Ricardo recognises that the value of the standard of money itself can change in exercising influence on the monetary system, in saying at the beginning of section III of *Proposals* as follows:

> While a standard is used, we are subject to only such a variation in the value of money, as the *standard* itself is subject to; but against such variation there is no possible remedy, and late events have proved that, during periods of war, when gold and silver are used for the payment of large armies, distant from home, those variations are much more considerable than has been generally allowed.
>
> (IV/62)

Ricardo seems to have drafted these sentences in considering the comments or criticisms from Malthus since his letter of 15 October. Though it is difficult to determine precisely the moment of writing of a particular part in *Proposals* as it was actually published, the passage quoted above may be inferred to have been added or rewritten in a relatively later phase in the revising process Ricardo continued till the end of 1815.

16 Deleplace says in Deleplace (2008) as follows:

> Deux questions sont posées: ces deux plans sont-ils compatibles? Pourquoi Ricardo passa-t-il de l'un à l'autre? Les réponses à ces questions sont recherchées dans la défense présentée par Ricardo au Parlement en 1822–1823, lorsqu'il y fut accusé d'être responsable de la déflation ayant suivi le retour à la convertibilité. Je suggère que le passage d'un plan à l'autre s'explique par sa conviction que la Banque d'Angleterre avait torpillé la mise en œuvre du premier.
>
> (p. 13)

But, as seen above, though not a named plan, the latter plan had already existed in the thinking of Ricardo, before the former plan was somehow put into execution and friction with the BoE arose. This will become clearer when examining chapter 27 of *Principles*. And the 'two plans', in no way contradicting each other, were conceived rather as something to be finally unified. Therefore, a compatibility between them or a passage from one to the other are out of question.

17 Cf. note 16 above.

18 McCulloch had published a review on the first edition of *Principles* in the issue of August 1818 of the *Edinburgh Review*. It accelerated the sale of remaining copies of the first edition, and in November, only three months after that, Ricardo was asked by Murray to prepare the second edition. It was published on 27 February 1819 ('Introduction' to *Principles*, I/1).

19 In the last part of Bonar (1923), bearing in mind the failure of the 'Ingot Plan' and comparing England at the end of the Bank Restriction Period and England after World War I moving toward recovering the gold standard system, Bonar says as follows: 'The English people in the mass are better instructed economically than a hundred years ago; and this time they may prove to have been really weaned from their fondness for gold coins, and a dear currency' (p. 300).

5 Peel's Act of 1819 and subsequent changes in monetary circulation

5.1 Decision on the resumption of cash payment (vote on Peel's Bill) and its aftermath

5.1.1 'The triumph of science, and truth, over prejudice and error'

Peel, president of the Secret Committee deliberating on the resumption of cash payments, submitted the first report to the House of Commons on 5 April 1819 after the examination of witnesses, and submitted, after its deliberation in the House, the second and final report on 6 May . This report adopted Ricardo's plan in outline, with some revisions. Peel proposed, on 24 May , the Bill of resumption of cash payment on the basis of this final report. On the same day Ricardo delivered a speech for the adoption of the Bill, which played an important role in its enactment and was also his first important speech after he sat in Parliament. On 26 May , two days after that, the Bill passed and on 2 July 1819 it received the Royal Assent of King George III. The Act was then to come into force on 1 February 1820. The outline of the Resumption Act (Peel's Act) is as follows (cf. V/7–8. The text of this Act is reproduced in Bonar (1923, pp. 301–3).

The payment of banknotes in bullion is a temporary measure over three years and three months from 1 February 1820 to 30 April 1823, from 1 May payment in coin would become obligatory. In addition, bullion payment was to begin at 4*l.* 1*s.*, i.e., at a price superior to the mint price by 4%, the current price of bullion in March 1819, and from 1 October 1820 it would be lowered to 3*l.* 19*s.* 6*d.*, i.e., to the level superior to the mint price by 2%, and further from 1 May 1821 bullion payment at the legal mint price would begin (cf. No. 78 in the questions and answers of the examination in the House of Lords, V/439–40). Within the range determined here, the date of lowering in the bullion price and its extent could be regulated at the discretion of the BoE, but the price should move always downwards, upward movement was prohibited (cf. No. 79 supra. V/440). The payment at these different prices would be made with bullion cast into a bar or ingot of 60 ounces (equivalent to about £240). That is, bullion would be paid only against banknotes of a face value equivalent or superior to 60 ounces of bullion and with this weight as a

DOI: 10.4324/9781003498322-6

unit. And from 1 May 1822, one year after that, the BoE would be permitted to choose payment in bullion or in coin. But from 1 May 1823, one year after that, bullion payment would be abolished and the BoE was obliged to pay in coin. The coin thus obtained could be freely melted and exported. This measure was indispensable for bullion as a commodity to be able to function as the standard of value of the currency of a country, and so to contribute to stabilise the value of this currency.

In this way, Ricardo's plan of bullion payment was integrated into the Act, not as a permanent regime, but only as a provisional measure for preparing for a real resumption of convertibility (i.e., cash payment). He was of course content with this in hoping that the advantage of his plan would be widely recognised, if it was executed even for a few years, and it would finally be adopted as a permanent regime (his letter to McCulloch of 7 April 1819, VIII/20). But, as was shown above on two points, in the examination of witnesses in March concrete measures for implementing bullion payments proposed by Ricardo (or by one of his questioners) were adopted. However, the procedure shown above, while aiming at dissolving the depreciation of currency and restoring its equivalence with gold as its standard, did not include any consideration about the instability of the value of currency in the contrary direction. In his plan Ricardo always foresaw that the BoE would purchase bullion (or coin) at a price slightly inferior to the mint price, every time when the value of currency would rise above its standard and the bullion price would fall below the mint price. In his letter to Trower of 28 May, two days after the passing of the Bill, he expresses almost unreserved pleasure as follows:

> I am every day rejoicing with increased satisfaction at the triumph of science, and truth, over prejudice, and error. You will perceive by the Newspapers that Parliament has at length decided that we should revert to a sound currency. The feeble resistance, in point of argument, of the Bank Directors, was easily overcome.
>
> (VIII/31. cf. also the letter to Say of 11 January 1820, VIII/150)

But at the same time he did not forget to add: 'I regret that the Committees have not adopted the measure of obliging the Bank to buy gold at £3 17. 6, whenever it is offered to them at that price' (VIII/32). Ricardo himself was aware of the omission of this point at the moment of the passing of the Bill, but the members of the committees may not have felt it necessary for the moment to take into consideration the risk of excessive contraction of the currency, obsessed by the urgent need of contracting it in excess issue. But, if the Bill had included this point and the mechanism had worked properly, the course English currency a few years after the adoption of the Bill would have been fairly different from what actually was.

On the sentence appearing at the beginning of Ricardo's speech of 24 May 'the difficulty was only that of raising the currency 3 per cent in value' (V/10), Sraffa adds a following note: 'On 4 March, to the Commons' Committee,

Ricardo had given the figure as 5 or 6 per cent [V/385]; on 24 March, to the Lords' Committee, as 4 per cent [V/417], and now, on 24 May, 3 per cent. The variation in these figures reflected the falling market price of gold' (ibid., editor's note 2). This proves that Ricardo obtained numerical data, continuously observing by very small steps the chronological variations, and gave them properly at each moment. According to these figures, the rate of depreciation of the banknote of the BoE, i.e., its rate of excess had fallen to half from 6 to 3% over less than three months preceding the passing of the Act of Resumption. If this evolution was due solely to the contraction of the total amount of banknotes in circulation, the BoE, aware of the sense of crisis, would have begun the recovery of its notes (through diminution or limitation of the discount of commercial bills or sale of securities it held) very early, as soon as Parliament began to move toward the resumption of convertibility at the beginning of February. In addition to this, as we have seen at the beginning of Subsection 4.5.2 in the previous chapter, the BoE was continuing a partial conversion. The most part of the banknotes recovered by this operation did not circulate in the form of coin, but were melted and exported, which may have been an additional important factor leading to the contraction of the total amount of currency in the country and so to the fall in the price of gold.

But the adopted Act contained a device sufficient for checking such a rapid contraction in the quantity of paper notes and the accompanying rapid fall in the price. As it would take one year and three months to bring down these indexes by 4%, beginning with selling bullion at its current market price, the BoE should have had no need to be in haste to recover currency or to try to buy as much gold as possible, since there would be no reason to demand convertibility once the depreciation of currency disappeared.

> Till October 1820, the Bank need make no reduction, and then a slight one [hear!]; and he had no doubt that if they were cautious they might arrive at cash payments without giving out one guinea in gold. The Bank should reduce their issues cautiously; he only feared they would do it too rapidly [hear!]. If he might give them advice, he should recommend to them not to buy bullion, but even though they had but a few millions, if he had the management of their concerns, he should boldly sell. Every sale would improve the exchanges, and till gold fell to 3*l.* 17*s.* 6*d.* there would be no necessity for the Bank to make any purchases[1].
>
> (V/13)

This speech of Ricardo made a large contribution to the passing of the Bill two days later. And, after having reported in the letter to Trower of 28 May of the circumstances up till its passing and of his satisfaction about it all, he ceased to speak about the problems of currency for a time.

On the situation relative to the currency from 2 July, on which Peel's Bill was given the Royal Assent, to September of the same year, when the Bill had not yet come into force, Ricardo tells briefly his view in two letters addressed to Trower.

In the letter of 8 July, he says, repeating the same words as in the letter of 28 May quoted above, 'the triumph of science and truth', that the 'great satisfaction' it gave him 'is not a little increased by observing the present state of the price of bullion and the foreign exchanges' (VIII/44). The market price of bullion Ricardo gives here is above its mint price only by 1.5 pence (at the rate of 0.16%), they are already in quasi-conformity. Since in his speech on 24 May this rate was 3%, the price of bullion fell by about 3% during the subsequent one and a half months. This rate of fall is about twice as rapid as the fall from 6 to 3% observed during a little less than the preceding three months. In spite of such a rapid fall in the price of bullion, Ricardo stated that 'the permanent price of bullion will settle at the present rate'. This was an extremely optimistic view. In order to check the fall of bullion price below the mint price, the issuing bank should purchase gold passively and unlimitedly. But, as seen above, such a measure had slipped from the Resumption Act adopted a little earlier. And even if there had been no such omission, the BoE should not yet have been obliged by the provisions of law to undertake any transactions stabilising the price of bullion, since the law had not yet come into force. If a similar situation had invariably continued, at that time it would have already become necessary to review Peel's Act, to be implemented half a year later in supposing the price of bullion superior to its mint price by 4%. Considering such circumstances, Ricardo's view on the present state of currency may be said to have been too optimistic.

Another source informing of Ricardo's view on the present state of currency during a time from his parliamentary speech of 24 May to the beginning of 1821 is his letter addressed to Trower on 25 September, two and a half months after the above letter. He says there as follows:

> I have pretty nearly discarded the subject of bullion from my mind. Everything regarding its price and the foreign exchanges is going on so much to my satisfaction that I have nothing to wish for. I repose in full confidence on the wise checks which have been put on the Bank Directors – if they had been unrestrained they would again have mistaken the object which they ought to have in view; instead of taking measures to equalise the value of paper and gold they would have been thinking of the public good, and under a mistaken idea of promoting that, they would have administered an increased dose of paper.
>
> (VIII/79)

Here he is as if completely feeling at ease in view of a law adopting his plan in outline. The only worry of which he still remains conscious is the excessive issue of banknotes which actually occurred for a long time in the past. But now it is impossible it should recur.

Originally, the BoE could issue its banknotes in excess and expand its income interest, only because it was exempted from the obligation of convertibility. But even if exempted from this obligation, for the first one or two years after the enactment of the Bank Restriction Act, the BoE contained the quantity of issue and was applying itself to hoarding gold reserve, for 'fear' of convertibility possibly being resumed. Subsequently, toward the turn of century when such a fear faded away, the BoE began to increase its issue, taking advantage of its exemption from convertibility (cf. IV/99–100). Judging from such 'timid' behaviour of the directors of the BoE, of which Ricardo was clearly aware, there would have been no possibility of an excess issue of currency at a time when, though not yet enforced, a law stipulating the resumption of convertibility undeniably existed. On the contrary, it was rather its excessive contraction that should have been worried about. He was talking about such worries in his parliamentary evidence in March, etc. Once the Bill was voted on, did he forget that? At least in the above quoted letter, he seems to have lost every sense of caution in this regard.

But in fact, a few years later Ricardo was clearly aware of the fact that, while he was absorbed in such satisfaction and optimism as seen above, the BoE was to set about an excessive recovery of banknotes and an equally excessive accumulation of reserve gold. In his speech of 11 June 1823, his last parliamentary address on the currency problem, Ricardo presents a view on the situation that existed four years before, entirely different from that expressed in the above quoted two letters.

> The Bank, from the moment of the passing of the bill in 1819, set their faces against the due execution of it. … Instead of maintaining an amount of paper money in circulation, which should keep the exchanges at par, they so limited the quantity as to cause an unprecedented influx of the precious metals, which they eagerly bought and coined into money.
>
> (V/312)

Because the BoE started such actions contrary to the enforcement of the Resumption Act long before Ricardo became aware of it, the step-by-step procedure of the execution it stipulated from 1 February 1820 to 1 May 1823 was obliged to adopt a large amendment halfway. Ricardo could have noticed its symptoms as early as in summer or autumn 1819. In the same parliamentary speech quoted above, he acknowledges his error on this point as follows: 'this, then, was the error which he (Mr. Ricardo) had been guilty of: he had not foreseen these unnecessary, and, as he must add, mischievous operations of the Bank' (ibid.).

Peel's Act stipulated the bullion payment with 60 ounces (corresponding to about 1800g) of it as unit to begin from 1 February 1820. To prepare for this obligation of payment, the BoE brought bullion of a certain weight and fineness to the Mint to make it cast into ingot stamped with a seal composed of the initials of the King George (R.G.) and of the design of a crown. As

Ricardo's plan of bullion payment became known in and out of Parliament in the first half of 1819, and an Act adopting this plan was expected to be approved soon, the fabrication of the ingot for this purpose was also expected. As early as in May, in advance of the passing of the Bill, this ingot was named 'Ricardoes' after the name of the proponent (cf. 'Notes on the evidence on the resumption of cash payment' by Sraffa, V/368–70). But it was only a commonly used name, not the official name. Till the beginning of 1820, the Mint cast 2,028 Ricardoes in total and delivered them to the BoE. This quantity of Ricardoes amounts to a little less than £500,000, i.e., to about one tenth of the total quantity of bullion the BoE held at that time.

The bullion payment with Ricardoes (their sale for banknotes) was begun according to the law, at first with the rate of 4*l.* 1*s.* per ounce, but at that time the price of bullion was below its mint price, and there was virtually no one who would buy Ricardoes (be paid in bullion from the BoE) at a loss. Afterwards, according to the stipulation of Peel's Act, the price of Ricardoes was lowered, but it still remained higher than the market price of bullion. Finally, only a very few rich collectors bought them out of curiosity, and over one year and three months from 1 February 1820 to 1 May 1821, not more than 13 were sold at the respective current prices. The rest of 2,015 were sent back to the Mint to be melted to bullion or minted to coin. 'It is unfortunate but not surprising that neither at the Bank nor at the Royal Mint nor at the British Museum is there any sample of the Ricardian bars. Sixty ounces of gold, with no 'artistic merit' superadded, are a costly curiosity' (Bonar (1923), p. 297). The ingot was made only for the convenience of the business of bullion payment of the BoE without any other use, so that those who obtained it could not but change it into another form destined for respective uses. That is why only the stamp for the seal on the ingot has been handed down.

The fall in the price of bullion to under its mint price means an influx of gold from abroad. The BoE made a large purchase of gold which began to overflow in the country. In this way, compared to the level observed two years before, in May 1821 the gold reserve in the BoE had nearly tripled (which is the highest since before the Bank Restriction Period (cf. Feavearyear and Morgan (1963), p. 227–9). This is a level at which the cash payment would have been regarded as possible enough. In such a situation, the Bank Cash Payments Bill was approved on 13 April 1821 (the text of which is reproduced in Bonar (1923), pp. 303–4), according to which the freedom of choice (between bullion and coin) to be given to the BoE in Peel's Act from 1 May 1822 would be advanced by one year to begin from 1 May 1821[2]. In this Bill, cash payment was to become obligatory from 1 May 23. Though bullion payment was to remain legally possible for two years, the Ricardoes, especially conceived for this purpose, had already disappeared. Ricardo's plan of bullion payment virtually ended here. Furthermore, for the first year and three months till April 1821, the plan did not actually work even as a temporary measure. When the conversion began factually only in coin from 1 May 1821, it was carried out not only for banknotes with a face value equivalent and superior to

60 ounces of bullion, set as the minimum for payment, but the minimum unit of payment had to be the face value of small notes (£1 notes) corresponding to that of £1 sovereign coin newly issued from 1817.

5.1.2 Change in the state of currency and agricultural distress, pursuit of Ricardo's 'responsibility'

As seen in Subsection 5.1.1, as long as one year and a few months after he expressed an extremely optimistic view on the evolution of the state of currency and its future prospects in the letter to Trower of 25 September 1819, Ricardo made no mention of the problem of currency in his writings, as if he had truly 'pretty nearly discarded the subject of bullion from my mind' (VIII/79). Around this time, he was occupied with the drafting of *Funding System* (IV/149–200). And, after *Principles of political economy* of Malthus was published at the beginning of April of the following year 1820, Ricardo continued till toward the end of this year to write detailed 'Notes' on this new publication of Malthus (Volume II of *Works*), and during the latter half of this year, in the intervals from writing 'Notes', he was busy preparing the third edition of his *Principles* including a number of wide-ranging corrections, above all in chapter one 'On value'. During a time when Ricardo's attention was thus temporarily away from the 'subject of bullion', the state of currency was steadily evolving toward a direction widely different from what he had expected under Peel's Act. The first symptom of this evolution was the petitions repeatedly submitted to Parliament from landed and commercial interests coming from various districts. After the enactment of Peel's Bill, before the end of 1820, such petitions had been submitted, but the first of them Ricardo found it necessary to take seriously was 'Trade of Birmingham – petition of merchants'. It is shown in his speech delivered about this petition on 8 February 1821, one year after the enforcement of the Act.

The business conditions on which the merchants made appeal to Parliament were a slowdown and distress in the commercial activities caused by the general fall in prices. Moreover, such a situation was not limited to some particular towns, but spread over the whole of England. And the responsibility for this distress was attributed to Peel's Bill, which had decided a change in monetary regime two years before, and to Ricardo, its virtual proponent. Then, equally in Parliament, Ricardo was accused for the same reason. Compelled to plead or argue against it, he said as follows:

> The relative value of the two metals [gold and silver] had varied since the act of parliament; but what was the cause of that variation? It was this: the Bank being a timid body, seldom clinging to the true principles of circulation, had taken alarm, and had made great and unnecessary purchases of gold, although they found, by experience, that no person applied to them

for any. He [Ricardo] almost doubted whether a single bar [Ricardoe] had been demanded from them since the commencement of the new plan. (V/75–6)

Focusing on solely one point, a rise in the value of gold, Ricardo claims here that the cause of the distress described in the petition is not the proposal he himself had made but the erroneous acts of the BoE, saying that the true cause of the fall in price consists in the BoE's unnecessary large purchases of gold enhancing its value. After that, similar petitions were continuously submitted to Parliament and in Parliament a review of the procedure of execution of Peel's Act was repeatedly claimed. On each occasion, Ricardo was to stand in a position of the 'responsible author' to be accused and compelled to make pleadings.

In Peel's Act of May 1819, it was stipulated that from 1 May 1821 the price of bullion to be paid would be brought down to its mint price, and that from 1 May 1822, one year after that, cash payment (conversion in coin) would become possible along with bullion payment. However, at the opening of the parliamentary session of 1821, in addition to the submission of petitions seen above, two other situations came to the surface urging abolishing the bullion payment and carrying cash payment into execution. The first is that, as Ricardo spoke about in his speech quoted above, the BoE was buying an enormous quantity of gold to mint into coin to expand its cash reserve. The second is that the forgery of small notes, of one pound note to begin with, spread, a subject which quite suddenly came to the surface in this period.

As for the first point, the depreciation of banknotes had almost disappeared soon after the passing of Peel's Bill. But the BoE continued to contract the currency. Because of this, the bullion price fell below the mint price and the foreign exchanges rose. Exportation of cheap commodities from England expanded, and on the contrary a great amount of gold flew in from abroad. The BoE bought this gold in large quantities and hoarded it as gold reserve. Indeed, during the year from February 1820 when Peel's Act came into force, the quantity of bullion in the coffers of the BoE increased more than twice, and its amount attained the highest level since 1790, prior to the suspension of convertibility (Feavearyear and Morgan (1963), pp. 227–9). And, to prepare for the conversion in coin from 1 May 1822, the BoE cast it into coin in the Mint. As the BoE prepared this reserve of coin sufficient to resume cash payments as early as toward the beginning of 1821, it went so far as to demand of Parliament a measure allowing it to advance by one year the resumption of cash payments originally foreseen to begin in May of the following year.

As for the second point, Ricardo says in his letter to Trower of 2 March 1821 as follows: 'I am sorry that no security can be found against the forgery of Bank notes, – the recalling of the one pound notes cannot fail to enhance the value of the currency' (VIII/350). Here he is claiming the maintenance of one pound notes in circulation so as to prevent the price from falling further, but he seems not yet to be worried about the circulation of coin in place of the recovered one pound notes. To this passage Sraffa adds a following note:

> On 20 February it was stated in the House of Commons that the Commissioners appointed to inquire into the means of preventing the forgery of Bank Notes had so far failed to discover a process which would produce an inimitable Bank Note. Vansittart on 19 March pointed to these disappointing results as a circumstance which justified the anticipation of the period in which the Bank should resume the issue of gold coins.
>
> (ibid., note 1)

And on the same day the Bank Cash Payments Bill was introduced to Parliament. The Bill was virtually intended to recover the small notes like one pound notes susceptible to forgery and to put into circulation in their place the sovereign, then sufficiently prepared in the BoE. If the forgery put serious obstacles to the circulation of small notes, an alternative means of small payment was indispensable. The only candidate for this was the sovereign.

In the condition of the suspension of convertibility and the depreciation of currency during the Bank Restriction Period, coin was not supplied anew, and at the same time the coin in circulation was melted down to be exported. Originally, the issue of small notes began from the end of the eighteenth century, to fill in the blank spaces in circulation for small payments. But subsequently the total amount of small notes gradually expanded, to drive out almost wholly coin and to replace it around 1810. The paper currency is used as 'money' of a value totally independent of the intrinsic value of its material, a piece of paper, virtually equal to null, with figures printed on it. Just as Ricardo says, the value of paper currency is entirely made up of 'seignorage [sic] (benefit for issue of money)' (cf. I/353, IV/114). But, as its face value is small, this benefit for the issue of money becomes small. In the case of one pound notes, this benefit per piece of paper is minimal. In addition, since the face value per piece is small, for a certain total amount the number of pieces to be issued is large, which makes the small notes a 'commodity of relatively high cost' for the issuing bank. Moreover, since the small notes are used by many people as a means of everyday consumption expense (income circulation), their rapidity of circulation may be generally high, and so the interval of their renewal rendered necessary by tear and wear may be generally short. This too becomes an additional factor, tending to increase the cost for issue of the small notes. In contrast, the contrary may apply to notes of high denominations.

As a result, the issuing bank will reduce to a maximum the cost for paper as material for the small notes, for their design and printing. In this way, they seem to have been likely to be of 'clumsy' (V/92) make, which may have made the forgery of small notes easy. Furthermore, since they were issued in a huge number to be used frequently by the general public, the forged small notes, once mingled into circulation, would be barely retraceable. On the contrary, this may have been a deterrent to the forgery of notes of high denominations.

But on the other hand, in view of the tiny benefit to be expected from the forgery and use of small notes for their troubles, the incentive may have also been small. If, in spite of this, their forgery spread, it may be because no highly technical procedure was needed for it and that it was an act of fraud 'relatively easily accessible to anyone'. But in any country and at any time, the fabrication and use of counterfeit currency, considered by the State monopolising the 'coinage prerogative' to be a violation of this power, to be an act disturbing the monetary (economic) order of a country, are in general very severely punished. It was the same for England at that time. In Ricardo's time, 'the numerous executions for forgery throughout the country' (V/201, see also IV/225–6) were carried out. If use of a counterfeit note, even if of only one pound, was worthy of the death penalty, people would have neither accepted nor used one pound notes never knowing whether a counterfeit note was palmed off as genuine. The circulation of one pound notes thus seems to have fallen stagnant. But in spite of this, some means of small payment corresponding to this face value was always indispensable. This was also one of the reasons for which the BoE demanded an early resumption of cash payment in order to stop the use of small notes and replace them with coin. Ricardo could not have bluntly refused this.

By the way, as we have said above, the small notes like one pound notes were already issued and circulating more than 20 years before the problem of their forgery became an item on the agenda in Parliament. If all through this period the conditions concerning the fabrication, issue and use (and also forgery) of the small notes remained the same, why did the problem of their forgery emerge suddenly toward the beginning of 1821 (as it appears to have done, at least judging from the materials included in *Works*) when the resumption of convertibility became an urgent subject? Why had not forgery spread before that time, or, if it was widely spread, why did not that lead to a cessation of their use? Were they to be used continuously in spite of the evils they implied (while Ricardo noticed only its advantages) for lack of other alternative means of circulation for a while (because of the continuation of inconvertible regime), even if their forgery never ceased? The answer to these questions could possibly not be found in Ricardo's texts. It is to be left to some future studies as a subject in suspense.

Now let us return from a digression, gone a little too far. The accumulation of reserves in cash by the BoE and the demand for an early resumption of cash payment because of the forgery of small notes were evidently contrary to the plan of bullion payment. The emergence of such a counter-current in the process of execution of Peel's Act would have given Ricardo a big shock. One factor in this counter-current had already become an established fact, and the other factor was difficult to object to, even for him. Ricardo's parliamentary speech of 19 March 1821, on which the Bank Cash Payments Bill was submitted, gives an impression that he was temporarily shaken in his strong hope and claim for legislation of his plan of bullion payment and its effectual enforcement, and weakened his position. Indeed, while always continuing to analyse the evolution of the situation after the enforcement of Peel's Bill and to criticise the BoE in his parliamentary speeches, he was no more to appeal to carry his plan into execution. In his speech of that day he affirmed that Peel's Act and himself were not responsible for the fall in price exceeding 5%, in showing that the current fall in price was due not only to the 5% rise in the value of currency foreseen by the Act, but also to the rise in the value of gold caused by the erroneous acts of the BoE and to real factors particular to the agricultural sector, and in conclusion he said of the then submitted Bill and of the future of the English currency regime as follows:

> It was perfectly clear, that whether the issues consisted altogether of Banknotes, or half in Bank-notes and half in sovereigns, the danger of forgery would be the same. The only effectual remedy against forgery would be, to hasten the period at which the Bank might commence payment in specie. He [Ricardo] should be perfectly ready to abandon his own plan, if by so doing that most desirable object could be effected; and he was quite satisfied that the Bank was at this time in such a state of preparation, that in a very few months they might provide the best and only effectual security against the imitation of their notes, by returning to the system of currency which existed in this country previous to 1797.
>
> (V/96–7)

He thus delivered a speech for the Bank Cash Payments Bill stipulating a resumption of cash payments to be commenced a little more than one month later and the virtual institutional cessation[3] of bullion payments. The deliberation on this Bill further continued and Ricardo delivered three other speeches. It passed the House of Commons on 13 April when he made the last speech on it, to come into force on 1 May. In this Bill too, cash payment was not obligatory until 30 April 1823, before this date bullion payment was to be included as one of the choices. But, as more than 2,000 Ricardoes 'left unsold' were sent back to the Mint, at the same time as the enforcement of this Bill to be changed into bullion or coin, bullion payment was also formally abolished. It is because of this that in the economic history the definitive end of the bank restriction and the resumption of convertibility are usually placed in 1821.

In his speech of 19 March, Ricardo says that to get rid of forgery there is no way other than to substitute coin for small notes by means of cash payment, and he estimates the BoE having prepared a sufficient reserve necessary for this (regardless of whether such was intended or not). And he goes so far as to declare that he is 'perfectly ready to abandon his own plan'. It was no more possible to return the situation to its initial state in order to insist on the execution of his plan. It may certainly be said that he abandoned the plan of bullion payment as a present practical programme. But he seems to have kept a sort of 'conviction' that it is the best possible monetary regime that can be theoretically thought. In a letter addressed to Trower on 5 March 1822, one year after this speech, he says that, in case of emergency, 'it might become necessary to adopt the Ingot plan of payment once more' (IX/176). After the above speech, Ricardo spoke about the execution of the plan of bullion payment only in this informal and private 'confidence' made to his reliable friend in correspondence from oldest times. Of course, during the remaining lifetime of Ricardo his plan was never reviewed or restored. But he seems to have kept a belief in the possibility of his plan recovering its validity and necessity at some future time.

Now, at the same time as the debates in and out of Parliament were going on, from 1 May 1821 began the payment of banknotes with coin on the basis of the Bank Cash Payments Bill passed just before, which brought about a wide change in a short time to the state of currency in England. During the whole of this period, Ricardo continued saying that 5% in the fall of prices expressed the rise in the value of currency just foreseen in Peel's Bill, while the other 5% represented the parallel rise in the value of gold itself as the standard of money, so that the price fall caused by the monetary factors was 10%. If these figures were obtained in relying on meticulous observations on empirical data as confirmed for his previous affirmations, it may be thought that, at least as long as he was adopting the calculation 5 + 5 = 10, the price of bullion was nearly equal to its mint price or did not largely deviate from the latter, hence there was neither international efflux nor influx of gold on an important scale (cf. Tooke (1838), p. 385). This means that the changes in the state of currency during this period were limited to changes in the state of domestic circulation, moreover to those not accompanied with changes in the value of currency (in the sense both of the price of gold and of the value of gold itself). In his letter addressed to Trower on 9 June 1822, about one year after the resumption of cash payment, in giving concrete figures on the situation of currency he says as follows:

> The whole amount of circulation, at the present moment, both in London and the country, does not probably much exceed 32 millions, of which there are nearly 16 millions of Bank of England notes of 5 pounds and above, 7,500,000 of sovereigns, and 9 millions of country Bank notes. If this be true there has been little or no falling off in the amount of Bank of England notes and coin together since 1819, but country Bank notes have diminished to the amount of 7,500,000£ .... By a return laid before the H of Commons more than 19 millions of sovereigns have been coined since 1817. During the period that the Bank so foolishly issued coin, when it was advantageous to export it, they got rid of 5 millions of sovereigns, so that if these were all exported more than 14 millions of sovereigns must now be in the country. Besides this quantity of gold it is probable the Bank may have a tolerable supply of bullion, and perhaps also some guineas.
>
> (IX/201–2)

According to the figures given here, the total quantity in circulation of the notes of high denominations, of sovereigns and of country banknotes is nearly equal to the total amount of currency in circulation. That is, the other kind of currency (small notes under five pounds[4]) was not in circulation at that time. This means that the small notes issued from the BoE were almost entirely replaced by sovereigns during the time of only a little more than one year from the beginning of cash payment. That is, after the resumption of convertibility the state of currency circulation returned shortly to that observed before 1797.

Ricardo says that the actual total amount of circulation made up of the total of the banknotes of the BoE of five pounds and above and of coin is nearly equal to that of 1819. But hasn't he affirmed since more than one year that the price fell twice as much as Peel's Act had foreseen (5 + 5 = 10%), because the BoE contracted the quantity of issue of currency and increased its value, inducing a massive influx of gold from abroad and raising its value in buying it in great quantities? But he affirms here the constancy of the quantity of currency in circulation in comparing the state of 1819 and that of 1821 and says nothing about how the quantity of currency has changed in the meantime. As we will discuss in detail in the next section, the quantity of banknotes issued by the BoE seems to have largely diminished for a time from 1819 and subsequently to have increased and recovered to the initial level (but then the small notes were changed into gold coin). Induced by the rise in the value of currency (fall in price) caused by the initial decrease, a large quantity of gold flowed in from abroad. The BoE was willing to obtain this gold to prepare for the conversion, and the exporters who had acquired gold from abroad would voluntarily sell it to the BoE with profits at the mint price superior to the current market price. The purchase of gold by the BoE was at the same time a new issue of banknotes, and in proportion to the amount of such a transaction the quantity of currency in circulation expanded again.

Further, the quantity in circulation of country banknotes also seems to have changed in parallel with the change in the quantity of banknotes of the BoE. The banknotes issued from the small country banks at that time maintained their value as currency by the guarantee of 'conversion' with the banknotes of the BoE. Hence, the evolution of their issue seems to have had a tendency to follow more or less that of the issue of the BoE. In the former phase mentioned above, the quantity of issue of the two kinds of banknotes may have equally diminished. But in the latter phase, only the BoE turned to an increase of issue to buy gold. Moreover, as the value of gold rose worldwide through the former phase[5], the quantity of currency necessary for mediating a certain amount of transactions must have diminished. Since Ricardo says in the above quotation that 'country Bank notes have diminished to the amount of 7,500,000£', the total amount of currency contracted from about 40 million to about 32 million, i.e., by circa 20% during the three years after 1819, and this contraction was wholly due to the diminution of issue of the country banknotes.

As was seen above, with the definitive ending of the Napoleonic War at the end of 1815, the BoE, foreseeing the conversion to be resumed before long, began to prepare a reserve of coin. As the conversion was not prohibited under the prolonged Bank Restriction Act, in December 1816 when the BoE judged its reserve of coin to have attained a level sufficient to respond to a certain extent to the demand for conversion, it began to accept the demand for conversion limited to the banknotes issued before a certain time, in order to avoid a demand going beyond its capacity. But the conversion was hardly demanded, as the price of bullion was below its mint price at that time. But when the BoE announced again an equally limited resumption of conversion in September 1817, this time there was a rush for conversion. Then the coin accumulated in the BoE continuously drained, but it had not to worry about a possible exhaustion of the gold reserve, because the conversion was limited to the banknotes issued during a certain period. In this way, the conversion with sovereigns continued till the execution of conversion before the passing of the Resumption Bill was prohibited in the reports of the Secret Committee presented in April and May 1819 for the preparation of the Bill. When he said in his letter to Trower quoted above that 'the Bank so foolishly issued coin, when it was advantageous to export it, they got rid of five millions of sovereigns', Ricardo meant what was happening at that time. For nearly two years from September 1817, the price of bullion was invariably above the mint price (Tooke (1838), p. 379). The aim of demand for conversion in such a situation was to get profits obtained from melting and exporting the coin drawn from the BoE. Therefore, the 'five millions of sovereigns' the BoE 'got rid of' 'were all exported'. This also may have been a factor in the continuous fall in the price of bullion throughout this period.

However, after such an 'anticipated' cash payment was temporarily suspended by the passing of Peel's Bill, and instead, from February 1820 the bullion payment with 'Ricardoes' was executed (virtually supposing from the outset the bullion used in payment to be exported), no substantial payment in accordance with Peel's Bill was made, as the price of payment was always above the market price of bullion, however little it might have been. And prior to the cash payment to be executed in advance from May 1821, almost all of 2,028 'Ricardoes', 'left unsold', were changed into bullion or sovereigns in the Mint and added to 'a tolerable supply of bullion [and coin]' for the BoE (IX/202). According to the calculation of Ricardo, of the sovereigns amounting to more than 19 million pounds minted since 1817, 5 million were reduced to bullion and exported, 7.5 million remained in domestic circulation, the rest of a little more than 6.5 million were hoarded in the coffers of the BoE. In adding to this 'tolerable supply' of old guineas and bullion, one can see how much gold in various forms the BoE was hoarding 'in vain'. Ricardo accuses the BoE of this in saying that 'how badly has this business been managed!' (ibid.).

One point was common to the several trials of resumption of exchange of banknotes for gold from December 1816 to April 1821, whether in coin or in bullion: it was only when the bullion price was above the mint price, that the holders of banknotes demanded payment from the BoE. Otherwise, the public would not want to get gold even if their banknotes could be exchanged for gold. This is precisely the behaviour of the banknote holders Ricardo theoretically supposed, and on the basis of this supposition he conceived a regime of 'economical and secure' currency. But ironically, the behaviour supposed by him drove, on the contrary, his plan of bullion payment into a temporary dysfunction, due to the unexpected intervention of the BoE.

When cash payment was resumed in May 1821, earlier than foreseen at first, the price of bullion stayed stable at about the same level as the mint price. If the holders of banknotes behaved always as before, the demand for conversion should have been virtually null, but this was not the case. Unlike in the Resumption Bill passed in May 1819, in the Act of the same name passed in April 1821, while the BoE was free to choose between coin and bullion for the payment of its banknotes, the provision stipulating the minimal sum of banknote the BoE would be obliged to pay was repealed (cf. Bonar (1923), pp. 303–4). Now, therefore, there was not such a high hurdle like a bullion payment with 'Ricardoes' as its unit, Ingot of a considerable sum of about 240 pounds applied till April 1821, and it was possible for all banknotes of every face value to be exchanged for sovereigns. In this way, 'the numerous executions for forgery throughout the country, had made the public clamorous for a metallic circulation so as in a measure to compel the Bank to precipitate the substitution of coin for their one and two pound notes' (words of a director of the BoE quoted by Ricardo in his speech of 12 June 1822 against the motion of Western, V/201). Many banknote holders rushed to the window of the BoE for their exchange for coin in order to avoid the use of small notes of which the forgery was spreading. The great demand for conversion at that time was different in its nature both from the 'run' caused by a panic when people rushed to the bank for conversion, suspicious about the value of paper currency, and from the ordinary act of conversion for the purpose of changing the depreciated paper into coin of the same face value in compensation for the loss due to the depreciation. At the moment of the resumption of cash payment, any action for one of these motives was not likely to occur. The public wanted only to avoid draconian punishments for the use of counterfeit currency, in changing from banknotes to coin as the means of small payments they were currently using. In addition, this conversion went on with such speed and on such a scale as to attain, in less than one year, 7.5 million pounds, an amount nearly equivalent to the total amount of the small notes in circulation till May 1821. On the other hand, for the holders of banknotes of high denominations, for which there was no rumour about the risk of involvement in criminal offense of currency forgery, there would have been no advantage in converting a small number of their notes into a large number of coins not always easy to handle. Almost the whole of the 7.5 million pounds of sovereigns Ricardo mentions in his letter of 9 June 1822 may be thought to have been in circulation as a substitute for the small notes replaced with them in little more than a year from May 1821[6].

5.1.3 Ricardo's pleading and analysis (section V of **On Protection to Agriculture** *and parliamentary speech in June 1822)*

The agricultural distress caused by the steep fall in prices, occurred during two to three years after the enforcement of Peel's Bill in February 1820,was imputed to be the responsibility of Ricardo as the proponent of Peel's Bill, who bore the brunt of attacks. Of course, he refused to be responsible for the evolution of the situation as a whole, and tried to refute this in Parliament on every occasion. Such activities of 'defence', so to speak, were repeated from toward the beginning of the parliamentary session in 1821 to the end of the session in 1823, i.e., for more than two years virtually till the end of his activities as a member of Parliament. During that time, he tried counter-attacks to all of the almost stereotyped attacks. After May 1821, as there was no substantial change in the legal framework of monetary regime and the situation was gradually evolving nearly in the same direction within the same framework, there were no important changes in the points in contest. For this reason, the debate was apt to fall into repetitions of similar arguments. But, in such a long-drawn-out war without a clear settlement, to be described rather as sterile, Ricardo made a pleading of his own position and a certain coherent theoretical analysis on the vicissitude of the situation after the passing of Peel's Act. In this subsection, we will confirm how he recognised the situation in taking up a part of *On Protection to Agriculture* (published on 18 April 1822) and of two of his parliamentary speeches (delivered respectively on 12 June 1822 and on 11 June 1823), belonging to the 'later' period of his activities during the four years after the enactment of Peel's Bill.

Soon after the opening of the parliamentary session in February 1822, an Agricultural Committee was set up to deliberate on the measures to cope with the agricultural distress and to present a report. Ricardo was nominated as a member. After the examination of witnesses a report was drafted. The report, to which 'the landlords on the committee had succeeded in adding a number of protectionist recommendations', 'was much more definitely protectionist' ('Note on 'Protection to Agriculture'' by Sraffa, IV/204) in comparison to the report of the previous year (not actually presented because of the expiration of the term). Immediately after that, Ricardo began writing a pamphlet attacking this 'Report'. The pamphlet was published on 18 April, after the 'Report' had been presented to Parliament on 1 April, and before the deliberation on it would begin at the end of the month after the recess for Easter. This is *On Protection to Agriculture* (hereinafter *Protection* for short), which was also a 'counter-proposal' of the dissident minority in Parliament in opposition to the official 'Report' presented from the Agricultural Committee (cf. IV/203). The subject of *Protection*, drafted in this way, was to analyse the current agricultural distress from the standpoint Ricardo had adopted in opposition to the Corn Laws, and to propose measures to protect English agriculture. The section V 'On the effect produced on the Price of Corn by Mr. Peel's Bill for restoring the ancient standard' aims at proving the unjustifiability of the attacks against the Bill and himself, in elucidating the extent to which the fall in agricultural prices which occurred during little more than two years after the enactment of Peel's Bill should be imputed to the influence of this Bill. For this purpose, he reveals in this section his fundamental views on the situation as a whole of the change in the currency circulation in England after the enactment of Peel's Bill, at times returning even to the preceding periods. What he says on the present state of currency in this section, seems to be a sort of synthesis of his repeated speeches delivered in Parliament before and after the time of writing this pamphlet and also the source of these speeches.

The attacks against Peel's Act or himself, against which Ricardo was obliged to repeat counter-attacks over about two and a half years from the opening of the parliamentary session in 1821, were like the following:

> When it is now said that money has been forcibly raised in value – 25 per cent, according to some; 50, and even 60 per cent., according to others, they do not refer to 1819, the period at which that bill passed, but to the period of the greatest depression; and they charge the whole increase in the value of the currency to Mr. Peel's bill.
>
> (IV/223)

In the period from 1813 to 1814 when the depreciation of currency attained its peak after the suspension of convertibility in 1797, the price of bullion rose to 5*l.* 10*s.*, hence the depreciation of currency went to about 41% compared to 'the ancient standard'. Even if taking this figure as a criterion, the above attack against Peel's Bill should be said to contain some exaggeration, but the criterion should be the current state of depreciation of currency at the moment of the enactment of the Bill. At that time, the price of bullion was about 4*l.* 2*s.*, i.e., the depreciation of currency was about 5%. 'In choosing to go back to the ancient standard' (ibid.), Peel's Act foresaw a rise in the value of money, and hence a general fall in prices by 5%. In showing thus the precondition and the objective of the enactment of Peel's Bill, Ricardo reminds the reader of the fact that the plan of bullion payment he had proposed was adopted in this Bill. This plan 'would have rendered the employment of any greater quantity of gold than the Bank then possessed wholly unnecessary', and 'if that plan had been adopted, not a particle of gold would have been used in the circulation' (IV/224). Therefore, if Peel's Act were implemented according to its provisions, the rise in the value of money should not have exceeded 5%. This is the fundamental position Ricardo persistently stuck to during the two and a half years of the debate (which implies at the same time that the price of bullion, once fallen to the 3*l.* 17*s.* 10½*d.*, the ancient standard, in May 1821, remained nearly stable all through the period in question, i.e., that the value of money measured by the price of bullion underwent virtually no change).

But in fact, two years after the enactment of Peel's Bill, the prices had fallen far beyond 5%, the range of fall in the price of bullion. Since the current price of bullion at each moment should have been given as empirical data, incontestable and easily accessible to anyone, in order to blame the rise in the value of money for this large fall in prices, one could not but affirm that the fall in the price of bullion caused by the Bill should have been equally large. The opponents of the Bill and Ricardo brought forward a comparison seen above on the criterion of the price of bullion exceeding five pounds in a time as far as several years before the passing of Peel's Bill, but this was evidently unjustifiable (moreover containing exaggerations). It was not so difficult to refute such a claim describable as an obvious demagogy, but apart from a refutation an answer was always required to the question of how to explain the fall in prices actually exceeding 5%. It is certain that the fall in the price of bullion that actually occurred during the two years from May 1819 was 5%. Therefore, the range of rise in the value of currency, calculated as the reciprocal of the market price of bullion, must have been also 5%. If during the same period of time the prices fell more than that, the cause of such a fall should be sought elsewhere than in the variation (rise) in the value of currency in the sense of its purchasing power over bullion.

As was seen above, in Peel's Bill adopting Ricardo's plan there was nothing 'which could cause a rise in the value of gold' (IV/224). The Bill stipulated that, after the execution of bullion payment as a temporary measure, the cash payment would be resumed in four years after its enactment. Therefore, till that time there should have been no need for the BoE to hoard coin in its coffers for preparing for the conversion. But the BoE, 'being a timid body' (speech of 8 February 1821, V/76) 'immediately commenced preparations for specie payments' (IV/225, cf. V/312), 'had taken alarm, and had made great and unnecessary purchases of gold' (V/76). Such an action of the BoE, wholly unnecessary according to the programme of execution of Peel's Bill (moreover begun 'immediately' after its enactment), raised the value of gold as the standard of money. And with the rise in the value of gold, the quantity of currency necessary for mediating the same scale of commercial transactions would contract. In this case, even if there had been no change in the quantity of currency issued, the currency becomes relatively excessive and the price of bullion rises reflecting the rise in the value of gold, but the prices of commodities with their values unchanged do not change. When the relative depreciation of currency risen in this way disappears and the quantity of its issue has decreased till the price of bullion conforms to its mint price, commodity prices will fall as much. While the price of bullion gets back to its initial level, only commodity prices have fallen. Here, therefore, if the 'value of currency' in the sense of its purchasing power over bullion does not change, the commodity prices fall. In contrast, the rise in the value of currency (the dissolution of its depreciation) means a parallel and equal fall in the price of bullion and in the prices of the other commodities in general. If these two processes to be distinguished can be shown to have occurred in parallel and simultaneously, it will become possible to explain the fall in prices exceeding 5%, the rise in the value of currency.

Then, by what means did the BoE 'purchase gold in large quantities' and bring about a price fall beyond 5%? On this essential point the explanation of Ricardo seems to be elliptical, not to show step by step each of the actions and of their results the BoE took and gave rise to immediately after the passing of Peel's Bill. To see how the rise in the value of gold Ricardo talks about took place, and what its meaning was, it would be necessary to reconstruct the whole of the process from his fragmentary explanations. While the variations in the value of currency can be confirmed as concrete figures (5% in the present case) by intertemporal comparisons of the domestic market price of bullion, easily known empirically, it is not easy to determine the value of gold and the range of its variations, these variables necessarily involving international relations in Ricardo's theory. We are going to examine equally by what procedures Ricardo draws answers on these points.

In section V of *Protection*, the rise in the value of gold is explained as follows:

> Their issues were so regulated, that the exchange became extremely favourable to this country, gold flowed into it in a continued stream, and all that came the Bank eagerly purchased at 3*l.* 17*s.* 10½*d.* per ounce. Such a demand for gold could not fail to elevate its value, compared with the value of all commodities. Not only, then, had we to elevate the value of our currency five per cent, the amount of the difference between the value of paper and of gold before these operations commenced, but we had still further to elevate it to the new value to which gold itself was raised, by the injudicious purchases which the Bank made of that metal.
>
> (IV/225)

Here the process is quickly described, beginning with the diminution of the quantity of issue of banknotes by the BoE and resulting in the rise in the value of gold itself, but some ambiguous points and gaps in logic seem to be contained in the intermediary steps (Humphrey (2004) mentions 'a heavy demand for gold in the world market' (p. 25) in this process, but in our view its explanation is rather cursory and therefore not sufficiently convincing (cf. also p. 26)). In the following, we will try to reconstruct the process, referring to similar explanations appearing in Ricardo's parliamentary speeches, and as for the parts which seem to contain logical gaps, in taking into account his other monetary writings.

The starting point is the reduction of banknotes issued by the BoE. It was of course carried out with a view to diminishing the quantity of banknotes, debt of the issuer, expanded during the Bank Restriction Period, so as to meet the obligation of convertibility, in preparation for this obligation soon to be imposed on it by virtue of Peel's Act. With this reduction going on till the price of bullion coincides with the mint price, the demand of conversion must come of itself nearly to null, as the banknote holders lose benefit from the conversion. Therefore, once this point is attained, both quantities of gold reserve and a further cut of issue will become unnecessary. This is self-evident for Ricardo, but the BoE, 'seldom clinging to the true principles of circulation' (speech of 8 February 1821, V/76), further pushed ahead with the reduction of issue. As a result, the price of bullion went down under the mint price and the commodity prices fell as much. With the rise in the value of currency, the foreign exchanges rise above the gold points. In this way the commodity exportation so increases, 'as to cause an unprecedented influx of the precious metals' (speech of 11 June 1823, V/312). Then, however, at the same time 'the currency would be at a very low level, the prices of commodities would fall, and great distress would be suffered. Something of this kind had, in fact, happened' (speech of 12 June 1822, V/199–200).

These quantities of precious metals were obtained from abroad by English exporters as the prices of exported cheap commodities. If they were originally foreign coins, in the domestic area of England they would be reduced to bullion or treated as bullion of equal weight and fineness. If the price of bullion was still remaining under the mint price, it would be more profitable to change it into coin in the Mint than to sell it on the market. But for minting, payment of a certain seigniorage would be required, so that the price of delivery of bullion would be lower than the mint price by this commission. But, if the BoE would buy this bullion at the mint price as in the above quotation, for the seller its sale to the BoE would be the most advantageous way of disposing of the gold obtained as the price of exports. Thus, it may be thought theoretically that 'all that came' (IV/225) from abroad were purchased by the BoE. But at the same time, this purchase of gold is also a new issue of banknotes from the BoE, and through this process the quantity of currency, once contracted, has expanded again. And Ricardo says that the purchase of gold in large quantities by the BoE constitutes so much demand for gold, which caused the rise in its value.

But can such an act of purchase of gold by the BoE be considered as being caused by demand for gold likely to raise its value 'compared with the value of all commodities?' In other places Ricardo repeats this point, for example, 'by their measures they [the BoE] occasioned a demand for gold' (V/312). As we have seen, the BoE would only buy all of the gold flowing into the country at the mint price, but would not obtain more at the cost of a price higher than that. And, did not the traders accept as sellers the sale of their bullion to the BoE at the mint price as the most advantageous way of disposing of it? In addition, as the BoE bought infinitely the bullion they brought in at an advantageous price, there seems to have been no reason for the sellers to still raise the price or keep bullion back for this purpose. It may have been an extremely easy and smooth transaction for both parties.

The 'demand for gold' which resulted in a rise in the value of gold can certainly be thought to have been caused by the act of the BoE beginning with an excessive contraction of currency, but this demand may not be caused by the BoE's purchase of gold in large quantities after its influx. In our view, this 'demand' should be understood as follows.

The starting point of the process was a change in the quantity of banknotes in the domestic circulation of England. According to Ricardo's theory of international distribution of money gold, probably inherited from Hume (*High Price*), gold is distributed among the countries participating in international commerce, in proportion to the relative weight the scale of commercial transactions within each of these countries occupies in the total amount of transactions in the world. Then gold has an equal value in every country, i.e., the quantity of commodities exchanged with a certain quantity of gold is equalised in every country. But, when this proportion of international distribution of gold is disturbed for some reasons, the equality in the value of gold between countries is also disturbed and the value of gold becomes different from country to country. Then gold moves among countries so as to dissolve this difference, various commodities move in opposite directions. After a certain time, a proportional distribution will be restored, and along with this the value of gold functioning as money will be again equalised everywhere in the world. And, the value of gold as a commodity is determined by the difficulty of its production, i.e., by the cost of mining it from gold mines (the quantity of labour required for this), just like any other commodity. If the quantity of gold circulating in the world as money is proportionate to its necessary quantity determined by the total amount of commodities in circulation in the world, the value of gold as money conforms with the value of gold as a commodity. But, as both the scale of transaction in the whole world and the proportion each country occupies therein never ceases to vary, both the total amount of gold to function as money in the whole world and the part of it assigned to each country must also constantly vary. But the production of gold is placed under heavy constraints by the natural conditions of the veins of gold as scarce resources, which makes it difficult to regulate the quantity of its supply promptly in response to the need of the economic state, like other industrial products in general. Therefore, the supply of gold does not correspond to the demand for it, in many cases it may be excessive or insufficient. Then, the current relative price at a particular moment (market price) of gold continuously deviates from its value, upwards or downwards. Even in the state of proportional distribution of gold to each of the countries in the world, such a deviation persists.

Ricardo then introduces the banknote as a means to regulate the supply of money rapidly and without quantitative limit. In Ricardo, the banknote was originally conceived as a means to really stabilise the value of money through regulation of the quantity of money, impossible with precious metals. However, unlike gold, the banknote is limited in its domain of circulation to the domestic area. Though within such a limited area, the banknote functions as virtual gold, understood as a part of the gold in the world circulation. If now half of the commercial transactions in the whole world is being carried out in England, its international commercial relations will recover their balance when half of the money in the world will be allotted to the domestic circulation in England. And if in England only the banknote circulates as the representative of gold, the quantity of the banknote (in fact the quantity of gold represented by it) at that moment will be determined in the same way. Then the foreign exchanges will be at par. If now the BoE, the issuing bank, diminishes this quantity of money by half, it would mean that it became half of its former quantity in England and the quantity of money in the world circulation would fall to ¾ of the former level. And, the proportion the money then circulating in England occupies in the whole amount of money in the world would have become ⅓ (= (½×½) ÷ (½+½×½)). In England the prices of commodities fall to ½, but in the rest of the world they do not change for the moment. For this reason, the exportation will surge and quantities of money (bullion) will flow into England from abroad. This process will continue until the quantity of gold in England will have increased to ¾ of the former domestic level, i.e., to ⅜ of the former quantity of money in the whole world (corresponding to ½ of the new quantity of world money), and then with the recovery of the balance in the international distribution of money as before, this movement (exportation of commodities from England and influx of gold in England) will cease. In this way, though it is certain that gold will flow into England, the quantity of money the BoE has brought down to half will not return back to the former level. While the quantity of money circulating in England will be half of the total amount of money in the world after the change as before, its quantity now circulating in England will have become ⅜ (= ¾ × ½) of the former total amount in the world (i.e., diminished by ⅛ compared to ½ of the former total amount), because the current total amount of money in the world will remain diminished to ¾. The quantity of money will be diminished in the same degree to ¾ both in the world as a whole and in England. If, in spite of this contraction of money, the total amount of transactions in the world does not undergo any variations, the value of gold as money will rise to 4/3 of the former level, reciprocal of the ratio of contraction of money, i.e., it will rise by a little more than 30%[7]. This is what Ricardo calls the rise in the value of gold caused by the erroneous acts of the BoE.

In the above example we have taken extreme figures to simplify the calculation, but in taking different figures (to express the place of England in the world economy and the extent of the contraction of banknotes by the BoE), the same result will be obtained. In other words, after 1821, however large the influx of gold into England may have been induced by the contraction of currency, and even if the gold thus flowed in were exchanged for banknotes to expand again the quantity of currency in domestic circulation, the quantity of currency would remain somewhat below the initial level, according to Ricardo's theory. The influx of gold to England means that the 'insufficiency in the supply of money gold' initially occurring in England was diffused worldwide to become an insufficiency in the supply (i.e., excess in demand) of money gold in the world, a redistribution from this 'insufficient' total amount will be newly brought into effect. Ricardo's affirmation that the value of gold has risen because the demand for it increased should be understood like this (this is based on our interpretation of what Ricardo says about the quantity and value of money in the world market in the first part of *High Price* (III/52–64).). The insufficiency in supply (excess in demand) taking place in such a process is naturally of relative character, so that there is no reason to suppose prior to this process a balance between demand and supply. Rather, considering the difficulties particular to the adjustment between supply of and demand for gold, it would be appropriate to think that a similar process has been added to the original situation of excess in supply or in demand. It is not the BoE that raised the value of gold in trying to buy gold in the domestic market as much as possible. This interpretation does not, of course, change the fact that the rise of the value of gold is finally the result of the act of the BoE.

As seen above, while the rise in the value of gold has finally taken place through the successive two processes of contraction and expansion of the currency circulating in England, Ricardo seems to have omitted almost wholly the explanation of these double processes, in saying only as follows: 'This [massively imported] bullion would be ultimately coined into money, and would replace the paper-money which had previously been withdrawn; but, before it was so coined, while all these operations were going on, the currency would be at a very low level' (V/199–200). He gave hardly any explanation on how 'these operations' went on. This seems to have been the source of the misleading explanation on the demand for gold.

At the same time as saying as if the value of gold was raised by the BoE's purchase of it in the domestic market, on the other hand Ricardo points out that the rise in the value of gold is a phenomenon of the world economy in saying that the BoE raised 'the value of gold in the general market of the world' (V/312). 'This rise in the value of gold it must always be remembered is not confined to this country, it is common to all [where the BoE did not buy gold in quantities]' ('Draft of a letter to a newspaper on the effects of Peel's Bill', V/520). This is a phenomenon brought about by an international redistribution of money (contraction of currency in England → fall in the quantity of money in the world → influx of gold in England), not a phenomenon caused by the purchase of this gold by the BoE. Ricardo continued to affirm that the range of rise in the value of gold induced by the improper acts of the BoE was 5%, i.e., equal to that of the rise in the value of currency after the enforcement of Peel's Bill. How does he give foundation to this affirmation?

On how to calculate the range of rise in the value of gold he says as follows: 'to estimate what the effect of this demand for gold had had upon its value in the general market of the world, he [Ricardo] contended, that we should compare the quantity actually purchased, with the whole quantity used in the different currencies of the world' (V/312–3). Here the 'quantity actually purchased' means the quantity of gold which flowed into England due to the contraction of currency in this country. For Ricardo, the exchange between gold and the other commodities is in a symmetrical relation, hence there is no distinction between sale and purchase. To export (sell) commodities is at the same time to import money, i.e., to buy money. The quantity of money bought in this way is determined by the position of England in the world economy, and by the proportion of contraction of banknotes. If in addition to these data 'the whole quantity [of gold] used in different currencies of the world' (V/313) is given, it will be possible to calculate concretely how much the value of gold has risen. This amounts to the same as the way of calculation we have given above with extreme numerical examples. But as it was practically impossible to procure such numerical data, Ricardo shows only the procedure of calculation as above, but does not concretely calculate the figure. Instead of calculating himself in showing empirical data, he adopts as they were the results of calculation by Tooke in saying that:

> Mr. Tooke, one of the most intelligent witnesses examined by the Agricultural Committee [of 1821], came to the conclusion that the eager demand for gold made by the Bank in order to substitute coin for their small notes, had raised the value of currency about five per cent. In this conclusion, I quite concur with Mr. Tooke.
>
> (IV/228)

Ricardo himself arrives in this way at the following conclusion: 'the whole increased value of our currency since the passing of Mr. Peel's bill in 1819, may be estimated at about ten per cent' (ibid.). He maintains this conclusion to the end, but the rise in the value of gold and the rise in the value of currency are two phenomena of different nature. While the latter is easily observable, the former can be obtained only in referring to many numerical data and by means of complicated calculations. For the former, results which can be commonly recognised may not be easily obtained.

Indeed, the range in the rise in the value of currency and of gold became readily an object of dispute: while Ricardo was 'now ready to admit, that Mr. Peel's bill had raised the value of the currency 10 per cent', 'the hon. member for Essex [Western] estimated it at 30 per cent' (V/312). And the attacks on Ricardo concentrated on this point. It was not to deny that the corn price had fallen about 30%, far beyond 10%, during the three years from May 1819 (Tooke (1838), p. 390). Ricardo would explain this difference in the rate of fall not by the rise in the value of currency, but by real factors particular to the agricultural sector.

> The hon. member for Essex said, that the currency had altered 30 per cent in value; but his chief proof rested on the altered price of corn. The true cause of the greater part of this alteration was, not the change in the currency, but the abundance of the supply. The stimulus to agriculture had been great during the war, and we were now suffering from a reaction, operating at the same time with the effect of two or three abundant crops. Could the agricultural interest be ruined by an alteration in the value of money, without its affecting, in the same manner, the manufacturing and commercial interests of the country? If corn fell 30 per cent from an alteration in the value of money, must not all other commodities fall in something

> like the same proportion? But, had they so fallen? Was the manufacturing interest so distressed? Quite the contrary. Everything was flourishing, but agriculture.
>
> (V/314–5)

'Many of the landed interest', headed by Western, who attack Ricardo, claim that 'all the distress in agriculture is to be ascribed' 'to one cause alone', which is 'alteration' 'in the value of the currency' (IV/228–9). As Tooke's empirical data show (see supra), it is certain that the corn price did not cease falling during the three or four years after the passing of Peel's Bill, then it would not be strange if, in the eyes of the landed interest thrown into hardship by this price fall, the Bill and Ricardo as its proponent appeared to be the origin of their distress. Ricardo tries to respond to the attack in showing that the causes of the actual agricultural distress are elsewhere than in the variation in the value of currency, and that the price variation brought about by the change in the value of currency is of a character entirely different from the price variation by other causes.

To face the difficulty of importing corn (more generally of procuring food) during the period of the Napoleonic War, agricultural production in England was promoted by extending the arable land, etc., but with the end of the War such obstacles disappeared, and the importation of agricultural products increased. And, English agriculture enjoyed a succession of good crops for three years from 1819, just overlapping the time of passing and enforcement of Peel's Bill. These circumstances caused a chronic oversupply of agricultural products. But, since agriculture too is a sector of capital investment, a reallocation of capital will take place, if it is not possible to sell the commodity at a 'remunerative price' (IV/210) and so to yield profits equal to those in other sectors. And, since good or bad crops depend mainly on the climatic conditions, good crops cannot continue infinitely even if it can continue for some time. In this way, Ricardo explains that the current distress will be soon mitigated or dissolved because it is brought about by real factors particular to the agricultural sector, which are all of temporary character.

> The peculiar hardships which the landed interest are suffering, are of a temporary character, and will continue only while the supply of produce exceeds the demand. A remunerative price is impossible while this cause of low value continues; but the situation of things which we now witness cannot have any permanence.
>
> (IV/230)

The variation in the price of commodities caused by variation in the value of currency is nominal, arising uniformly to every commodity irrespective of the variation in the value of commodities themselves, and it does not influence the relative value of the commodities to each other. The large fall in price, as high as 30%, which occurred after the enactment of Peel's Bill, is particular to one industrial sector, agriculture. This is evident if one compares the price of agricultural products with the price of other commodities. The large price fall of the former includes elements of real variations simultaneously accompanied with a fall in their relative price. 'If the real efficient cause of the distress of the landed gentlemen was the increased value of money, it ought to have produced similar distress in other quarters; it has not done so' (IV/231). The situation in agriculture was rather exceptional, other industries being in prosperity, says Ricardo.

As a result of these analyses Ricardo concludes as follows: 'agriculture has been depressed by causes of which the currency forms only a little part' (IV/230). If the price has fallen 30%, the part to be attributed to the monetary cause is 10% and the rest of 20% is due to the real causes particular to the agricultural sector. In addition, of the 10% of fall caused by the monetary factor the part to be attributed the 'responsibility' of Peel's Bill hence of Ricardo is 5%, a half of it, and the rest of 5% belongs to the responsibility of the erroneous acts of the BoE. And, the real causes, the largest, consist in the natural conditions or the transition from war to peace, the responsibility of which cannot be imputed to particular individuals or institutions. In this way, Ricardo divides the large price fall into three parts with different provenance and nature, and in affirming that only a minor part of it was caused by his plan, he tries to show the unjustifiability of those who attack him in mixing up everything together.

But, although its proponent continued such a pleading in the debates for more than two years, the plan of bullion payment cannot be said to have been carried into execution even as a temporary measure as foreseen. In insisting to the end on its adoption as a permanent measure (cf. IV/225), Ricardo was obliged to recognise that the execution of Peel's Bill, 'experiment[8]' of his plan, finally ended in failure. He aimed at unifying the domestic circulation to a paper circulation in expelling from there precious metal money. But he could not attain this aim for two reasons: difficulty in maintaining the circulation of small notes, and the BoE's act contrary to the provisions of Peel's Bill rendering possible both the withdrawal of small notes and the reinjection of precious metal coin into circulation. As for the latter of these two reasons, hitherto we have seen in detail that Ricardo repeatedly stated his position on the basis of economic analyses and would not stop attacking the BoE. But as for the former, though he made a parliamentary speech on 19 March 1821 as if to accept it voluntarily (cf. V/96–7), or, a little earlier than this, in his letter to Trower of 2 March 1821 he said 'I am sorry' (VIII/350) when any measures against the forgery of small notes turned out to be virtually impossible to take, he never made clear his view and position in Parliament about the cessation of circulation of small notes because of the problem of forgery followed by a resumption of circulation of the great amount of gold coin. But, in section V of *Protection*, he exceptionally mentions this issue. This seems to be the only place where he stated his view on this issue after the metallic circulation was resumed. In the following we will try to introduce and examine this place.

While recognising the change in the circulation of currency after May 1821 as unavoidable, Ricardo accuses the BoE of the inappropriateness of the measures it had taken up to that time. He expresses his fundamental position as follows:

> The Bank Directors urge in defence of the measures which they have pursued, the complaints which were made against them, on account of the frequent executions for forgery, which rendered it indispensable that they should withdraw the one pound notes from circulation, for the purpose of replacing them with coin. If they could not substitute a note better calculated to prevent forgery, than the one which they have hitherto used, this plea is a valid one; for the sacrifice of a small pecuniary interest could not be thought too great, if it took away the temptation to the crime of forgery, for which so many unfortunate persons were annually executed.
>
> (IV/225–6)

The small notes, represented by one pound notes, had been issued since the time of suspension of convertibility more than 20 years before, and afterwards replaced gradually the gold coin, almost driving it out of circulation toward 1810. After that they were circulating in quantities till the resumption of convertibility in May 1821. Why then, in spite of this, did their forgery suddenly emerge as a problem so serious as to be the cause of so many executions, only toward the beginning of this year when the resumption of cash payment was going to be an item on the agenda? As far as in referring to the materials included in *Works*, such an impression and doubt seem to be unavoidable.

However, it might be possible to infer as follows. During almost all the Bank Restriction Period before May 1821, the banknote was in depreciation due to its over-issue, and the gold reserve the in BoE was generally at a low level. Even if there existed serious problems about one pound notes, it would have been neither possible to recover them by means of conversion, nor had the BoE had any such intention. For a time from 1817, with a certain recovery of the gold reserve a limited conversion into coin was carried out, but then the price of bullion was always above the mint price, so the coin obtained from conversion was melted and flowed out as bullion (cf. letter to Trower of 9 July 1822 (see supra), IX/202). In such a situation, it was impossible to recover one pound notes, to put coin into circulation in their place, because, if coin did not remain in the country and circulate as currency, some other substitutive means of small payments was indispensable. If so, although the forgery of one pound notes spread for a long time before 1821 and was so serious a problem as to cause many executions, it was left as it was for the lack of any effective measures. Ricardo suggests that the problem of forgery had been known to many including himself, and also its seriousness recognised many years before, in saying in the above quotation that for 'the crime of forgery' 'so many unfortunate persons were annually executed'. If so, with the note printing technology applied at that time, the circulation of small notes may have had to contain such serious problems. Around the year 1820, with the appearance of a new situation in which a law stipulating the resumption of convertibility was approved and the BoE accumulated an amount of coin sufficient to render possible cash payments, a problem hidden for a long time may have suddenly appeared.

In any case, 'on 20 February it was stated in the House of Commons that the Commissioners appointed to inquire into the means of preventing the forgery of Bank Notes had so far failed to discover a process which would produce an inimitable Bank Note' (VIII/350, editor's note 1). Ricardo recognised that there was no measure against this problem, in saying that 'I am sorry that no security can be found against the forgery of Bank notes' (ibid.), in his letter to Trower of 2 March, immediately after that statement. In such a situation he seems to have had to choose between the following : (1) to insist on the continuation of circulation of one pound notes with their unresolved serious problem in opposition to the cash payment; or (2) to agree all the same with the circulation of coin in the current situation where, in addition to the accumulation of sovereigns in the BoE, the price of bullion had fallen almost to the mint price so that there was no more possibility for coin to flow out as during the time from 1817 to 1819. The above quotation from *Protection* was written a year after that. Here Ricardo recognises finally the measure the BoE took as 'valid' (IV/226) knowing that there was no means to prevent forgery, while saying that the BoE pleaded for the recovery of small notes (i.e., conversion with coin) as if taking advantage of the problem of forgery.

In spite of this, he still claims that the BoE, in preparing a great amount of coin committing an erroneous act, advanced the convertibility in coin at its convenience, in saying as follows:

> The Bank of England, who did not discover the importance of preventing forgery by the issue of coin till 1821, after they had made such large purchases of gold, were under the necessity of applying to Parliament for a bill [Bank Cash Payments Bill, proposed on 19 March, approved on 13 April 1821], to enable them to issue coin in payment of their notes, which, by Mr. Peel's bill, they were prevented from doing till 1823.
>
> (IV/226)

While recognising as unavoidable the anticipated cash payment from May 1821, Ricardo nevertheless continues to ridicule the BoE in this way. It may be because of his persistent commitment to the plan of bullion payment and of the regret for its halfway failure. But, as seen above, it was not solely due to the 'ignorance and cowardice' of the BoE that his plan had to end in such a result. After all, the deadlock in such a situation was not brought to an end till the last moment in his activities as a member of Parliament (his second speech against the motion of Western on 11 June, at the end of the session of 1823).

Probably in aiming at breaking such a deadlock, and retired to Gatcombe after the end of the session, Ricardo wrote a new manuscript for the reform of the monetary regime with a simple title 'Plan, &c.'. This was to be the last document he left to posterity on monetary matters. In the next section, we will examine the content of this new plan to reflect on its relation to the plan of bullion payment hitherto examined from various points of view.

5.2 Conception of the establishment of a national bank in the manuscript 'Plan, &c.' and the wither of bullion payment

5.2.1 'Renewal of Charter' of the BoE

In his first speech after the recess delivered on 29 April 1822, Ricardo had to discuss, along with the agricultural distress, a problem newly arisen on the renewal of the charter of the BoE. This was because 'the Government proposed to extend the charter, which was due to expire in 1833, in order to induce the Bank of England to consent to a relaxation of its provisions' (V/156, editor's note 3). Since its foundation in 1694, the BoE had been allowed its business as issuing bank by virtue of the Bank Charter granted from the Government, and in return for this the BoE extended loans to the Government. The Charter had to be renewed at a certain interval. 'The charter of the Bank was renewed in 1800 for twenty-one years, from its expiration in 1812; consequently it will not now terminate till 1833' (*Proposals*, IV/88). The renewal was proposed at that time, still more than ten years before the term, as a return for relaxing the conditions of business management of small joint stock banks in amending the provisions stipulating *de facto* monopoly of the BoE in prohibiting the establishment of every bank with more than six partners in London and in the surrounding areas. From the beginning critical of the management of the BoE, in hearing of this proposal Ricardo firmly objected to it. 'He solemnly protested against prolonging the charter of the Bank. ... He had hoped never to have heard of their charter being renewed. The benefit of the paper currency ought to belong to the public. No advantage could ever be derived from the Bank lending money to the public' (V/156).

This problem of renewal of the Charter went on smouldering up to the following year. On 18 February, just after the opening of the session of 1823, Grenfell demanded the disclosure of information in proposing again a motion 'for a return of the balances of public money in the hands of the Bank of England'. As if in response to this motion, Ricardo stated that 'the chancellor of the exchequer would be particularly careful that they [the BoE] did not overreach him. Before any such bargain should be made, it would be the duty of the right hon. gentleman to consult the House as to the terms of it' (V/247), warning the Government and the BoE in their negotiations for the renewal of the Charter. Ricardo did not further speak about the matter till the end of this parliamentary session. The problem of extension of authorisation of the business of the BoE, arisen coupled with that of new small banking business, was left in suspense for the time being. However, for Ricardo and Grenfell who were against the extension, this meant that there would be no knowing when the matter would come back on the agenda again and the renewal of the Charter would be definitely decided.

As we have seen in the previous chapter (Subsection 4.4.3), Ricardo had conceived a fairly clear idea of placing the currency issue under the competence of the State in abolishing the BoE since the time when he began writing *Proposals* in autumn of 1815. First expressed in his letter to Malthus of 10 September, this idea is shown in the last paragraph of *Proposals* (IV/114) and in chapter 27 of *Principles* (I/361–3, text of the first edition), which makes us know that it was not a simple passing idea. And the related passage in *Principles* comes just after the long quotation from *Proposals*, drawn from the core part of the plan of bullion payment, which shows that Ricardo considered the plan of bullion payment and the nationalisation of currency issue not as two separate subjects, but rather as one set to be understood in continuity. The direct motive which pushed Ricardo at that time to conceive an issuer alternative to the BoE was that he came to know concretely the reality of their management from various sources of information offered by Grenfell (earning of enormous unjust profits, non-disclosure of information, monopolisation of benefits, above all inappropriate policy of their distribution). But at the same time, he said that 'my views respecting the Bank are entirely prospective' (the letter to Malthus of 17 October 1815, VI/306), considering it impossible to bring into question the subsistence of the BoE before 1833, the term of the Charter granted to it. Probably because of this, in the bitter blame and onslaught on the BoE during about two and a half years, from the beginning of the parliament session of 1821 when Ricardo became aware of the 'erroneous' acts of the BoE to the end of the session of 1823, Ricardo never said a word about the abolition of the BoE. But when the question whether or not to let the BoE exist after the next term to come in ten years appeared to him as an imminent matter to be settled, he could not think about an issuing bank alternative to the BoE simply as something 'entirely prospective', as before. He may have thought it indispensable to block the renewal of the Charter at any cost. And, the parliamentary session of 1823 already closed, for him the next target would be the following session to begin in February 1824. Soon after the closure of the session of 1823 on 19 July, he retired to Gatcombe to begin the work for this purpose 'with a view to publication[9]' (IV/275).

The manuscript with a simple title 'Plan, &s.' written in this way seems to have been completed as early as at the beginning of August. Of this work Ricardo made report to Malthus, J. Mill and McCulloch one after another (respectively on 3, 7 and 8 August). But this time, unlike when he wrote similar manuscripts before, he did not show the manuscript to anyone of them to ask comments or whether or not to publish it. Only McCulloch said in his response of 11 August that 'I am extremely glad to learn that you have written your Essay on a National Bank, and I shall be most anxious to see it' (IX/345), but this seems not to have been realised. Ricardo may have thought it necessary to review and rewrite the manuscript drafted in a hurry before he could show it to others and ask their opinions. But in the summer of that year, he had not time for this. About Malthus (1823), published in April, the debate continued between them in correspondence. And just from the time when Ricardo finished writing 'Plan, &s.', a severe debate in correspondence with McCulloch himself began on some fundamental theoretical problems of the theory of value (cf. Section 2.5 of Chapter 2 in this book). On the debate with these two correspondents, Ricardo continued to write a manuscript from the beginning of August till the appearance of symptoms of the fatal disease at the beginning of September, in order to give an organised form to his thinking (originally untitled, published for the first time entitled '[Absolute Value and Exchangeable Value, A Rough Draft]' in the volume IV of *Works*)[10]. In this way, 'Plan, &c' was left in the initial state of its rough draft, discovered after the death of the author and edited and published by one of his younger brothers, who made considerable revisions to some parts of the manuscript preparing it for publication. Given the state of the manuscript as a rough draft, such measures may have been unavoidable, but in some places revisions seem to have been mingled with editor's interpretations on the text of the manuscript. In *Works*, the original manuscript is judged as agreeing 'with the text of the posthumous edition' 'to a large extent', and the posthumous edition of 1824 is reproduced. But, as 'the chief variants are given in footnotes' (IV/274), in the following we will consider Ricardo's plan for establishing a national bank according to this original manuscript.

5.2.2 'Plan for the Establishment of a National Bank' and 'Economical and Secure Currency'

Since Ricardo had presented his conception on the establishment of a national bank in various forms since many years before, some of the elements in the idea brought forward in 'Plan, &c' have been already examined in this chapter. In examining 'Plan, &c', we will focus on the points newly added in 1823, in particular on the points related to the plan of bullion payment Ricardo had conceived since 1811.

The point presented at the outset had never been advanced before and is in this sense very innovative. It is well known as one of the most important influences of Ricardo on Peel's Bank Charter Act 1844 (see Sayers (1953), p. 49). 'Plan, &c.' opens with the following words:

> The Bank of England performs two operations of banking, which are quite distinct, and have no necessary connection with each other: it issues a paper currency as a substitute for a metallic one; and it advances money in the way of loan, to merchants and others. These two operations of banking … might be carried on by two separate bodies.
>
> (IV/276)

In Peel's Act 1844 the BoE was actually separated into the issuing department and the banking department. But Ricardo claimed to separate the issuing department from the BoE and concentrated the following arguments mainly on banknote issue. The issuing organ, placed in this way under the State, would carry out its business on the same principles as the current BoE, except that it would not be a private company. Ricardo did not conceive an issuing organ of a wholly new type.

> Suppose the privilege of issuing paper money were taken away from the Bank, and were in future to be exercised by the State only, subject to the same regulation to which the Bank is now liable, of paying its notes, on demand, in specie; in what way would the national wealth be in the least impaired? We should then, as now, carry on all the traffic and commerce of the country, with the cheap medium, paper money, instead of the dear medium, metallic money.
>
> (ibid.)

This is the fundamental idea of Ricardo's 'Plan, &c', in which there is no change except that the interest actually obtained by the BoE as a private company in lending money to the state will belong to the state and become a public benefit. 'All other classes in the community would be exactly in the same position in which they now stand. It is evident too, that there would be just as much money in circulation' (IV/277, cf. IV/279–81). But, in what he says at the outset of 'Plan, &c.' he seems to intermingle the current state of currency after the enforcement of the Bank Cash Payments Bill approved in April 1821 and the plan of bullion payment he has recommended for a long time. That is, on the one hand he says that the future issuing organ placed under the State will pay 'its notes, on demand, in specie'. But on the other hand, according to him, it will 'as now, carry on all the traffic and commerce of the country, with the cheap medium, paper money, instead of the dear medium, metallic money'. Therefore, on the one hand, he approves the fact that the circulation of gold coin (sovereigns) in place of small notes has been established as a result of the execution of convertibility in coin after a lapse of more than two years, and he neither criticises nor negates the conversion in coin. But in the face of such a reality it would be difficult to regard as feasible the latter point. For this to be actually carried out, it will be necessary to reproduce beforehand the state of currency not 'as now' in recovering 'the dear medium, metallic money' and restoring in its place the circulation of 'the cheap medium, paper money' (i.e., of small notes). The latter part of the above quotation seems to show Ricardo still sticking to his plan of bullion payment in the situation where there was neither bullion payment nor exclusive circulation of paper currency. It seems to be because of such a position of his (conscious or unconscious), that there arose certain ambiguities and self-contradictions in the details of working of the new issuing organ (its installation, start of its business, liquidation of the ancient organ, i.e., the BoE, treatment of the country circulation and regulation of paper issue by the new issuing organ), stipulated in the provisions of the 14 'regulations' appearing in the latter part of 'Plan, &c.'[11]. We will examine this point later.

After having shown as above that the BoE as it is now is earning unjust profits from the public in engaging itself in the business of paper issue not to be entrusted to a private company, and that this business can be transferred to the State without problem, Ricardo argues against the renewal of its charter: 'Let it not then be said that the Bank Charter ought to be renewed, for this reason – that if it be not, the merchants will suffer inconvenience, from being deprived of the usual facilities of borrowing' (IV/278). And, as if to rub the directors of the BoE up the wrong way on purpose, Ricardo calmly speaks about how to dispose of the material and human resources it actually possesses, when the charter will not be renewed and the BoE will not be able to subsist as issuing bank (cf. IV/290).

If the power of issuing money belongs not to a private organ placed under the control of Government but to Government itself, this power may be abused because of the absence of an entity placed above the Government and endowed with the competence of control and punishment. Such a worry was once entertained by Ricardo, who was hence negative to the State issuing money (cf. his letter to Say of 24 December 1814). But afterwards he changed his mind when he had serious doubts about the issuing business of the BoE and thought up a device to prevent such a risk. In this 'Plan, &c.' a similar idea is repeated.

> If Government wanted money, it should be obliged to raise it by the issue and sale of exchequer bills, by public loans, or by borrowing from any of the numerous banks which might exist in the country; It should be a part of the constitution of the board which I propose to establish that they should at no time and under no circumstances lend money to Govern.t , but that if their funds were so ample as to permit them to dispose of money they should purchase govern.t securities in open market, and if on the contrary they had occasion to reduce their floating securities they should in like manner sell them in open market.
>
> (IV/283–4, including variants in the original manuscript given in editor's note 6)

The issuing organ, competent to increase or decrease the quantity of currency in domestic circulation, cannot make direct transactions with the Government (loan to it or direct purchase of public securities). For this purpose, the Commissioners must be independent of the Government, out of its control and only responsible to Parliament. But, in the open market, the transactions of Government securities are recognised as a means to regulate the quantity of money. Ricardo advances an idea which would be called today 'open market operations' for the first time in 'Plan, &c.' of 1823.

The National Bank can regulate the quantity of money by selling and purchasing Government securities in the open market, in addition to the way mentioned in Ricardo's preceding writings: payment of notes in gold and purchase of gold.

> In London the circulation can always be increased either by means of the sale of gold bullion to the commissioners for paper money to be issued on the demand of the seller of the bullion or by the issue of notes by the commissioners in payment of gov.t securities which they are authorised to purchase in the market.
>
> (IV/297, variants in the original manuscript given in editor's note 1)

The regulation of quantity of issue is mentioned only in the sense of its increase, but with the operation in the opposite sense the currency can be contracted equally in two ways.

As a dealer in securities, Ricardo had experience of transactions of Government securities along with stock exchange and currency dealing, and he is said to have gotten huge benefits from these transactions. The principle of these transactions is extremely simple: buy cheap, sell dear, and the sole aim of the transaction is the positive difference of selling from buying price. The securities are traded in this way in the general (open) market. The open market operation means an intervention of the issuing bank in such a market. But the purchase and sale of Government securities by the issuing bank, as Ricardo mentions above, aim at a quantitative regulation of currency in circulation but not at benefits. The transaction of securities carried on with a criterion different from the current prices of securities may be made at a loss (if not necessarily), or on the contrary it may not be made even if missing opportunities for benefit. Thus, Ricardo says following the above quotation:

> By this regulation a very trifling sacrifice would be made, amounting to the turn of the market, which may be supposed to be gained by those whose business it is to employ their capital and skill in dealing in these securities; but in a question of this importance such a sacrifice is not worth considering.
>
> (IV/284)

The open market operation no doubt entails a certain 'sacrifice', but if it plays only a secondary role in the regulation of the quantity of currency issue by the issuing bank, this 'sacrifice' may be even more trifling. On this point he says as follows:

> It must be recollected that these transactions would be few in amount, as the circulation would be kept at its just level by being exchanged for coin and bullion when it exceeded its proper proportion, and by the sale of gold bullion or of coin to the commissioners when the amount of paper money was below that proportion.
>
> (IV/284, variants in the original manuscript given in editor's note 2)

If the cash payment and purchase of gold is executed without fail, the quantity of currency will never deviate from the proper level. If so, the open market operation will hardly be necessary. Why then is it discussed here?

From the time before 1797 the BoE had always held various sorts of securities, public and private, and made of their transaction one of the pillars of its business for profits, along with the issue of currency. The amount of various sorts of securities it held as an item of its assets could sometimes exceed even the total amount of the banknotes it issued at the same time (Feavearyear and Morgan (1963), p. 227–9). Ricardo also says at the beginning of 'Plan, &c.' that the Government lends 'many more millions, which are advanced on Exchequer bills, on half-pay and pension annuities, and on other securities' (IV/277). The transactions of securities the BoE were carrying on on a large scale for profits may have destabilised the value of currency, about which it may not have been worried. A new issuing bank to succeed the BoE will equally succeed to the transaction of securities the latter is now making, but at the same time it will become 'a part of its regulations' by the new organ in charge of this transaction to change its aim fundamentally, from obtaining benefits, to secure the stability of the value of currency as its most important task as issuing bank. But, in this case, since this essential task is fundamentally accomplished by the operations of cash payment and purchase of gold, the open market operation will be limited both in its scale and frequency, and even if it is at a loss, the loss will be negligibly trifling. But on the other hand, as the cash payment and purchase of gold are both done by the issuing bank responding passively to the demand from banknote holders or holders of gold, they may not be sufficiently responsive to need at times. In contrast, the open market operation is executed on the judgement and initiative of the issuing bank itself to regulate actively the quantity of currency. In this sense, the open market operation can have its *raison d'être* as a supplementary means for regulating the quantity of issue. Since the quantity of currency to be injected in circulation from the issuing bank varies incessantly, to respond quickly and promptly to such a need, a means of active quantitative regulation on the part of the issuer will be required.

> It would be only when, from the increasing wealth and prosperity of the country, the country required a permanently increased amount of circulation, that it would be expedient to invest money in the purchase of securities paying interest, and only in a contrary case, that a part of such securities would be required to be sold.
>
> (IV/284, words in the edition of 1824 changed from the original manuscript by Moses)

The above is a summary introduction to the former part of 'Plan, &c.', at the end of which Ricardo says that 'I would propose, then, some such plan as the following, for the establishment of a National Bank' (IV/285), to pass to the latter part, where he enumerates the 14 'regulations' and explains them one by one. The title given to the manuscript by the brother when he published it in 1824 *Plan for the Establishment of a National Bank* may come from this sentence. Incidentally, the term 'National Bank' is employed in the original manuscript of 'Plan, &c.' only twice other than in this place: in 'regulation 14' (IV/289) and its explanation (IV/294). All the other examples of use of this term are included in the parts added or rewritten by the editor.

In the latter part of 'Plan, &c.', Ricardo determines the establishment of a National Bank 'on the [the date, left blank] 1833, the day on which the Bank charter expires' (IV/285, variant of regulation 2 in the original manuscript) and fixes minutely every one of the measures necessary for the new bank to issue a new currency to commence its operation in place of the BoE. Ricardo would determine from then on what was to be carried into execution ten years later in order to start up a fictional bank existing still only in his mind. In so doing, he wanted to take measures to block, at any cost, the renewal of the Bank Charter which had already become an item on the agenda. The Commissioners 'appointed for the management of the paper circulation of the country' issue the necessary amount of new paper at the expiration of the Charter, pay with it the debt of the Government to the BoE, and with the rest 'purchase gold and silver bullion', 'pay the Bank for as many Exchequer bills as they may think proper to take' (IV/285–6, from the variant in the original manuscript given in editor's notes). All of these measures will have to be executed in one day. In this way, on the day of the establishment of a National Bank, every debtor–creditor relationship between the Government and the BoE will be completely liquidated, and the new currency replacing the banknotes of the BoE will be delivered to the BoE as redemption of the debt. And 'for the substitution of the new paper money for the old' (IV/292), 'the Bank shall be obliged to use its best effort, within six months of the expiration of its charter, to redeem all its notes in circulation, by the payment of them in the new notes issued by government' (IV/286). 'The notes of the Bank of England shall be current for six months after the expiration of the Bank charter, after which they shall no longer be received by government in payment of the revenue' (IV/287). In this way, on [the date, left blank] 1833(4), both the BoE as issuing bank and its banknotes will completely disappear.

This is a summary of the first five regulations. Though the question is about what will take place in ten years, the details described here seem to be based on the state of management of the BoE and of currency in 1823, at the time of drafting of 'Plan, &c.'. At that time small notes did not circulate and the conversion was in coin. Probably small notes like one pound notes were not included in the new notes of a National Bank to be issued as substitution for the banknotes of the BoE. The composition of face values of the new notes may have been conceived after that of the notes of the BoE in 1823. And nothing is said about the then widely diffused circulation of coin, there is no clear mention of the recovery of coin. The circulation of coin was probably to be left intact. Further, for the stability of the value of currency, like the BoE at that time, a National Bank to be newly established should naturally respond to the demand for payment in gold from the banknote holders. But it is not clear whether the payment should be made in cash or in bullion, since it is always indicated in two forms at the same time such as 'cash and bullion' (IV/279) or 'coin and bullion' (IV/284). In 'Plan, &c.' Ricardo is very ambiguous about how he thought of the way of payment of banknotes after the liquidation of the BoE would occur[12]. While on the one hand recognising as it is ongoing cash payments, on the other Ricardo seems to still remain committed to the already disappeared bullion payment. Without sweeping out the precious metal circulation by means of bullion payment, it is not possible 'to dispense with the use of a great quantity of a very valuable metal which as money produces nothing[13]' (IV/298). In order to carry this out, the issue and circulation of small notes to be substituted for gold coin are indispensable. But, as seen above, the bank notes to be issued from a new National Bank seem not to include small notes. Ricardo speaks about the one pound notes, representative small notes, only in 'regulation 14' and in its explanation, i.e., in the latter of the last two regulations (13 and 14) inserted subsequently after he had ended the first manuscript with 'regulation 12' (IV/288, editor's note 1). We will examine this point later.

The next 6 regulations (from 7 to 12, regulation 6. lacking) determine in detail the relation between the circulation in London and that in the country. The domain of circulation of the banknotes issued from the BoE was limited to London and its surrounding area, and in the country a number of small country banks issued their proper notes. The value of these country banknotes was linked to that of the banknote of the BoE through 'conversion' of the former into the latter, and the issue of the former varied according to that of the latter. With the abolition of the BoE and the establishment of a new National Bank, a restructuring of the current relation of note circulation between London and the country would be required. The above six 'regulations' stipulate in detail the procedures to be taken for this purpose (still ten years later!). Through these six 'regulations', Ricardo seems to have intended to construct a system concentrating in London the decision-making on currency circulation all over England with a subordinate country system. For our purpose that is all that is to be said on these 'regulations'.

As seen above, in the original manuscript of 'Plan, &c' the 'regulations' on the establishment of a National Bank terminated with 'regulation 12'. But afterwards, as if recalling something important, Ricardo inserted additional two regulations, 13 and 14. These last two regulations are somewhat different in their character from the preceding 12. They seem to stipulate provisions relating to the essentials of his plan for the reform of the monetary regime: how should the new National Bank supply an 'economical and secure currency' after the completion of all the necessary procedures during the transitional period just after its establishment?[14]

The text of 'regulation 13' is as follows:

> The Commissioners in London shall be obliged to buy any quantity of gold of standard fineness, and exceeding hundred ounces in weight, that may be offered them at £3. 17. 6 – they shall be at liberty to give a price as high as £3. 17. 10½ if they think proper to do so. The Commissioners shall be obliged to give gold coin of the standard weight on demand for any notes issued in London or for any bill drawn from the country.
>
> (IV/288–9, including variants in the original manuscripts given in editor's note 6)

Here is determined simultaneously the obligation to be assumed by the issuing bank of purchasing gold and selling gold (conversion). The buying price can be discretionarily fixed within the range of 4½ pence of difference between the mint price and 3*l.* 17*s.* 6*d.* slightly inferior to the former, on the other hand, the selling price is fixed at the mint price. Through both transactions the quantity of currency issue is regulated toward both directions of increase and decrease, its value being confined within a narrow range between the purchasing price as upper limit and the selling price as lower limit. And, as the price of gold cannot largely deviate from the mint price, the issuing bank will not be faced with the necessity of making any gold transactions on a large scale, hence of having a large amount of gold as reserve. About 'regulation 13' the following explanation is given.

> If the commissioners regulate their issues by the comparative value of gold and paper they cannot err and they might carry on the whole business of currency with a very small quantity of gold by merely increasing or diminishing the quantity of paper according as its value was high or low compared with gold.
>
> (IV/294, variant in the original manuscript shown in editor's note 1)

Such an idea is familiar to Ricardo from the time when he presented the plan of bullion payment for the first time in 'Appendix' to the fourth edition of *High Price*. In the former part of 'Plan, &c', Ricardo added to this idea the open market operation as a means for 'merely increasing or decreasing the quantity of paper' without involving any transactions of gold, but the 'regulations' in the latter part of 'Plan, &c' contain no mention of the open market operation. Maybe for Ricardo the quantitative adjustment of currency should be carried out mainly by minor gold transactions.

Equally, since 1811, a certain minimal limit has been imposed on the gold transactions the issuing bank implements for regulating the quantity of currency. In 'Appendix' of 1811, the minimal sum for the payment in bullion was fixed at 20 pounds. Subsequently this sum was modified several times, but it was always imposed on the payment in bullion the issuing bank makes in response to the demand from banknote holders. However, in 'regulation 13' quoted above, this minimal limit for the gold transaction is fixed, on the contrary, for the purchase of gold by the issuing bank. The limit is 100 ounces (a little more than 3kg), expressed in terms of weight of bullion (amounting to the sum of a little less than 400 pounds). Why does such a change suddenly happen here? And whence comes this figure of 100 ounces (in the bullion payment with Ricardoes tentatively carried out till April 1821 this minimal limit was 60 ounces)? Such a question naturally arises, but the explanation on 'regulation 13' gives no answer. If Ricardo had fixed with some clear intention an unprecedented high hurdle to the purchase of bullion, he should have given a due explanation. The reason for which such a provision is included in the 'regulation 13' may be inferred as follows.

Purchase of gold will be demanded from the issuing bank when the currency issue is insufficient, the price of bullion falls, exportation of commodities (importation of gold) expands, and the exchange of gold flowed in from abroad for domestic currency is profitable. Those who want to sell gold (bullion or foreign currency) not on the market but advantageously to the issuing bank are merchants engaged in foreign trade, whose transactions may be generally above a certain scale. Ricardo may have estimated 'a certain scale' at 100 ounces of gold. And if such an international transfer of gold induced by insufficiency in the quantity of domestic currency is absorbed by the issue of banknotes, i.e., if the issuing bank purchases gold of not less than 100 ounces of weight, the insufficiency of currency can be dissolved without falling into excessive issue. Of course, there may exist those who possess gold of less than 100 ounces of weight for various reasons. But, while not responding to every demand for purchase of gold from such persons, in accepting its purchase only above a certain amount demanded from a small number of them, the issuing bank will soon be able to calm the demand for purchase of gold itself without bothering itself with many small deals. Probably such may have been Ricardo's idea. And, though these transactions would be limited in both frequency and scale, the issuing bank would obtain from them some profits, since it purchases gold at a price under the mint price. And, as seen above, the quantity of gold flowing in from abroad because of the insufficiency of currency will be theoretically a little inferior to the quantity to make up for the insufficiency, hence the state of insufficiency of currency will subsist even if the banknotes corresponding to this quantity are issued. But, since the National Bank will always try to maintain the proper level of quantity of currency, there can be neither a large contraction of currency nor an influx of large quantities of gold, so that the remaining insufficiency will be trifling.

In contrast to the purchase of gold, no limit is set for the payment of banknotes with gold. Demand for purchase of banknotes is made to the issuing bank when the currency is in excess, and the price of bullion is above the mint price. Then, though the banknotes and the coin of the same face value remain equivalents in law, the latter is substantially higher in value than the former. Because, in melting coin and reducing it to bullion, it can be exchanged for banknotes of higher face value. In assuming the obligation of convertibility in such a situation, the issuing bank would incur potential loss ('potential', because the bank may not make of itself the above operation.). But, just like the purchase of gold, the deals in this case will also be very limited, both in scale and frequency, and the loss incurred will be compensated with the equally trifling benefit obtained by the purchase of gold seen above. The melting of coin and export of bullion being no longer prohibited under Peel's Act of 1819, it will be more advantageous to melt and sell coin on the market or export it than to use it as currency when the currency depreciates and the price of bullion rises. A legal act like this is possible even with one piece of coin, without collecting a certain number of them. As an official organ, the issuing bank cannot discriminate coin and banknotes, but must regard them as a currency both nominally and substantially equal (hence it must pay banknotes with coin of the same face value even at a substantial loss). This may be the reason why no minimal limit is set for the amount of banknotes to be paid in cash. What is essentially more important than this is, however, the provision that the payment of banknotes must be necessarily implemented with 'gold coin of the standard weight'. Prior to this 'regulation 13', Ricardo always mentioned the bullion payment in addition to cash payment, but here he mentions only the cash payment, as if abandoning the bullion payment. From his position this may be called a major concession. Probably 'in exchange for' this 'concession', he discusses the issue and use of small notes (one pound notes) in the following 'regulation 14'. In 'Plan, &c.', the small notes appear only in this 'regulation 14' and its explanation.

The text of the last 'regulation 14' is as follows: 'notes of one pound shall be issued at the first establishment of the National Bank, and shall be given to anyone requiring them in exchange for notes of a larger amount, if the person presenting them prefer such notes to coin' (IV/289). The issue of one pound notes will be made not on the first day of the establishment of the National Bank but after that as early as possible. Therefore, among the new banknotes to be issued at the same time as its establishment the small notes will not be included, as was actually the case at the time of drafting of 'Plan, &c.'. If one pound notes are issued soon after the establishment of the National Bank and they take root in circulation, coin in circulation will diminish or disappear. And when banknotes depreciate in such a situation, the payment of banknotes will be made in bullion, but no more in cash. But, in 'regulation 14', it is not clear whether one pound notes will soon begin to circulate in place of coin supposed to circulate for a certain time just after the establishment of the National Bank. The choice between coin and paper for use as currency is entrusted to the users of money. And one pound notes too will be injected into circulation via the right of choice the banknote holders are to exercise when converting notes of high denominations. Each particular money user will not prefer paper to coin, although the former is economical from the standpoint of national economy, as Ricardo thought it to be. They may choose considering the facility of use of each of them as currency. Ricardo explains this 'facility' with concrete examples in saying that 'another advantage attending the use of paper money is the extreme facility with which payments are made by its means' (IV/298, from fragment of the manuscript of 'Plan, &c.'). An argument of this kind may be far more effective for persuading the public. But in this case the question is limited to the choice of the means of small payments as a part of currency (though an important part to be daily used for many people) in supposing the use of notes of high denominations.

Ricardo could do nothing but expect the notes to be widely accepted in place of coin by the public recognising its conveniences, who would hopefully demand the exchange of coin for paper. But the choice between paper and coin depends not only on the comparative conveniences of each of them, but also on the attachment of the public for coin as a means of circulation which had been used for a far longer time in history than paper. Ricardo was well aware of this. After the deliberation in the Secret Committee on the Resumption Bill in spring of 1819, he made the following comment on it: 'they [members of the Committee] had to contend with public prejudice, and perhaps too with prepossessions which they themselves felt in favour of coin' (his letter to McCulloch of 8 May 1819, VIII/27). And, for 'the English people in the mass' to 'prove to have been really weaned from their fondness for gold coins' (Bonar (1923), p. 300), still a lapse of time of 100 years was necessary. Indeed, the sovereign, issued from 1817, continued to circulate as the sole unlimited legal tender for 100 years till the time of the First World War, 1917. Apart from this result, there seems to have been a serious lack in 'regulation 14'. The one pound notes had been withdrawn after having circulated for a long time during the Bank Restriction Period because of their widespread forgery raising serious social problems. To try to issue and inject into circulation the same kind of paper again after such a hard experience, it is indispensable to think about sufficient measures to prevent the recurrence of similar problems. But in 'regulation 14' no consideration of this point can be found. In the explanation of 'regulation 14', Ricardo writes that 'the fourteenth regulation provides for a supply of one pound notes for the country circulation' (IV/294), but the text of 'regulation 14', containing no mention of the country circulation, can be taken as stipulating the issue of one pound notes in London. And in the explanation on this regulation, in determining minutely the way for supplying one pound notes to the country, he says that 'the security for the detection of fraud is nearly perfect' (IV/295), as if no problem of forgery existed with regard to the use of one pound notes in London. Could Ricardo think of any preventive measures to be taken by the National Bank itself? But, in any case, the last two 'regulations' in 'Plan, &c.' may have been the results of his final 'concession and resistance' he tried in expecting to put into practice once again his plan of bullion payment, while recognising the reality of restored circulation of coin.

5.3 Afterword

Ricardo continued thinking about money and finance both as abstract theoretical and actual current problems during the whole of his lifetime as an economist. But except for *High Price* belonging to the earliest period in his career, his writings about these topics were left in the form of a set of minor works not to be described as systematic, like pamphlets on current issues, manuscripts or letters. For this, Ricardo's economic theory has been regarded mainly as a 'theory of value and distribution' embodied in the first several chapters of *Principles*, has made a lasting mark as such on the following history of political economy, and is actually discussed from various points of view. But his theory of money is ordinarily (mis-)understood in an extremely simplified form as a 'quantity theory of money'. In addition, a group of the minor works he wrote as an intervention in the debates over current issues on currency appear today to be almost forgotten, apart from the fact that they have been taken up sporadically in the studies on the 'bullion (-ist) controversy' involving a number of economists including Ricardo. The same can be said of *Proposals*. In spite of its importance, almost decisive for understanding his monetary thought, this work seems to be taken up less and less with time, because of its close entanglement with the concrete situation of the time on money and finance, rendering it less and less easily accessible with increasing distance from the time of its writing.

Chapter three of this book discusses Ricardo's theory of money with the aim of searching for a relation between his 'theory of value and distribution' and his 'theory of money', considered for the most part as two separate theories, or even theories contradictory to each other. For this purpose, aiming at 'abstracting' his 'general and abstract' theory of money, comparable to the first theoretical chapters in *Principles*, from the historical context in which were embedded almost all of his monetary writings, we tried to remove the 'impurities' of the past. Such a way of their study may of course not be meaningless for some particular purpose, but in evidence this is not to comprehend sufficiently his theory of money advanced in his struggle with the problems of money of the time. For the purpose of supplementing the study made in chapter three in considering Ricardo's theory of money from a wider point of view, we have tried to concentrate on the aspects intentionally put aside there. The points in chapter four and five presuppose the interpretation on the fundamental issues in Ricardo's theory of money brought forward in chapter three.

To approach such an objective, we have tried to trace and analyse in detail how Ricardo came to conceive his plan for the reform of the monetary regime, what was the destiny that plan had to follow in his lifetime. For this reason, we had to enter into the concrete situation of currency of the time. In particular, the discussion was extended to the problems concerning the interrelation between the paper circulation and the circulation of coin, to the problems particular to the latter circulation, which have hardly been taken up in the foregoing studies on Ricardo's theory of money. And mentions were made of minor debates and personal relations at that time which exercised some influence on the evolution of his arguments about money. These are mainly based on the materials included in *Works*, but also the related minor literature of the time was referred to as far as possible.

It is one of the main points in chapters four and five, to bring into question the usage of the term 'Ingot plan', likely to give some fixed image to the whole of the conception of the reform of the monetary regime Ricardo kept, extended or at times modified over a long time. Ricardo himself continued to call simply 'plan' the proposals he made from 1811 to 1823, and also his friends like J. Mill understood the 'plan' as Ricardo did. Therefore, we have adopted a general wording 'plan for the reform of monetary regime', vaguer hence apt to admit various interpretations. Ricardo himself called both 'plan of bullion payment' and 'plan of the establishment of a National Bank' equally and simply 'plan'. These two were seen by him as only two different aspects or phases in his plan. There were not two different plans, and he did not, in abandoning (or resigning) the one, 'pass' from the one to the other for some reason. Besides, the fact that the manuscript he had drafted just before his death was posthumously published by one of his younger brothers under the title *Plan for the Establishment of a National Bank* contributed to give rise to the impression that Ricardo got the idea of the establishment of a national bank only in the last months of his life, in place of the plan of bullion payment he had proposed a long time before. On the contrary, we emphasised that the establishment of a national bank was conceived by Ricardo from earlier times, in continuity with the plan of bullion payment.

Though the plan of bullion payment failed because of two difficulties simultaneously arisen in abolishing metallic circulation and in maintaining small notes in circulation to replace the former, Ricardo never ceased to the end thinking about measures for realising these two objectives, indispensable to an 'economical and secure currency'. As a result, his plan was never carried into execution as he had expected, but his conception continued to exercise great influence on the Currency Controversy and the planning of banking system in later years. And, as a small number of researchers like Boner affirmed, the Gold-Exchange Standard adopted in India at the end of the nineteenth century, the monetary thought of Keynes who esteemed it highly, and further the International Monetary Fund (IMF) after the Second World War[15], a sort of its modification, all these could neither be understood nor estimated correctly without the monetary thought Ricardo brought forward in his plan. Money in the contemporary world after the Nixon shock has been repeating unstable evolutions without a clear anchor in the past 50 years and more. Can the monetary thought of Ricardo still give any suggestions to such an actual state of money?

Notes

1 The record of parliamentary speech is written in the third and not first person of the speaker, and voices in the conference room are included. About these points, cf. 'IV. How the Speeches were Reported' and 'V. The Speeches in the Present Edition' in Sraffa's 'Introduction to the Speeches in Parliament', V/viii–xxxiv.

2 In fact, in addition to this, the Bank Cash Payments Bill was enacted for another reason, the spread of forgery of small notes, typically of one pound notes, emerged in this period (see infra). The trend, contrary to what Ricardo aimed at, toward recovering small notes, inevitably involving the inconvenience of spread of forgery, and toward replacing them with coin, was one factor pressing on to its enactment (cf. V/91–2).

3 It had ceased in fact. Or rather it did not work from the outset. If it ever worked, it was only for postponing cash payments.

4 The change in the state of currency in England after May 1821 Ricardo analyses in this letter naturally include the withdrawal of small notes from circulation (and the spread of forgery as its cause) and the recovery of the great amount of Ricardoes 'left unsold'. In neglecting these elements, it is impossible to evaluate his analysis, but he does not mention them at all.

5 If any change took place either in the state of currency in the other countries or in the scale of world commerce, the contraction of banknotes in England, occupying an important place in the world (in fact West-European) economy, meant, according to Ricardo's theory, also a contraction in a lesser proportion of the total amount of money in the whole world composed of gold and banknotes (cf. III/54–7). This must have raised the value of gold as much.

6 About the situation in which the plan of bullion payment of Ricardo failed thus, Laidler says as follows:

> Counterfeiting of bank notes had been virtually unknown before 1797, but the increased circulation of low denomination Bank of England notes thereafter had offered considerable temptation to forgers. ... Hence Ricardo's ingot plan was dropped, and when resumption was finally implemented in 1821, gold coin replaced small denomination notes in circulation.
>
> (Laidler (1987), p. 293)

Laidler says as if the forgery of small notes began at the same time as their circulation after 1797, but this explanation leaves open the question why the problem of their forgery became so serious only in 1821 and so suddenly as to put an end to their circulation.

7 Even if the total quantity of the gold flowed in England circulates in the form of coin or banknotes, the increase in the total amount of currency does not go beyond this total quantity. As seen above, the bullion was 'all' purchased by the BoE at the mint price and its whole value was changed into banknotes, equivalent to the bullion. And, to change the purchased bullion into coin and to inject it into circulation, the BoE could not but exchange coin with banknotes of the same face value, i.e., convert the banknotes. This operation (recovery of small notes and injection of gold coin into circulation, carried out and ended in a short time from May 1821) cannot change the quantity of currency in circulation. And it is hardly thinkable that the BoE, voluntarily contracting the quantity of issue of banknotes for preparing for the cash payment, would issue the note beyond it would be necessary for the purchase of bullion and anticipated conversion.

8 'That bill he had always considered as an experiment, to try whether a bank could not be carried on with advantage to the general interests of the country, upon the principle of not being called upon to pay their notes in coin, but in bullion' (V/200).

9 Words employed by Moses, one of the younger brothers, in his 'Preface' to the pamphlet, published by him after the death of Ricardo in February 1824 under the title *Plan for the Establishment of a National Bank* from Murray. In his 'Note', Sraffa says that Ricardo showed on his deathbed the manuscript to this younger brother. Probably Ricardo said to him then that the manuscript was written 'with a view to publication'.

10 While making report of the manuscript of 'Plan, &c' during and immediately after its writing to his three friends one after the other in a short time (as if very eager to spread it about), to the end he never spoke to anyone of the writing of the manuscript on 'absolute value and exchangeable value'.

11 In the latter part of 'Plan, &c.', a style suggestive of a letter of the law is adopted. It may be for the purpose of preparing for the possible parliamentary discussion on the renewal of the charter of the BoE, in publishing this manuscript in time for the following session of 1824. But it may also be because Ricardo intended to propose himself a Bill of establishing a 'National Bank' in abolishing the BoE at the expiration of its current charter in 1833. He may have been familiar with documents of a similar style, but has never drafted in such a style. As a polemist out of office or a dissident in minority, he used to take a firm stand for or against in his own free style.

12 As the explanation about regulation 3 containing the above quoted phrase 'purchase gold and silver bullion', Ricardo says as follows: 'the third regulation provides for a store of gold coin and bullion without which the new establishment could not act' (IV/291, variant in the original manuscript given in editor's note 1). Here he also writes 'gold coin and bullion' as if a new National Bank would make bullion payment along with cash payment, but it is not at all clear in what relation these two ways of payment stand, whether they can ever be compatible.

13 From a fragment of the manuscript. From the letter of the text, this appears to be a part of the first draft of 'Plan, &c.' in which is expressed Ricardo's fundamental idea. Equally in the first part of this fragment, he emphasises 'the advantages of a paper money provided security be taken to fix its value on a basis as permanent as the metals themselves' (ibid.). His conception of an 'economical and secure currency' had to be applied as it was to a new National Bank.

14 In the edition of 1824, 'regulation 12' in Ricardo's original manuscript was moved to the end of 'regulation 11' by the editor. At the same time, 'regulation 13' in the original manuscript was divided into two parts, of which the first was inserted into the empty space of the former 'regulation 12' and 'regulation 13 came to be made up only of the initial latter part. Moreover, the editor revised both parts. He also rewrote the subsequent explanations of these regulations in consequence of the former revisions. In *Works* the edition of 1824 is reprinted, but at the same time all the differences from the original manuscript are indicated in editor's notes with the corresponding original texts. In principle, our following examination is based on Ricardo's original manuscript.

15 Cf. 'Papers on Money and Banking' by Deleplace in Kurz and Salvadori (2015), p. 395.

6 An aspect of Ricardo's theory of money

Monetary issue and economic dynamics

6.1 Foreword

In the second volume of the work of his later years (Wicksell (1935)), Wicksell examines in detail Ricardo's theory of money as a historical source of his cumulative process theory. What Wicksell noticed most is the thesis Ricardo advanced in chapter 27 of his *Principles* 'On Currency and Banks', according to which the discount rate of bills (more generally the bank rate of interest) below the profit rate (or the market rate of interest), levied by the Bank of England, induces an unlimited expansion of bank loans (and hence of monetary issue), resulting in an infinite rise in prices (I/364, cf. pp.89-90 in this book).

Up to now, for the most part, Ricardo's theory of money has been characterised as a quantity theory based on Say's law, which does not recognise any structural divergence between supply and demand, with the conception of neutral money exerting no effect on the real economy, its quantitative variations doing nothing but pulling up or down uniformly the prices of commodities[1]. However, in the recent literature there exists (under the influence of Wicksell?) a tendency to situate Ricardo not in the tradition of the concept of neutral money, but in that of its non-neutrality[2], the origin of which can be traced back to English economic thought from the end of the eighteenth century to the beginning of the nineteenth century (Thornton, Bentham, Malthus, etc.), a concept which was going to play an important role in the monetary theories of the business cycle developed by German and Austrian authors in the twentieth century (cf. for example, Humphrey (1986)).

The objective of this chapter is to shed some light on an aspect of Ricardo's theory of money in examining his reactions to the arguments brought forward by the three contemporary authors named above – the so called 'forced saving'[3] theory, according to which the increase in monetary issue by the bank not only uniformly raises the prices of all commodities in proportion to the increased quantity of money, but also this increase has the effect of expanding production through a redistribution of wealth and modifications brought about by it to the relative price system, as well as on the view he had on the relation between the interest rate and the profit rate, the driving force of monetary issue allegedly triggering such a process. Ricardo was quite aware of these

DOI: 10.4324/9781003498322-7

points brought forward by these three authors at the time when he began his activities as an economist in 1809. And these points were among the most important themes of his theory of money, so much so that they appeared as subjects of his parliamentary evidence and discussion after 1819[4] (but only as responses to criticism and questions, not as elements of his positive opinion).

The theory of economic dynamics, which has as its driving force the variations in interest rate and the monetary issue by the bank, was developed by heterodox economists such as Wicksell, Schumpeter, Hayek, Keynes. This theory belongs to an extremely important theme for reflecting on the historical current of monetary theory. Therefore, it is only by making comparative examinations including these authors that it would become possible to make clear Ricardo's historical place. But in this chapter, we aim only to clarify the position Ricardo took on this theme in comparing his viewpoints with those of his three contemporaries enumerated above.

As the question here is about Ricardo's position on this theme, we are not going into details on the writings of Thornton, Bentham, Malthus. They will be examined *ad hoc* insofar as necessary to understand Ricardo's viewpoints. All of these three authors discussed the effects of 'forced saving' in the historical conditions in which the Bank of England, after the suspension of cash payments, was increasing its note issue and thus raising prices. It's just the same situation as that Ricardo was observing in order to develop his theory of money. In other words, the theory of 'forced saving' was not simply a theory based on some abstract theoretical suppositions, but it was conceived of giving a certain interpretation and evaluation to the increase of monetary issue and to the consequent depreciation of banknotes, a real situation of the time that they all witnessed. In this sense, it can be said that the theory of 'forced saving' is a product of the bullion controversy. It is worth noting that after the controversy this theory was almost forgotten in the middle of the nineteenth century except by J.S. Mill and Walras, and that with the rise of prices observed from the end of the nineteenth century and the breakdown of the gold standard system after the First World War the theory of 'forced saving' was rediscovered and developed anew by economists of this period (and at the same time the bullion controversy was also revived).

Among the three authors enumerated above, Thornton was the first to bring forward the idea of 'forced saving' in a detailed and systematic way (Thornton (1802)). Two years after the publication of his book, Bentham, though in a less ordered form, discussed 'forced frugality' in his manuscript mentioned above. But, in one of his letters supposedly written after the writing of this manuscript, he gives priority to Thornton on this idea (cf. Hayek (1939)). Bentham developed the idea he had expressed in this manuscript further in one part of his unpublished work 'Sur les prix' (probably in referring to the book of Thornton[5]). Malthus, on the other hand, addressed this problem in Malthus (1811a).

When and how did Ricardo become aware of their arguments and how did he react to them? Thornton was perhaps the first author among these three whom Ricardo read. Having published in 1809 two newspaper articles entitled 'Price of Gold', Ricardo pursued during the autumn of this year intensive studies of English literature on money and finance, going back to Locke (III/7, editor's note 2)[6]. The work of Thornton was included there. However, Ricardo never explicitly mentioned the arguments of Thornton to make clear his point of view on them. Ricardo encountered the arguments of Bentham when he read (from the end of December 1810 to the beginning of January 1811) the manuscript of his unpublished work 'Sur les prix' (in the French version made by Dumont, his French editor, from the original English manuscript) requested by J. Mill. Ricardo made, on this occasion, detailed comments on this work (III/269–341) and expressed his point of view on this subject (also in his letter to J. Mill of 01 January 1811, in the course of writing these comments Ricardo reports his views on this work). On the other hand, having read Malthus's review article immediately after its publication in the *Edinburgh Review*, Ricardo wrote his reply which was to be published in 'Appendix' to the fourth edition of *High Price* (April 1811), and he continued epistolary discussions after this first exchange of views.

The theory which would be called in the twentieth century the theory of 'forced saving', is made up of a combination of particular hypotheses on the increase of monetary issue by the bank and the rise in prices caused by this increase.

Supposing that the variations in the quantity of money in circulation pulls up or down uniformly (and perhaps instantly) all prices, and that the quantities of money held by all vary uniformly in proportion to its quantitative variations, the rise in prices by the increase of monetary issue will leave the system of relative prices of commodities on the market unchanged, including labour (power), and thus the quantitative variations of money would be in themselves neutral to the economy. But, if the increase of monetary issue by the bank brings about unequal changes in the quantities of money held by all, or if the range or the speed of the rise of prices is divergent according to the kinds of commodity, the quantitative increase of money will have severe economic consequences, and money will become non-neutral to the economy. The theory of 'forced saving' is based on this effect of monetary changes to affirm that the fall in the value of money caused by its increase expands economic activity. For these arguments it is further necessary to add some particular hypotheses. But, in any case, all the theorists of 'forced saving' have in common the viewpoint according to which the increase in monetary issue results in its depreciation. In this sense they all adopted the quantity theory of money in the conditions of circulation of inconvertible banknotes, and in the context of the period they were bullionists, as Ricardo was.

The starting point of this movement, which goes from the increase of issue to depreciation, is the bank's issuing action, which is the fundamental precondition of 'forced saving'. And the disturbance in the system of relative prices will become all the more certain if the quantity of money does not cease changing (increasing in the present case). Under what conditions does such a continued increase take place? Bentham and Malthus do not raise this question. The questions they raise are only about the results of the rise of prices consequent upon a monetary expansion. For their arguments the action of bank of issue is a given fact. Thornton is the only author who brought forward a clear theory on this point. Here the interest rate charged by the bank for loans (discount on bills) plays a decisive role. Ricardo, on his part, gave an impressive discussion on the relation between the rate of interest and the trend of bank loans in a passage of *Principles*, though not in direct response to Thornton. It is on this passage that the arguments of those who estimate Ricardo as the precursor of the theory of cumulative process of Wicksell are based. We will examine in the following what Ricardo brings forward concerning the continued expansion of monetary issue with the level of the rate of interest as a fundamental factor, taking into account the theory of Thornton.

As was seen above, there is first the bank's action of issue, and then there will be changes in the relative quantities of money held by each and in the system of relative prices, which causes the 'forced saving' resulting in an expansion of investment activities and production. That's the scenario of the theory of 'forced saving'. Therefore, logically our discussion must begin with examining the expansion of monetary issue. But, in view of the importance of this problem, which is in close relationship with the history of the theory from Thornton, Ricardo to Wicksell, we will see first how Ricardo reacted to the arguments brought forward by his contemporaries on the effect the monetary expansion would have on economic activities.

6.2 'Forced saving'

6.2.1 Depreciation of money and transfer of wealth

The BoE in Ricardo's time was issuing inconvertible notes in discounting commercial bills brought to the Bank, or in paying the price of government bonds it accepted. The banknotes newly issued in this way enter into the National Treasury or pass into the hands of those who were able to benefit from the discount in the Bank. But these banknotes do not fall into the hands of those who are not in commercial relationships with the Bank. Thus, the part each holds of the total amount of banknotes changes so as to reduce the relative quantities held by those who are not able to benefit from the Bank's loans. Given the reduction of purchasing power of the banknotes held by all, in proportion to their increased quantity, there is a transfer of wealth from those who don't have access to banknotes newly issued by the Bank to those who do have it, a transfer carried out by monetary operations.

From the outset of his participation in the bullion controversy, Ricardo was well aware of the fact that the increased issue of inconvertible banknotes has, as its effect, not only rise of prices, but also changes in the distribution of the total amount of banknotes, and for this reason such an increase transfers the purchasing power from certain categories of the population to others. The transfer does not increase the wealth for the whole of the population, it being a zero-sum game, he says:

> However abundant may be the quantity of money or of banknotes; though it may increase the nominal prices of commodities; though it may distribute the productive capital in different proportions; though the Bank, by increasing the quantity of other notes, may enable A to carry on part of the business formerly engrossed by B and C, *nothing will be added to the real revenue and wealth of the country*. B and C may be injured, and A and the Bank may be gainers, but they will gain exactly what B and C lose. *There will be a violent and unjust transfer of property, but no benefit whatever will be gained by the community*[7].
>
> (III/93, emphasis added)

It is such a point of view on the influence of the increase of monetary issue which had been the target of Malthus' critique in [Malthus] (1811a). We are going to see in the following the theory of 'forced saving' developed by Malthus in this article, and Ricardo's refutation in the 'Appendix' to the fourth edition of *High Price*[8].

Malthus shares with Ricardo the view that the increase of banknote issue is accompanied entirely by transfer of wealth. And it can be said that they have in common the same viewpoint on which categories of the population gain or lose wealth. That is to say, they equally thought that 'considerable portions of the currency were taken away from the idle, and those who live upon fixed incomes, and transferred to farmers, manufacturers and merchants' ([Malthus] (1811a), p. 364). Ricardo supposed that the transfer of one part of the wealth among social classes of different nature does nothing but change the subjects who spend it, without changing the fact that the transferred part of wealth is, in any case, allotted in its totality to direct or indirect investment. But Malthus thinks that this transfer produces a radical change in the way in which one part of the wealth is spent. From here their opinion diverges.

According to Malthus, the question of which part of the circulating medium will be invested for the production of wealth, and which part of it will be allotted to the unproductive consumption ('the proportion between capital and revenue' (ibid.)) is dependent on the question of what are the types of people to whom the circulating medium of a country are distributed, and of how they are distributed. And if the increase of monetary issue lowers the purchasing power per monetary unit and brings about the transfer of wealth:

> the proportion between capital and revenue would be greatly altered to the advantage of capital; and in a short time, the produce of the country would be greatly augmented. Whenever, in the actual state of things, a fresh issue of notes comes into the hands of those who mean to employ them in the prosecution and extension of a profitable business, a difference in the

> distribution of the circulating medium takes place, similar in kind to that which has been last supposed; and produces similar, though of course comparatively inconsiderable effects, in altering the proportion between capital and revenue in favour of the former. The new notes go into the market, as so much additional capital, to purchase what is necessary for the conduct of the concern. But before the produce of the country has been increased, it is impossible for one person to have more of it, without diminishing the shares of some others. ... On every fresh issue of notes, not only is the quantity of the circulating medium increased, but the distribution of the whole mass is altered. A larger proportion falls into the hands of those who consume and produce, and a smaller proportion into the hands of those who only consume.
>
> (ibid.)

Thus, Malthus considers the increase of monetary issue and the consequent depreciation as having the effect of coercive transfer of wealth, which is in favour of expansion of production by diminishing unproductive consumption to increase the part allotted to accumulation[9]. Malthus supposes here that 'the idle, and those who live upon fixed incomes' allot the whole of their revenues to spending for consumption[10]. Ricardo's refutation consists of bringing to light the illegitimacy of this supposition[11].

'They [Reviewers] appear to take it for granted, that those who live on fixed incomes *must* consume the whole of their income, and that no part of it can be saved and annually added to capital. But this is very far from being the true state of the case' (III/122, emphasis in original). Ricardo affirms that the transfer of wealth through the depreciation of money never changes the amount of investment of a country as a whole, in saying as follows. If, previous to the depreciation of money, the stockholders gave 'a stimulus to the growth of national wealth by saving half their incomes and investing it in stocks, thereby liberating capital which will ultimately be employed by those who consume and produce', the extent of this stimulus would be the same as that which would be given to its growth, while 'their incomes were depreciated 50 per cent by the issues of banknotes, and the power of savings were in consequence entirely taken from them', if 'the Bank should lend to an industrious man an amount of notes equal in value to the diminished income of the stockholder' (ibid.).

The coercive transfer of a part of wealth through the depreciation of money does not have the effect of promoting production, but its only possible result is unjust redistribution of the fortune, and unjust conversion of beneficiaries of the interest on investment. It is nothing but a harmful operation. Such is Ricardo's position.

> The difference, and the only difference appears to me to be this, that in the one case the interest on the money lent would be paid to the real owner of the property, in the other it would ultimately be paid in the shape of

> increased dividends or bonuses to the bank proprietors, who had been enabled unjustly to possess themselves of it.
>
> (ibid.)

'I see no reason why it should diminish the idle and add to the productive class of society. At any rate the evil is certain' (III/123).

According to Ricardo's viewpoint, the money held by each is necessarily expended in its totality, either for consumption or for investment (the whole of saving is allotted to the latter). In such a situation as described above, former investors, and so beneficiaries of profit, will be replaced by others. This is the only possible change. Consequently, it must be considered that as for the consumers and the amount of their consumption, there is no change through this process. That is to say, the unproductive classes receiving fixed revenue are certainly victims of the diminution of their real revenues caused by the depreciation of money, but nevertheless they still maintain their real consumption as before. In order to do this, they increase their monetary spending in proportion to the rise in prices (in the above example, from the half of their revenues to their totality). If they can increase their monetary spending despite the constancy of their revenues, it is because they did not allot the whole of their revenues to consumption. In other words, their revenues were divided into consumption and saving, and the latter was allotted in its totality to direct or indirect investments (in the above example, purchase of stocks). This invested part is eroded by the increase of spending for consumption (in the above example, it disappears). This eroded part is now transformed into purchasing power in the hands of those who have had access to newly issued banknotes to acquire a certain quantity of existing capital goods.

Consequently, if saving means, as in its ordinary sense, the abstinence of consumption, the increase of monetary issue in Ricardo's theory is not likely to increase the saving allotted to new investments, but this increase in issue does only transfer from certain categories of the population to others a part (or totality) of the purchasing power of the classes receiving fixed revenue, a part which was saved for the sake of investment. In this case there is no saving, and in consequence no 'forced saving' either. Therefore, as for this aspect of the problem, Ricardo denies the 'forced saving'.

But, if one extends the example given above to admit the case where the increase in monetary issue and the consequent depreciation progress further to such an extent that even spending the whole of the fixed revenue does not maintain consumption as it was before this process, not only the saved part of the revenue but also its consumed part will have to be transferred to those who could borrow newly issued banknotes. If such a case occurs, Ricardo will have to recognise, according to his own logic, that the unproductive classes are reduced to give up a part of their consumption which will be allotted to investment by other classes to promote the production of wealth of the country (i.e., 'forced saving'). Some years later, Ricardo says as follows in one of his letters addressed to Malthus:

> Depreciation of money may be beneficial because it generally favours that class who are disposed to accumulate, but I should say that it augmented riches by diminishing happiness, that it was advantageous only by occasioning a great pressure on the labouring classes and on those who lived on fixed incomes.
>
> (VI/233, letter to Malthus of 27 June 1815)

Here he evidently recognises 'forced saving' and its effects, which shows that there was a lack in the logic Ricardo made use of in order to deny it[12]. Nevertheless, he does not share Malthus' viewpoint in his review article, who estimates these effects positively and considers that the consequent pains certain classes must suffer are only temporary.

In the letter cited above, it is 'the labouring classes' and 'those who lived on fixed incomes', who encounter difficulties in their lives. In the theory of 'forced saving' the wages of labourers are an important factor. But, in Malthus' discussions we have just seen (and Ricardo's critique of them), this factor played no role and the 'saving' was exclusively that imposed with 'force' upon the classes of 'the idle'. But, if the wages are also a kind of fixed revenue, the 'forced saving' will not spare the wage labourers, and also in this respect it will have the effect of expanding production. We will examine Ricardo's reactions concerning this aspect of the theory of 'forced saving'.

6.2.2 Wages and prices of commodities in general

Until now it was implicitly supposed that the increase in the issue of currency raises the prices of all commodities at the same time (or instantaneously), and in the same degree. Does the increase of monetary issue and its depreciation bring about transfer of wealth among classes? Has this transfer in turn the effect of expanding production? If we have concentrated on these questions till now, it is because the above supposition was not brought into question. In this case, the effect of stimulating production could come only from the limitation of consumption of classes which are deprived of a part of their wealth. But, if the increase in money brings about rises in prices in unequal degrees and at divergent paces, even if admitting a uniform rise of all the prices in the long run, the system of relative prices will be disturbed during the intermediary period ending up with the cessation of a rising movement of all prices, we will have such consequences on economic activities, as Hume had already pointed out in the eighteenth century[13]. This divergence in the rise of prices will have particular importance in the case of wages, which are an object of purchase and sale on the market as a kind of commodity. Hume talks of the effect of temporary disturbance on the system of relative prices only generally. But, in the work published 50 years after Hume (1752), Thornton affirms that the effect of 'forced saving' arises because of a fall in real wages and of the consequent limitation of a part of consumption of labourers when wages as a kind of price rise more slowly than the prices of other commodities in general (cf.

Thornton (1802), p. 239). Neither Bentham (1804) nor [Malthus (1811a)] bring into question this side of 'forced saving'. But, in a part of his unpublished work 'Sur les prix', Bentham emphasises, probably under the influence of Thornton, the effect of 'forced saving' based on the characteristics of the movement of wages in the situation of general price rises.

Having been requested by J. Mill to read the manuscript of this work and to express his opinion on it, Ricardo read the French translation of the manuscript during the fortnight from the end of 1810 and wrote here and there detailed comments (III/269–341). At the same time, in his letter of 1 January 1811, in the middle of this work, he informed J. Mill of his general impression. In these documents he showed clearly his viewpoint on the problem above indicated. In his letter to J. Mill he says:

> There appears to me only one way in which any addition would be made to the Capital of a country in consequence of an addition of money; it would be this. Till the wages of labour had found their new level with the altered value of money, the situation of the labourer would be relatively worse; he would produce more relatively to that which he consumed, or rather he would be obliged to consume less. The manufacturer would be enabled to employ more labourers as he would receive an additional price for his commodities; he might therefore add to his real capital till the rise in the wages of labour placed him in his proper sphere. In this interval some trifling addition would have been made to the Capital of the community[14].
>
> (VI/16–7)

Ricardo thought that under the conditions of inconvertibility the price of every commodity rises uniformly in the long run proportionately to the monetary expansion, and that the system of relative prices remains unchanged. However, he never expresses his opinion on the possibility of change in a short (or temporary) term in the relative prices consequent upon variations in the quantity of money. The only point he brings into question concerning this possibility is, as can be seen in the text quoted above, the case in which the rise in wages is slower than that of other commodities. Even in this case, he does not affirm positively a relative slowness in the rise of wages, but he admits it only in response to Thornton and Bentham who had emphasised the effect of 'forced saving' based on this point. Thus, for him, it is only a matter of consequences which would be possible if it was supposed that the rise of wages may be slower for whatever reason. If this supposition is justified, the wage labourers would certainly be obliged to limit their consumption, wages being devoted to spending for consumption as a whole. The purchasing power 'saved' in this way will be transferred to employers who can sell their commodities at prices which have risen more than wages. And if this purchasing power is allotted to investments, the 'forced saving' realised at the cost of consumption of labourers will enlarge investment of the whole of society and promote production, which will result in a greater production of wealth in comparison with the case where there was no such 'saving'. Thus, Ricardo admits the possibility of the effect of 'forced saving' in a particular supposition about the rise of wages.

But this amounts to limiting the consumption of the labourers who lived around the minimal subsistence level, i.e., to lowering real wages below its 'natural rate'. Even if temporarily possible, such a state of things cannot endure for long. 'Labour is paid not by money but by the money's worth therefore if prices rise it will not occasion any increased production because more money must be given to the labourer to enable him to obtain the same amount of commodities' (Ricardo, 'Notes on Bentham's "Sur les prix"', No. 51/1, III/329). The monetary depreciation can lower the level of the 'natural rate' of real wages determined by the cost of subsistence of labourers in a larger sense of the word, but this real wage cannot but restore its initial level through the relation between supply and demand on the labour market. The effect described above is therefore temporary and lasts only till then. The fall of real wages consequent upon monetary depreciation diminishes the supply of labour, and the expansion of employment by the investment fund levied at the cost of real wages increases the demand for labour. This is how the tendency to invalidate the effect of 'forced saving' is all the more reinforced as this effect is strong. It follows that in the long run the 'forced saving' is not possible and it has no effect either, even if it is admitted that the rise of wages is slower in comparison to the prices of commodities in general.

6.3 Monetary issue and interest rate

In the previous section we examined Ricardo's point of view on the theory of 'forced saving' brought forward by his contemporary authors emphasising the positive effect the rise of prices caused by the increase of monetary issue exercises on the activities of production. On the whole, Ricardo was rather negative about the possibility of this effect. And when he recognised it, he stressed not its advantages, but rather its evils for the entire society. This effect is realised by the limitation of a part of consumption certain social classes undergo with monetary depreciation, and by the transformation of this part of consumption in a fund for investment by other classes. He admitted (or could not positively deny) the possibility of expansion of production by monetary causes in the two cases: (1) the rise of wages is slower than that of prices of other commodities; and (2) the monetary depreciation progresses so as to erode not only the saved part of fixed revenue of the 'idle' classes, but also a part of their revenue allotted to consumption. The former case is only a supposition with no justification. Besides, the fall in real wages is only temporary even if it was possible. The latter case is not to be denied as a possibility, but it is not very likely. That was Ricardo's general point of view on 'forced saving'.

Now, the increase in money is the result of the operation of loans by the bank of issue. So, there must first be its action of increasing money for the process described to start. Nevertheless, in the previous section, we deliberately neglected this point. Although logically in inverse order, we examine in this section Ricardo's viewpoint on this monetary issue as the starting point of the process in the theory of 'forced saving'. This procedure is justified by the fact that his arguments concerning the rate of interest and the monetary issue by the bank have a profound relation with the place of his theory of money in the history of thought, which have been the subject of repeated debate in literature.

The BoE had been in the state of suspension of convertibility since 1797, and the notes of the Bank became inconvertible. The theory of 'forced saving' was born in this situation and it is inseparable from the mode of issue of currency as inconvertible notes. The two main forms of monetary issue of the BoE of that time are the loans to government via the purchase of government bonds mainly for financing the war with France, and the discount of bills granted to London merchants.

The BoE is a private enterprise in the form of a joint-stock company established with a royal license. Its notes were commodities (*de facto* with no cost of production) this enterprise sold in exchange for the price, which was the rate of interest it fixed. Its operating benefit was determined by the product of the sum of issued notes and this interest rate. The Bank, exempt from the obligation of conversion, could increase the quantity of issue without considering its gold reserves. It had a natural tendency to issue its notes liberally (accommodating its attitude with respect to the loan requests of government, and the liberal policy of bill discount). In addition, by the law put into effect since the eighteenth century prohibiting usury (Usury Laws), the upper limit of the rate of interest of loan was fixed at 5%. The BoE, a joint-stock company like every other company, but at the same time a public institution on a large scale, had to observe strictly this limit of legal interest rate in fixing its discount rate, which remained constantly at the upper limit of 5% during the whole period of the suspension of convertibility (cf. Homer and Sylla (2005), p. 183). However, there existed on the financial market medium- and small-sized money lenders other than the BoE, and the interest rates they applied during the same period were for the most part above the upper limit fixed by the law[15]. In other words, the BoE carried on its discount operation always at a rate under the interest rate on the market while respecting the law against usury, whereas the other medium- and small-sized money lenders applied, in violation of the law, variable interest rates determined according to the relation between supply and demand on the financial market[16]. The discount rate of the BoE was thus fixed constantly at a level under the rate of interest on the market, making use of the usury laws as an excuse so to speak. Ricardo's arguments on the interest rate and monetary issue by the BoE are to criticise such a situation of the time, and must be read in this context.

6.3.1 Increase of monetary issue and rate of interest

Ricardo adopts Smith's theory, according to which the rate of interest for the purpose of financing industrial or commercial investment cannot exceed the rate of profit obtained or expected from this investment and varies according to this rate of profit as its upper limit. In this sense the rate of interest is ultimately determined by the rate of profit. From *High Price* to *Principles* Ricardo maintained this point of view. And also, this is all he says clearly about the determination of the rate of interest. That is to say, it is possible to fix a maximal upper limit, but as for a rate of interest concretely determined at a given moment and placed between this limit and zero, it can only be said that it is 'the result of the fair competition in the market between the lenders and the borrowers' (I/365). Unlike the case of the theory of value (or price), nothing can be said on what depends the relation itself between the supply and demand on the financial market. On the other hand, Ricardo had a clear theory on what determines the evolution of the rate of profit. Consequently, it is only the evolution of the rate of profit that can be pointed out as the cause of the evolution of the rate of interest. Thus, all that does not change the rate of profit through whatever may be the process is not likely to modify the upper limit of the rate of interest.

> The interest which a man agrees to pay for use of a sum of money is in reality a portion of the profits which he expects to derive from the employment of a capital which that sum of money will enable him to obtain. In the interest which he is willing to pay he is guided solely by the probable extent of those profits. His profits are necessarily totally independent of the abundance or scarcity of the money which circulates commodities in the country.
>
> (III/374–5)

In the same manner he says in *Principles*: 'the interest for money ...[is]... regulated by the rate of profits which can be made by the employment of capital, and which is totally independent of the quantity, or of the value of money' (I/363).

What is thus regulated is the upper limit of the rate of interest of the money borrowed for investing to obtain profit. But the real rate of interest on the market can vary between this upper limit and zero according to the relation between the demand and supply. But Ricardo does not raise the question of what this relation depends on, about what determines the rate of interest at a certain level lower than this upper limit. The quantity of money has nothing to do with the rate of interest either. Inconvertible notes can be absorbed in circulation in any quantity and only changes their value (in terms of the 'standard of money') in inverse proportion to the absorbed quantity, and their quantity has no influence on the relation between the supply and demand of money and on the rate of interest either. Ricardo repeatedly says thus, but in one passage in *High Price* he exceptionally recognises that increase in the quantity of money lowers the rate of interest in making the supply of money excessive in relation to its demand.

> I do not dispute, that if the Bank were to bring a large additional sum of notes into the market, and offer them on loan, but that they would for a

> time affect the rate of interest. … If the amount were large, the Bank … might not be able to lend the notes or the money at four, nor perhaps, above three per cent; but having done so, neither the notes, nor the money, would be retained unemployed by the borrowers; they would be sent into every market, and would everywhere raise the prices of commodities, till they were absorbed in the general circulation. It is only during the interval of the issues of the Bank, and their effect on prices, that we should be sensible of an abundance of money; interest would, during that interval, be under its natural level; but as soon as the additional sum of notes or of money became absorbed in the general circulation, the rate of interest would be as high, and new loans would be demanded with as much eagerness as before the additional issues.
>
> (III/91)[17]

Wicksell paid attention to this text and recognised Ricardo as having shown the influence of monetary issue on the rate of interest. And at the same time Wicksell saw the limit of the theory of Ricardo in that he had not recognised it without temporal limitation. The 'Bank' in the above quoted text seems to mean the BoE, the sole bank of issue, which had fixed permanently the rate of interest at 5%. Then here the question is about the situation in which this BoE would be obliged for the moment to admit a reduction of its rate of interest and to lend its notes at 4% or 3% instead of 5%, if the Bank wanted to create and lend a quantity of notes exceeding the demand. The conditional mood applied to the whole of the above quoted text suggests that it is simply a quite impossible hypothetical situation. As the rate of interest of 5%, with an upper limit fixed by the Usury Laws, applied by the BoE was under the interest rate determined on the market by the relation between the supply and demand for loans, the Bank must not be in want of demand for money, it had nothing to do but accept passively the demands for discount on the basis of 'real bills doctrine' without being obliged to take pains to search for clients in reducing the discount rate. If the rate of interest was to fall because of an increase in money supply, it would be rather the interest rate on the market. But, even if it were possible that the increase of money should lower this rate of interest on the market, the newly issued money would already be in circulation far apart from the Bank of issue and widespread on the market. So, the effect 'proper' to the increase of money should be considered as having already manifested itself, i.e., the rise in prices has started. Consequently, even if a fall in the rate of interest on the market arose, it would be minimal and of limited durability.

At any rate, in the above quoted text Ricardo does not positively affirm the relation between the increase of monetary issue and the movement of interest rate, but here it is only a matter of concessive discussion made under the wholly imaginary hypothesis on the rate of interest of the BoE. And even in this framework, the conclusion Ricardo draws is the following: as the increase of note issue will finally raise prices proportionally, and thus the demand for money will increase as much as its supply, the rate of interest will rise till its initial level, i.e., the quantitative variation of the sum of banknotes in circulation does not change the relation between their supply and demand.

Now, the more important problem for Ricardo is the variation in the rate of profit which is behind that of the rate of interest and manifests itself as the latter. The question is then whether the increase of money supply is accompanied by the variation in the rate of profit. In *High Price*, Ricardo adopted Smith's vague theory on the fall in the rate of profit, according to which this fall results from increased competition among capitals (and not of the rise of the prices of wage goods, especially of corn). What increases this competition, is the increase in capital. The problem raised in the above quoted text ultimately boils down to the question whether the increase in money brings about that of capital which is at the root of the fall in the rate of profit, which lowers in turn the rate of interest, in other words, whether the increase in monetary issue has the effect of expanding production[18].

In the paragraph following that which was quoted above, and which has not so much attracted the attention of commentators as the preceding one, Ricardo clearly expresses his opinion on this point. Apparently difficult to understand, this paragraph seems to allow a certain interpretation if read in relation to the preceding paragraph.

> To suppose that any increased issues of the Bank can have the effect of permanently lowering the interest, and satisfying the demands of all borrowers, so that there will be none to apply for new loans, ... is to attribute a power to the circulating medium which it can never possess. Banks would, if this were possible, become powerful engines indeed. By creating paper money, and lending it at three or two per cent. under the present market rate of interest [it is just the thing the BoE was doing], the Bank would reduce the profits on trade in the same proportion ... . No nation, but by similar means, could enter into competition with us, we should engross the trade of the world. To what absurdities would not such a theory lead us! Profits can only be lowered by a competition of capitals not consisting of circulating medium. As the increase of Bank-notes does not add to this species of capital [real capitals], as it neither increases our exportable commodities, our machinery, or our raw materials, it cannot add to our profits nor lower interest.
>
> (III/92)

If the 'borrowers' invest the borrowed money expecting profits, we can think that 'permanently lowering the interest, and satisfying the demands of all borrowers' is the expression of the situation in which the fall in the rate of profit accompanied by that of the rate of interest reduces the gap between these two rates to zero or around zero, or the rate of profit falls to a level so low that there remains no more sufficient margin of gap between these two rates to motivate borrowing. That such a state of things is the consequence of the increase in monetary issue by the BoE means that this increase brings about that of the quantity of capital and progress the competition among them which lowers the rate of profit. This is indeed 'to attribute a power to the circulating medium which it can never possess'. According to Ricardo, circulating medium is not in itself capital, but the material goods of production ('our exportable commodities, our machinery, or our raw materials') bought with this circulating medium are capitals. Since those who are capable of borrowing money from the bank can raise capital, for them the increase in monetary issue can mean as much increase in their capital. In this way, each individual investor would possibly have the illusion that the increase in monetary issue were equal to as much creation of capital. But, as we have seen in the last section, from Ricardo's standpoint, it is nothing but a redistribution (violent and unjust moreover) of the whole of the capital goods existing in a country, redistribution of which has nothing to do with any positive increase of capital goods. In consequence, the bank capable of issuing inconvertible notes without limit cannot be 'powerful engines' of industry.

6.3.2 Rate of interest and expansion of monetary issue

We have examined above on passages drawn from *High Price*, Ricardo's view on the determination of the rate of interest and the (no-)relation between the increase of monetary issue and the rate of interest. We have seen, at the same time, that his point of view on this subject comes from the perception he has of capital, according to which money is not capital, and the increase in money does not mean in itself any increase in capital. We will summarise our examination on the nature of the connection of money and economic dynamic in Ricardo referring to a passage in chapter 27 of *Principles*, where he expresses his points of view on the relation between the bank rate of interest and the quantity of monetary issue, particularly on the unlimited expansion of issue by regulating this rate of interest. This passage has been mentioned many times by a number of commentators since Wicksell, with the object of situating Ricardo's theory of money as the precursor to the cumulative process theory.

> The applications to the Bank for money, then, depend on the comparison between the rate of profits that may be made by the employment of it, and the rate at which they are willing to lend it. If they charge less than the market rate of interest, there is no amount of money which they might not lend, if they charge more than that rate, none but spendthrifts and prodigals would be found to borrow of them. We accordingly find, that when the market rate of interest exceeds the rate of five per cent, at which the Bank uniformly lend, the discount office is besieged with applicants for money; and, on the contrary, when the market rate is even temporarily under five per cent, the clerks of that office have no employment.
>
> (I/364)

The factors which determine whether the application for loans to the bank enlarges infinitely or reduces to zero are three in number: the rate of profit; the rate of interest on loans of the BoE (discount rate); and the market rate of interest. The rate of profit is the maximal upper limit for every rate of interest when anyone other than 'spendthrifts and prodigals' want to borrow money. Those who apply for discount to the Bank make a comparison not between the rate of profit and the discount rate, but between the discount rate and the rate of interest on the market. Here, Ricardo calls into question the lower level of the discount rate of the BoE not with regard to the rate of profit (it is evident), but with regard to the market rate of interest determined by the relation between the supply and demand (free competition). That is to say, the borrowers make a comparison not between the rate of profit, the revenue expected from the borrowed money, and the rate of interest on the borrowed money, which represents for them the cost (decisive point in the Wicksellian theory of cumulative process), but in fact between the two rates of interest (two different prices given to the money as a commodity, so to speak) which have for them the same meaning as cost.

Now, in classical theory including Ricardo's, for the relation of lending and borrowing with the object of investment to be established, it is necessary that the rate of interest should be constantly lower than the general rate of profit. Does this mean that there can exist permanently an infinite demand for money, and that if the bank is capable of unlimited monetary issue the monetary circulation can expand without limit? In other words, is it a universe where is eternalised the Wicksellian cumulative process of increase of monetary issue? For such a situation to materialise in the framework of Ricardo's theory, in addition to the suspension of convertibility exempting the bank from the obligation of cash payment, it is necessary that the bank should adopt a loan policy of accepting passively and indefinitely every application for loans, without setting certain quantitative criterion for monetary issue. In Ricardo's judgement, such a possibility really existed in the period when banknote issue was continuing on the basis of the 'real bills doctrine' under conditions of the suspension of convertibility. But, if the resumption of cash payments imposes on the bank the obligation of conversion, the monetary issue will be blocked at a certain quantitative limit independently of the relation between the rate of interest and the rate of profit. An infinite monetary expansion will be impossible. Or if the bank continues to control the quantity of its monetary issue to assure the convergence of the market price of bullion with its 'mint price', instead of accepting passively and indefinitely the applications for discount on the basis of the 'real bills doctrine', the unlimited increase in issue will not be inevitable. However, for this it is necessary that the directors of the bank of issue act in conformity to their public duty of stabilising the value of money without regard to their own particular interest (gaining the revenue of interest in selling as much as possible their commodity, banknotes). 'Experience, however, shows, that neither a State nor a Bank ever have had the unrestricted power of issuing paper money, without abusing that power' (I/356), so that it is almost impossible to expect from the administration of the bank such behaviour. In any case, infinite monetary expansion was possible only in the 'abnormal' situation of the time Ricardo constantly criticises. It is not necessarily inherent in the universe of the classical theory of money. That is to say, even if the bank rate of interest is situated below the general rate of profit (or 'natural rate of interest' *à la* Wicksell), this will not automatically cause an indefinite increase in monetary issue.

When Ricardo spoke of the possibility of unlimited expansion of the quantity of notes in the above quoted text, the cause of this movement was the level of the discount rate of the BoE set under the interest rate on the market. 'The discount office is besieged with applicants for money', because in borrowing from the BoE they can pay interest less than if borrowed from other medium- and small-sized money lenders on the market. In taking advantage of its monopolistic position as the only bank of issue, and in using the Usury Laws as an excuse[19], the BoE secures a certain number of privileged as its clients to offer them its commodities cheaply and without restriction. In addition, unlike the loans given by other financiers, the loan of the bank of issue can bring about expansion of the quantity of money in circulation and its liberal loan policy can result in an indefinite increase of monetary issue. But such behaviour of the bank of issue allows the bank itself to earn all the more interest revenue and the borrowers to secure cheap funds of investment to finance their enterprises, and to make even more profits. The increase of monetary issue under the conditions of suspension of convertibility was thus a kind of alchemy with a 'magic effect' (IV/36) favourable both to the bank of issue itself and to its clients. Both sides rallied to a solid community of interest against the resumption of convertibility. This is 'the reason … why for the last twenty years [1797–1817], the Bank is said to have given so much aid to commerce, by assisting the merchants with money' (I/364).

But, whereas a certain number of clients of the Bank derive benefits made possible by the forced transfer of wealth through the depreciation of money, there are others who suffer as much loss at the same time by the diminution of their monetary assets because of the depreciation. The monetary expansion and the consequent depreciation, though redistributing existing capital[20], do not have in themselves the effect of promoting the increase of capital. 'Of what benefit would it be to the community? It would not extend our trade' (ibid.). In this way Ricardo clearly denies the effect of economic expansion by the swelling of credit.

If such is the case, does the swelling of credit never further production, according to Ricardo's logic and not to his letter? As we have seen in the last section, he recognised the effect of 'forced saving' for the following two cases: (1) the case of limitation of the consumption of labourers because of the lower speed of the rise in wages in comparison to the rise of the prices of general commodities; (2) the case in which monetary depreciation advances so far that the real consumption of those who live on fixed incomes must diminish, even if they spend the whole of their revenues, a large part of which was allotted to their saving (= investment). As for the first case, even if it were possible, it would only be temporary, real wages having to be restored sooner or later. Concerning the second case, it cannot be realised with such monetary depreciation as actually took place during the period of the suspension of convertibility. Consequently, only if an immense increase in monetary issue never stops and the depreciation progresses infinitely, a part of the wages and fixed revenues will be transferred to those who can take advantage of newly-issued banknotes and it will be assigned constantly to activities of investment which will thus enlarge and further the production of wealth. Then real wages will constantly fall and soon reach the level of starvation wages, and those who live on fixed revenues will be deprived of a considerable part of their real revenues by the depreciation of their monetary revenues.

Such would be, according to Ricardo's logic, the only possible scenario of a divergent economic expansion to be triggered by the swelling of credit[21]. But, if the BoE continues accelerated monetary expansion, prices will never cease rising and a new 'excess of money' will permanently arise, at the same time as the dissolution of the preceding 'excess of money'. The fall in the market rate of interest owing to this excess of money will not be temporary, but it will continuously fall. And 'when the market rate is even temporarily under 5 per cent, the clerks of that office have no employment', i.e., the increase of issue will cease at this point[22]. In consequence, the continual increase without limit of banknotes is impossible, since the fall in the rate of interest sooner or later stops the monetary issue.

That is the course of the 'forced saving' inferable from Ricardo's logic, but not from his letter. It would be a terrible consequence of the expansion of banknotes under the conditions of the suspension of convertibility. But, apart from the 'cessation' of issue by the fall in the market rate of interest we have just seen, this consequence is not an automatic (or inevitable) outcome of the adoption of the policy of a reduced rate of interest by the bank of issue. The reduced rate of interest induces applications for loans, but results will be very different according to the reaction of the bank. Ricardo always emphasised the possibility of indefinite expansion of banknotes and of unlimited monetary depreciation, and its dangerous consequences. The outcome would be the above situation. For Ricardo it was not to be welcome as progress of wealth but to be avoided at all costs.

The destabilisation of the value of money caused by the suspension of convertibility is the most important issue in Ricardo's monetary writings. Thus, he aimed ultimately to propose measures for stabilising the value of money. In this context, he acted as a kind of political agitator in his discourses on the expansion of monetary issue, recommending the resumption of convertibility by showing the dangerous possibilities of its suspension in their extreme forms. As we have just seen, in his theory the relation between the level of the rate of interest of the loans by the bank of issue and the general rate of profit is not the only determining factor of the evolution of monetary issue. A lower level of the former in comparison to the latter is only one factor. In

Wicksell, the stability of prices (therefore of the value of money) is attained by the adjustment of the rate of interest carried out by the bank aiming to conform to the natural rate of interest, while for Ricardo this stability is attained not by regulating the rate of interest but by adjusting the sum of loan (of issue) so as to remove the gap between the 'mint price' and the market price of the standard commodity (bullion), the rate of interest of bank loan should not be the object of artificial regulation, but it should conform to the market rate of interest determined by the relation between the supply and demand for money. If convertibility is ensured, this adjustment will be made automatically, but if convertibility is suspended, this adjustment will rest with the delicate sense of responsibility (moral) on the side of the bank administration charged with the management of the value of money.

In conclusion, it is not possible to characterise Ricardo's theory of money as a theory of monetary dynamics, according to which the evolution of money supply dependent on the movement of interest rate leads economic activities to increase or decrease, and historically it is not possible to place Ricardo's theory in the tradition ending up with the cumulative process theory of Wicksell[23].

Notes

1 Cf. on this point Blaug (1995), p. 41, 'Gold' by Quadrio and Rotond in Kurz and Salvadori (2015), p. 176.
2 Ahiakpor (1985) stresses the non-neutral character of money in Ricardo's theory, in particular the short run impact its quantitative variations may have on economic activity in the conditions of the suspension of cash payments during the Bank Restriction Period.
3 This term is the English translation of the German term 'erzwungenes Sparen' forged by Mises in the twentieth century. Historically, it was Bentham who used for the first time the synonym 'forced frugality' in his manuscript written in 1804 (Bentham (1954), p. 343). On historic matters about 'forced saving', see the following documents: Hayek, 'Theories of the Influence of Money on Prices' in Hayek (1931), Do. 'A Note on the Development of the Doctrine of "forced saving"', in Hayek (1939).
4 'Minutes of Evidence taken before the Lords Committees', on 26 March 1819, Nos. 97–9 (V/445–6). 'Speeches', 10 July 1822 (V/237).
5 Bentham left detailed comments on the work of Thornton. The manuscript of these comments was deciphered and published in French. 'Jeremy Bentham, Discussion sur le papier-monnaie, à propos d'un ouvrage d'H. Thornton, (manuscrit inédit, Bibliothèque publique et universitaire de la ville de Genève, Ms. 50, f.440–452)', *Cahiers d'Économie Politique*, no. 32, 1998, pp. 149–57.
6 Excerpts from the related documents Ricardo read in this epoch and his sparse comments are published in Ricardo (1932).
7 Here the monetary expansion transfers a part of wealth in a certain direction, but in the case of monetary contraction a transfer in the opposite direction will take place (those who have gained will lose as much) and at the moment when the quantity of money comes back to the initial level, (*ceteris paribus*) the prices and the distribution of wealth will be in the same state as they were before the change (cf. III/135).

Throughout this process the wealth of the country as a whole undergoes no quantitative change. Ricardo thus supposed that monetary expansion and contraction can result in reversible movements of the prices and of the state of distribution of wealth. What he foresaw later when the resumption of convertibility and a monetary contraction were going to be realised, was symmetrical movements in the opposite direction exactly in the same degree as before following the suspension of convertibility. However, as not all the conditions actually remained the same, he was obliged to give diverse explanations on the part of the fall of prices which far exceeded his prognosis (from 5 to 6 per cent, cf. the previous chapter in this book).

8 On this point both Thornton (cf. Thornton (1802), Chapter X, pp. 236–9) and Bentham (cf. Bentham (1804), pp. 343–51) make similar discussions. But because it is only to Malthus that Ricardo gave coherent responses and also because Malthus' discussions raise more interesting problems, we confine ourselves to examining the debates between Ricardo and Malthus.

9 The process which goes from the increase of banknote issue to the expansion of production via depreciation of money is perceived as a process through which a kind of disequilibrium between commodities and money is brought back to the equilibrium state by the expansion of production (quantitative increase of commodities). There is no factor likely to activate the same process anew.

> The increased command of the produce transferred to the industrious classes by the increase of prices, gives such a stimulus to the productive powers of the country, that, in a short time, the balance between commodities and currency is restored, by the great multiplication of the former, and prices return to their former level.
>
> (Malthus (1811a), p. 365–6)

Malthus does not think that the rise in prices and the expansion of production progress in a cumulative way. And according to him, such a transfer of wealth is certainly contrary to justice and reduces a part of social classes to economic distress, but this pain suffered by certain classes is only temporary. 'The evil ... is so inconsiderable, and so strictly limited, as probably to be more than counterbalanced, even to him [the possessor of a fixed income], by the advantage which the country derives from it' (ibid.). With the fall in prices, the substantial conditions of life of those who sustained temporary damages would be restored. In this way, Malthus affirms that the injustice and pains of 'forced saving' dissolve finally. But, even if the increase of production brings the quantity of disposable means of subsistence back to the initial level, the part of the whole of the national products allotted to the classes with fixed revenues will have fallen. On the other hand, the classes which sustain the injustice and pain in this process are 'the idle, and those who live upon fixed incomes', more concretely landowners, renters, moneylenders, pensioners, etc. (so-called leisure classes). The class of wage labourers has no place in this context and the movement of wages is left out of the question.

10 Though Malthus does not make it explicit here, even if one supposes that the revenue is not always allotted as a whole to unproductive consumption but a part of it is reserved for saving without being expended in any way (without forming effective demand), his argument holds only if no part of this revenue is allotted to investment.

11 In view of Malthus's position in economic theory, his theory of 'forced saving' briefly presented above seems to raise the following serious problems. In the first place, his position is not in accordance with that of bullionism which is against the increase of banknote issue. He certainly does not recommend this increase. But there is no positive reason to oppose it for him who affirms that the increase of banknotes is favourable to the production of wealth, and in addition that consequent evil is only momentary. Also, even if he had other reasons to oppose it, his theory of 'forced saving' would weaken his opposing position as a whole. On the other hand, Ricardo's attitude toward this theory is certainly determined first by his position in the economic theory, but it can also be consequent on the consideration that this theory of 'forced saving' may give support to the anti-bullionism (cf. Hudson (1965), p. 245, Humphrey (1974), p. 6). Secondly, some years later Malthus would contend that the spending for consumption of unproductive classes receiving fixed revenue creates demand and thus has the effect of stimulating the activities of production, while here the pecuniary wealth allotted to such spending for consumption is 'saved' under coercion and transferred to social classes ready to invest it productively. This is not in accordance with his theory of effective demand. In other words, according to the position he was going to take in economic theory, 'forced saving' must result in an irremediable overproduction, since it means diverting the source of demand which was to compensate for the fatal insufficiency of demand toward further productive investment. In short, Malthus seems to be completely unaware of the question of demand in his discussion about 'forced saving'. However, the point of view Malthus adopted in 1811 on the meaning of effective demand is to be found in his writings of this epoch, but this is a subject beyond the scope of this chapter.

12 However, this can be justified only within the limits of abstract theory. Ricardo had the following point of view on those who lived on fixed incomes: 'My opinion however is that by no class are greater savings made than by those who are in possession of fixed monied rents and annuities. As far as they have come under my observation, and I have seen a good deal of monied men, they are amongst the most accumulating of the community' (Letter of Ricardo to J. Mill of 1 January 1811, VI/16). According to the theory of Ricardo, those who save a greater part of their revenue do invest as much as their savings and have at their disposal a large margin for nominal expansion of their spending for consumption when money depreciates, and so they do not easily come to diminish their real consumption (i.e., to accept 'forced saving'). It can be thought that such a point of view was in the background of his response to Malthus. But on the other hand, since Ricardo affirmed repeatedly that monetary operation can progress infinitely, theoretically it is not impossible to suppose a depreciation of money which goes beyond this large margin and erodes real consumption. There will then be an increase of investment at the cost of real consumption ('forced saving'). The problem is thus left undetermined. 'Whether those who are enriched will employ their additional income more economically or more advantageously than those who before possessed of it, must be matter of speculation only' (ibid.). Ricardo could only say so. This is what he said in his letter reporting his impressions after having read Bentham's manuscript, addressed to J. Mill, with whom Ricardo was not in controversy, but the answer to Malthus made a little later was (since this was a retort to him) in a pretty different tone. It is not simply because Ricardo made use of different logic alternately according to

the situation. Ricardo's attitude should be understood in relation to his above viewpoint (the 'forced saving' is little probable).

13 'Since the discovery of the mines in AMERICA, industry has encreased in all the nations of EUROPE' (Hume (1752), p. 52).

> To account, then, for this phenomenon, we must consider, that though the high price of commodities be a necessary consequence of the encrease of gold and silver, yet it follows not immediately upon that increase; but some time is required before the money circulates through the whole state, and makes its effect be felt on all ranks of people. At first, no alteration is perceived; by degrees the price rises, first of one commodity, then of another, till the whole at last reaches a just proportion with the new quantity of specie which is in the kingdom. In my opinion, it is only in this interval or intermediate situation, between the acquisition of money and rise of prices, that the encreasing quantity of gold and silver is favourable to industry.
>
> (ibid., p. 47)

Cf. Hicks (1967), chapter 9. 'Monetary theory and history – an attempt at perspective'.

14 The part quoted here of the letter to J. Mill seems to be an orderly paraphrase of one of the comments on the manuscript of Bentham. Cf., 'Notes on Bentham's "Sur les prix"', No. 34, III/318–9. See also the following passages of the same comments in III/302, 325, 329.

15 Homer and Sylla (2005). Cf. particularly chapter 13, which contains a historical description of the evolution of the interest rate in England during the nineteenth century. Ricardo discusses the evolution of the rate of interest in England of his time in relation to the Usury Laws. Cf. I/296–7, in chapter 21, 'Effects of Accumulation on Profits and Interest'.

16 But it is only the former that is officially registered, and the latter is known only in unofficial documents or market information. Ricardo notes also this point in the passages indicated above.

17 Although not so explicit on the possibility of fall in interest rate as in the text quoted here, in chapter 21 of *Principles* Ricardo equally indicates that the rate of interest is temporarily influenced by the increase in the quantity of money until the prices rise so much. Cf. I/298.

18 Contrary to Wicksell's theory in which the fall in the rate of interest is the cause of expansion of production, in Ricardo the fall of the rate of interest is the indirect consequence of the expansion of production.

19 Ricardo's position concerning this law, like Thornton's (cf. Thornton (1802), pp. 253–4), is as follows:

> But in all countries, from mistaken notions of policy, the State has interfered to prevent a fair and free market rate of interest, by imposing heavy and ruinous penalties on all those who shall take more than the rate fixed by the law. In all countries probably those laws are evaded, but records give us little information on this head, and point out rather the legal and fixed rate, than the market rate of interest.
>
> (I/296–7)

Ricardo claims the repeal of the Usury Laws which were serving, according to him, for the Bank of England as the pretext to lower its rate of interest. And he affirms that the Bank had to adopt the market rate of interest, which is 'the result of the fair competition in the market between the lenders and the borrowers' (I/365).

20 'The whole business, which the whole community can carry on, depends on the quantity of its capital, that is, of its raw material, machinery, food, vessels, &c. employed in production' (I/365). The money is not included in this 'quantity of its capital'.

21 Ricardo might suppose a similar situation when he says as follows:

> Depreciation of money may be beneficial because it generally favours that class who are disposed to accumulate, but I should say that it augmented riches by diminishing happiness, that it was advantageous only by occasioning a great pressure on the labouring classes and on those who lived on fixed incomes.
>
> (VI/233, his letter to Malthus of 27 June 1815)

22 It is also possible to suppose a case in which the BoE lowers the discount rate under 5%. But then the same process will be repeated starting from a new lowered rate, and the discount rate will at last reach a level so low that further falls will make the bank operations impossible. Soon afterwards the market rate of interest will catch up to this level of discount rate of the Bank, and the result will be the same as when the Bank fixed it at 5%.

23 In the preface of Thornton (1802 [1991]), the editor Hayek says that Wicksell's cumulative process theory is the result of combination of two elements contained in Thornton's work.

> A remarkable anticipation of the distinction between the market rate and the 'natural' or 'equilibrium' rate of interest which since the work of Knut Wicksell has played such an important rôle in the discussions of these problems. With this idea, along with the idea of forced saving, Thornton was for the first time in possession of the two main elements which it was left for Wicksell, nearly a hundred years later, successfully to combine into one of the most promising contributions to the theory of credit and industrial fluctuations.
>
> (ibid., p. 50)

In this chapter we have shown on each of these elements that Ricardo does not belong to the stream emphasised by Hayek (from Thornton to Wicksell).

References

Primary literature

[Bailey, S.] (1825) *A critical dissertation on the nature, measures, and causes of value; chiefly in relation to the writings of Mr. Ricardo and his followers*, London, R. Hunter.

Bentham, J. (1804 [1954]) 'Institute of political economy', in *Jeremy Bentham's economic writings: critical edition based on his printed works and unprinted manuscripts*, edited by W. Stark, vol. III, London, Allen & Unwin.

Bosanquet, C. (1810) *Practical observations on the report of the Bullion-committee*, London, J.M. Richardson.

Cannan, E. (1919) *The paper pound of 1797–1821. A reprint of the Bullion Report, with an introduction by E. Cannan*, London, P.S. King.

Galton, S.T. (1813) *A chart, exhibiting the relations between the amount of Bank of England notes in circulation, the rate of foreign exchanges, and the prices of gold and silver bullion and of wheat; accompanied with explanatory observations*, London, J. Johnson and Co.

Gilbart, J.W. (1837) *The history and principles of banking*, third edition, London, Longman.

Hayek, F. (1931) *Prices and production, Lecture I*, Abingdon, Routledge.

Hayek, F. (1939) *Profits, interest and investment*, Abingdon, Routledge.

Horner, F. (1811) 'Resolutions moved by Francis Horner ESQ., Chairman of the Bullion Committee', in *Substance of two speeches, delivered in the House of Commons, by the Right Honourable George Canning, On Wednesday the 8th, and Monday the 13th of May, 1811, in the Committee of the Whole House; to which was referred the Report of the Committee, appointed in the last session of Parliament 'to inquire into the cause of The High Price of Bullion, and to take into consideration the state of the circulating medium, and of the exchanges between Great-Britain and Foreign Parts'*, 190, Opposite Albany, Piccadilly, J. Hatchard, Bookseller to Her Majesty.

Hume, D. (1752) *Political discourses*, second edition, Edinburgh, R. Fleming.

Jevons, W.S. (1871 [1965]) *The theory of political economy*, London and New York, Macmillan and Co., reprinted on the fifth edition of 1957 by Augustus M. Kelley, New York.

King (1804) *Thoughts on the effects of the Bank restrictions, the second edition enlarged, including some remarks on the coinage*, London, Cadell and Davies.

King (1811 [1844]) 'Speech of the Right Hon. Lord King, in the House of Lords, on Tuesday, 2 July 1811, upon the second reading of Earl Stanhope's Bill respecting Guineas and Bank Notes', in *A selection from the speeches and writings of the late*

Lord King with a short introductory memoir by Earl Fortescue, edited by J. Ridgway, London, Longmans.

[Malthus, R.] (1811a) 'Article V: Publications on the Depreciation of Currency', *Edinburgh Review*, 2, pp. 339–72.

[Malthus, R.] (1811b) 'Article X: Review of the Controversy respecting the High Price of Bullion', *Edinburgh Review*, 8, pp. 448–70.

Malthus, T.R. (1820) *Principles of political economy: considered with a view to their practical application*, London, Murray.

Malthus, T.R. (1823) *The measure of value stated and illustrated, with an application of it to the alteration in the value of the English currency since 1790*, London, Murray.

Marshall, A. (1920) *Principles of economics, an introductory volume*, eighth edition, London, Macmillan [from Appendix I 'Ricardo's theory of value'].

Marx, K. (1859 [2010]) 'A contribution to the critique of political economy, Part one', in *Marx Engels collected works*, London, Lawrence and Wishart, vol. 29.

Marx, K. (1861–3 [2010]) 'Economic manuscript of 1861–63 (Theories of Surplus Value)', in *Marx Engels Collected Works*, London, Lawrence and Wishart, Vol. 31.

Marx, K. (1867 [2010]) 'Capital, vol. I', in *Marx Engels Collected Works*, London, Lawrence and Wishart, Vol. 35.

Marx, K. (1894 [2010]) 'Capital, vol. III', in *Marx Engels Collected Works*, London, Lawrence and Wishart, Vol. 37.

[McCulloch, J.R.] (1818) 'Article III: Proposals for an Economical and Secure Currency; with Observations on the Profits of the Bank of England, &c. by David Ricardo, Esq. 1816', *Edinburgh Review*, 12, pp. 53–80.

McCulloch, J.R. (1825a) *A discourse on the rise, progress, peculiar objects, and importance, of political economy*, second edition, Edinburgh, Archibald Constable & Co.

McCulloch, J.R. (1825b) *The principles of political economy: with a sketch of the rise and progress of the science*, Edinburgh, William and Charles Tail.

Mill, J. (1821) *Elements of political economy*, London, Baldwin.

Mushet, R. (1810) *An Enquiry into the effects produced on the national currency and rates of exchange, by the Bank Restriction Bill; explaining the cause on the high price of bullion; with plans for maintaining the national coins in a state of uniformity and perfection*, second edition, London, Baldwin.

Ricardo, D. (1932) *Minor papers on the currency question 1809–1823*, edited with an introduction and notes by Jacob H. Hollander, Baltimore, The John Hopkins Press.

Ricardo, D. (1951–2), *The works and correspondence of David Ricardo*, edited by Piero Sraffa with the collaboration of M. H. Dobb, Cambridge, Cambridge University Press, Vol. I–IX.

Smith, A. (1776 [1976]) 'An inquiry into the nature and causes of the wealth of nations', in *The Glasgow Edition of the works and correspondence of Adam Smith*, 2, Oxford, Clarendon Press.

Steuart, J. (1767) *An inquiry into the principles of political economy*, London, A. Miller.

Thornton, H. (1802 [1991]) *An enquiry into the nature and effects of the paper credit of Great Britain*, edited with an introduction by F.A.V. Hayek, New York, A.M. Kelley.

Tooke, T. (1838) *A history of prices, and of the circulation, from 1793 to 1837; preceded by a sketch of the state of the corn trade in the last two centuries*, vol. 2, London, Longman.

[Torrens, R.] (1818 [1984]) 'Strictures on Mr. Ricardo's Doctrine respecting exchangeable value', *The Edinburgh Magazine*, in *Robert Torrens, The economists refuted 1808*

and other early economic writings, reprints of economic classics, series 2, number 3, edited by P.D. Groenewegen, Sydney, University of Sydney, pp. 56–60.
Torrens, R. (1821) *An essay on the production of wealth*, London, Longman.
Wicksell, J.G.K. (1935) *Lectures on political economy*, translated by E. Classen; and edited with an introduction by Lionel Robbins, 'Money', London, Macmillan, vol. 2.

Secondary literature

Ahiakpor, J. (1985) 'Ricardo on Money: The Operational Significance of the Non-neutrality of Money in the Short Run', *History of Political Economy*, vol. 17, no. 1, pp. 17–30.
Arnon, A. (2011) *Monetary theory and policy from Hume and Smith to Wicksell: money, credit and economy*, Cambridge, Cambridge University Press.
Blaug, M. (1995) 'Why is the quantity theory of money the oldest surviving theory in economics', in chapter 2 in *The quantity theory of money from Locke to Keynes and Friedman*, edited by Blaug, M. et al., London, Edward Elgar, pp. 27–49.
Bonar, J. (1923) 'Ricardo's Ingot Plan: A Centenary Tribute', *Economic Journal*, vol. 33, pp. 281–304.
Bonar, J., Hollander, J.H. (1899) (eds.), *Letters of David Ricardo to Hutches Trower and others, 1811–1823*, Oxford, Clarendon Press.
Cassels, J.M. (1935) 'A Re-interpretation of Ricardo on Value', *The Quarterly Journal of Economics*, vol. 49, no. 3, pp. 518–31.
De Leo, M. (2017) '"Absolute Value and Exchangeable Value": A Key Element in Ricardo's Theory of Value', *Contribution to Political Economy*, no. 36, pp. 61–79.
Deleplace, G. (2008) 'Les deux plans monétaires de Ricardo', in *Cahiers d'économie politique*, no. 55, "David Ricardo 199 ans après", Paris, L'Harmattan, pp. 13–33.
Deleplace, G. (2017) *Ricardo on money, a reappraisal*, London, Routledge.
Deleplace, G. and Sigot, N. (2012) 'Ricardo's Critique of Bentham's French Manuscript: Secure Currency versus Secure Banks', *European Journal of the History of Economic Thought*, vol. 19, no. 4, pp. 733–64.
Depoortère, C. (2015), 'Two Unpublished Letters of David Ricardo on a Monetary Pamphlet by Samuel Tertius Galton', *Journal of the History of Economic Thought*, vol. 37, no. 3, pp. 341–61.
De Vivo, G. (1987) 'Ricardo', in *The New Palgrave: A dictionary of economics*, edited by J. Eatwell, P. Milgate and P. Newmann, London, Macmillan, vol. 4, pp. 183–98.
Feavearyear, A. and Morgan, V. (1963) *The pound Sterling: a history of English money*, second edition revised by E. Victor Morgan, Oxford, Clarendon Press.
Fetter, F.W. (1965) *Development of British monetary orthodoxy, 1797–1965*, Cambridge, Harvard University Press.
Hadori, T. (1972) *Kotenha Keizaigaku no Kihon Mondai* (*Fundamental problems of the classical economics*), Tokyo, Miraisha (in Japanese).
Hadori, T. (1982) *Ricardo Kenkyu – Kachi to Bunpai no Riron* – (Studies on Ricardo – theory of value and distribution –), Tokyo, Miraisha (in Japanese).
Hashimoto, M. (2013) 'Tendency of Settlement by a Merchant Banker in the Bank of Amsterdam: The Case of Hope & Co.', *The Economic Science* (University of Nagoya), vol. 61, no. 3, pp. 35–52 (in Japanese).
Hicks, J. (1967) *Critical essays in monetary theory*, Oxford, Clarendon Press.

Hollander, J. (1904) 'The Development of Ricardo's Theory of Value', *The Quarterly Journal of Economics*, vol. 18, no. 4, pp. 455–91.
Hollander, J. (1910) *David Ricardo, a centenary estimate*, Baltimore, The Johns Hopkins Press.
Homer, S. and Sylla R. (2005) *A history of interest rates*, fourth edition, Hoboken, Wiley.
Hudson, M.A. (1965) 'Ricardo on Forced Saving', *The Economic Record*, vol. 41, no. 94, pp. 240–7.
Humphrey, T.M. (1974) 'The Quantity Theory of Money: Its Historical Evolution and Role in Policy Debates', *Economic Review, Federal Reserve Bank of Richmond*, vol. 6, May, pp. 2–19.
Humphrey, T.M. (1986) 'Cumulative process models from Thornton to Wicksell', *Economic Review*, vol. 72, no. 3, pp. 18–25.
Humphrey, T.M. (2004) 'Classical Deflationary Theory', *Economic Quarterly*, vol. 90/1, Federal Reserve Bank of Richmond, pp. 11–31.
Kurz, H. (1994) 'Review of T. Peach, Interpreting Ricardo', *European Journal of the History of Economic Thought*, vol. 1, no. 2, pp. 411–20.
Kurz, H. and Mongiovi, G. (2002) 'Notes and Comments', *Cambridge Journal of Economics*, no. 26, pp. 371–80.
Kurz, H. and Salvadori, N. (2015) *The Elgar companion to David Ricardo*, Camberley, Edward Elgar.
Laidler, D. (1987) 'Bullionist controversy', in *The New Palgrave: A dictionary of economics*, edited by J. Eatwell, P. Newman, London, Macmillan, Vol. 1, pp. 290–3.
Laidler, D. (2000) *Highlights of the Bullionist Controversy*, Research Report, no. 2000–2, The University of Western Ontario, Department of Economics.
Marcuzzo, M.C. and Rosselli, A. (1991) *Ricardo and the gold standard, the Foundations of the International Monetary Order* (tr. from Italian), New York, St. Martin's Press.
Nakatani, S. (2006) 'Deposits of the Bank of Amsterdam and Foreign Trade (1610–1683)', *Bulletin of the Japan –Netherlands Institute*, vol. 31, no. 1, pp. 25–42 (in Japanese).
O'Brien, D.P. (1970) *J.R. McCulloch a study in classical economics*, London, Allen & Unwin.
Peach, T. (1993) *Interpreting Ricardo*, Cambridge, Cambridge University Press.
Peach, T. (2002) 'Interpreting Ricardo: a further reply to Sraffians', *Cambridge Journal of Economics*, no. 26, pp. 381–91.
Robbins, L.C. (1958) *Robert Torrens and the evolution of classical economics*, London, Macmillan.
Roll, E. (1938) *A history of economic thought*, London, Faber and Faber.
Sato, S. (2013) 'Japanese Studies on Ricardo after World War II', The History of Economic Thought (JSHET) 54(2), pp. 64–71.
Sato, Y. and Takenaga, S. (eds.) (2013) *Ricardo on money and finance, a bicentenary reappraisal*, New York, Routledge.
Sayers, R.S. (1953) 'Ricardo's Views on Monetary Questions', *Quarterly Journal of Economics*, vol. 67, no. 2, pp. 30–49.
Smith, M. (2013) 'Ricardo versus Tooke, On the enduring value of their respective monetary theories to classical economics', in Sato and Takenaga, pp. 179–97.
Stigler, G.J. (1958) 'Ricardo and the 93% Labor Theory of Value', *The American Economic Review*, vol. 48, no. 3, pp. 357–68.
Takenaga, S. (2018) 'Review of Ricardo on Money: A Reappraisal by G. Deleplace', *Cahiers D'économie Politique*, no. 74, pp. 171–85.

Index

FSC
www.fsc.org
MIX
Papier | Fördert
gute Waldnutzung
FSC® C083411

Kolibri 360 GmbH
Ferdinand-Jühlke-Straße 7
99095 Erfurt, Deutschland
produktsicherheit@kolibri360.de